C000056541

# A Celebration of
# Leeds

**People, Places, Pictures and Memories to mark
the 800th Anniversary of Leeds City Charter**

**by John Morgan & David Joy**

GREAT NORTHERN

Great Northern Books
PO Box 213, Ilkley, LS29 9WS
www.greatnorthernbooks.co.uk

First published 2006

© John Morgan & David Joy 2006


All rights reserved. No part of this book may be reproduced in
any form or by any means without permission in writing from
the publisher, except by a reviewer who may quote brief
passages in a review.

Except where otherwise credited, all photographs are courtesy
Yorkshire Post Newspapers Ltd. Every effort has been made to
acknowledge correctly and contact the copyright holders of
material in this book. Great Northern Books Ltd apologises for
any unintentional errors or omissions, which should be notified
to the publisher.

ISBN: 1 905080 21 2


Design and layout: David Burrill


Printed by Quebecor Ibérica, Barcelona


CIP Data
A catalogue for this book is available from the British Library

# Contents

*Chapter 1 is by David Joy. The remaining chapters are by John Morgan*

*The publishers gratefully acknowledge the help received during the preparation of this book from Yorkshire Post Newspapers, Leodis and Leeds City Council, especially Kate Vigurs, Celebrate Leeds 2007 Festival Coordinator.*

# First Lines
## from Freemen of the City of Leeds

When, in 1933, John Betjeman came to Leeds to report on the opening of the Civic Hall he came away thinking that it was the people who made Leeds. And that is still true. Despite the homogenising effect of television the Leeds voice - the Leeds 'twang' as my mother called it - hasn't changed and hearing it whenever I get off the train at what I still think of as the City Station something in me responds and, I suppose, relaxes. It's the sound of home. And that twang is now happily shared by the different races who live in Leeds seems to me an evidence of community and a sign of hope.

The look of Leeds has, of course, changed but I rejoice that so much has survived even though I find it hard to think that the Post Office in City Square now houses restaurants and the banks wine bars. Still I am happy that the Market is much the same and the Town Hall, the Art Gallery and the Reference Library – all of them scenes from my life.

Since Leeds is home, though, I feel entitled to criticise it and however proud the city is of its Victorian quarter I still mourn the loss of the Venetian Gothic buildings that once graced Park Row. They would never be pulled down nowadays but later buildings, which will one day seem every bit as notable, are still being lost and it's not merely piety that makes me think my old school, Lawnswood School (or Leeds Modern as was) to be one of them. So Leeds means that, too, to me – a short-sightedness about its architectural heritage that always has to be resisted. We are too anxious, it seems to me in Leeds, to get to the future.

But there is so much to be proud of, like the Grand, West Yorkshire Playhouse, Temple Newsam and even battered old Kirkstall Abbey, still, I imagine, in the minds of most people in Leeds, thought of as being demolished by Oliver Cromwell.

There is another survival from the Thirties which has come down to us almost intact and which deserves to be celebrated and that is the Green Belt. That, too, has to be defended on behalf of the community as a whole against the sectional interest that would nibble it away.

It might not seem the highest praise for a city that it is easy to get out of but Leeds people will know what I mean.

**Alan Bennett**

As a Leeds Member of Parliament for forty years, I was fascinated to see how the city developed from two-room back-to-backs in Hunslet to the houses with gardens on estates like Halton Moor to the luxurious villas in Alwoodley. I was also much impressed by Leeds's ability to accommodate different ethnic groups particularly Irish, Asian and Caribbean.

Most impressive of all was the contribution made by Leeds to the arts in Britain, which owed a great deal to the work of my close friends Bernard and Rose Gillinson, who gave much assistance to the Gregory Fellows. Leeds played a key role in encouraging artists in my time such as Terry Frost, Kenneth Armitage and Harry Thubron.

**Denis Healey**

As a native of the City of Leeds I have had a love affair with it for 86 years. I was born in a house which only had a cellar kitchen and no toilet, but I have no regrets as it influenced my moral values throughout my life.

My education started at Cowper Street Elementary School and later on at Chapel Allerton High School as it was then called. After winning a music scholarship to the Royal College of Music in London, where I studied with the great English pianist Cyril Smith, I returned to Leeds and have lived the rest of my life here with my late husband Dr. Geoffrey de Keyser. My weekend visits to our beautiful Roundhay Park as a child still live long in my memory and the Leeds Town Hall has played a significant part throughout my life. As a child I used to sit behind the orchestra and there I have heard Rachmaninov, Kreisler, Paderewski, Barbirolli, Sargent and most of the greatest international musicians of our time.

The University of Leeds honoured me twice with honorary degrees and I am still very involved with this great institution. I recall two former Vice-Chancellors, the late Lord Boyle of Handsworth and Professor Sir Alan Wilson who were very involved and supportive of my 1963 dream. The present Vice-Chancellor, Professor Michael Arthur, is a Vice-President of the Leeds International Pianoforte Competition and I am infinitely grateful to him for his interest and support.

The Leeds International Pianoforte Competition was born in 1963 (43 years ago) and, now in its fifteenth edition, it has become one of the greatest international piano competitions in the world. I am proud that I, with Marion (then Countess of Harewood) and Geoffrey, have given a significant cultural gift to this City which honoured me in 2004 with the Freedom of the City. No city in the world could have done more for one of its citizens than Leeds has done for me – I am truly proud and grateful to it.

**Dame Fanny Waterman DBE DMus FRCM**

The new settlement created by Maurice Paynel in 1207 was centred round what became Briggate and the Headrow – the row at the head of the town. It retained vestiges of its ancient character until as late as the early 1930s, when all was swept away to make room for today's broad thoroughfare. Here small shops await the demolition men, with J.R. Teale & Son – 'established over 150 years' – anxious for its furniture to be 'positively cleared'.

# 1. Eight Centuries of Change

## The Lord of Leeds

It was in November 1207 that the Norman lord Maurice Paynel founded a new town in his manor of Leeds. Celebrating its 800th anniversary in 2007, it was very much in the fashion of its time. Following the Norman Conquest, the king took over all land and claimed it to be the property of the Crown. He then granted vast estates to his 'thanes' – members of his household and part of his military elite – in return for services at court and in battle. These estates were administered as a series of manors, each of which had a definite hierarchy, descending from the manorial lord down through the villeins or tenants to the serfs. It was a new pecking order, ushering in a feudal society destined to epitomise English life for several centuries to come.

Maurice Paynel was one such manorial lord who decided to stamp his authority on his new territory by creating a 'planned' settlement. 'Planned' in this context should not be equated with the kind of utopia that was the original aim of today's new settlements such as Milton Keynes. Instead of concrete cows and countless roundabouts, the distinguishing feature was an all-pervading stench. The timber-framed houses generally had floors of beaten earth and walls formed from 'wattle and daub' – intertwined branches supporting a mixture of clay and mud. Smoke from the open-hearth fire mixed with the smell of body odour and dung to create an aroma far from fragrant.

The axis of Paynel's new settlement was what became the broad market street of Briggate leading up to the Headrow. The pattern of many of its thirty plots formed the basis of the long and narrow inn yards and the Victorian arcades that have survived to the present day. Paynel did not start with a virgin site but grafted his settlement onto the western side of what had been the Anglo-Scandinavian village of Loidis (or Leodis), centred on what is now Kirkgate. By the time of the Domesday Book it comprised a thousand acres tended by less than forty farmers supported practically by a grinding mill and spiritually by the Church of St Peter, still retaining a superb Saxon cross in its churchyard.

**Maurice Paynel grafted his new settlement onto the side of the earlier Anglo-Scandinavian village of Leodis, centred on what is now Kirkgate. This street also long smacked of an older era, as instanced by this marvellous jumble of premises that included a 'cut cake' shop, a tobacconist, a 'noted tripe shop' and a medical botanist. The last two are housed in the original home of the Ancient Order of Foresters, a body that provided insurance against sickness and death and grew to have almost a million members.**
**(Leeds Central Library)**

# The White Monks

On the opposite side of the new settlement was green and pleasant countryside with the then crystal clear waters of the River Aire bubbling eastwards on their way to the North Sea. It was sufficiently pastoral to appeal to Cistercian monks who had as one of their avowed aims the colonisation of remote tracts of land. Such land was usually of little value to Norman lords like Maurice de Gant, who had holdings far in excess of their needs. Warriors in battle they might have been, but they were also devout and only too happy to give surplus acres in return for what they perceived as spiritual benefits and perpetual remembrance.

So it was that a community of Cistercian monks, forced by thieves and unproductive land to desert their original settlement at Barnoldswick, established themselves at Kirkstall in 1152. A daughter house of the great Cistercian abbey of Fountains, near Ripon, with its million-acre land holdings, Kirkstall was a more modest affair. The derivation of its name is an unassuming 'church with cattle shed', but despite this handicap it grew to house thirty-six monks and considerably more lay brothers.

The Cistercians were known as the White Monks by virtue of their long white woollen robes. It was wool that formed the basis of life at Kirkstall, with sheep production expanding to the extent that the monks became international traders on a grand scale. In a system akin to modern-day dealing in 'futures', Florentine monks paid cash for the wool crop several years ahead of delivery. Inevitably this created occasional disasters and in 1284 the abbey was in debt to the tune of £5,250 (over £2 million in today's money). Over the next seventeen years this debt was whittled down to £160 and the livestock built up to an impressive 4,000 sheep and 160 head of cattle.

The sheep provided milk, cheese and butter as well as wool. They were normally milked by women – hence the term 'milkmaids'. An early Cistercian rule designed to maintain chastity, and one suspects not always honoured to the letter, stated: 'Let the women milk our sheep in the fields and not in walled houses, and let young and pretty ones be avoided as far as possible.'

Trade and temptation often got the better of the monks' vows of poverty and simplicity, but nevertheless the fabric of Kirkstall changed little after the initial period of expansion. Although its lead roofs were stripped and its bells ignominiously recast as cannon, the abbey escaped massive destruction at the Dissolution. Its Romanesque-style buildings survived in semi-ruinous form, eventually becoming a smoke-blackened monument in a much-expanded industrial city.

# Cloth and prosperity

The wool trade established by the monks provided a springboard for events destined to propel Leeds into one of the great urban centres of northern England. Wool prices rose almost continuously in the late sixteenth century, creating an era of growing prosperity that led to little short of social and economic revolution. Leeds soon became famous for the homes of its cloth merchants, driven westwards by the restrictive practices of guilds in York and the East Riding towns. They traded at a cloth market noted for handling broad cloths expertly finished by local dressers, croppers and dyers. By 1626 the 'planned' settlement of Norman times had expanded into a town of some 6,000 souls sufficiently confident to take the decisive step of placing the whole of its affairs under the jurisdiction of a new corporation. Today such a step would lead to a mission statement of largely meaningless phraseology, but happily the seventeenth century approach was a survey that has left us a clear and colourful picture of Leeds as it then existed. Loosely translated into modern English, a summary passage reads:

*Leeds is an ancient market town. It stands pleasantly in a fruitful and enclosed vale, on the north side of the River Aire over a stone bridge, from which a large and broad street paved with stone leads directly north and continually ascends. The houses on both sides are very dense and closely compacted together, being ancient, mean and lowly built. They are generally all of timber, although they have many stone quarries in and about the town. Only a few of the richer sort of inhabitants have their houses larger and more capacious, although even these are low and straight on their back sides.*

The substantial ruins of Kirkstall Abbey, founded in 1152 by Cistercian monks. They established the wool trade that was to underpin the growth of Leeds in succeeding centuries.

*In the middle of the street, towards the upper end where the Market Place stands, is the Court or Moot House. Upwards from here is the Shambles, with a narrow street on both sides, much annoying the whole town, but for their convenience and want of room they are not to be avoided or placed elsewhere.*

*This manor is all enclosed and has some parcels of land as small as half an acre and some two acres or more. Many houses are scattered frequently and throughout the whole lordship by reason of the great clothing trade on which the whole town chiefly depends.*

Blessed with its new status as a borough, the town continued to expand and above all sought peace so that its textile trade could flourish. Such hopes were initially doomed to disappointment, as the country in general and Yorkshire in particular became enmeshed in the Civil War. The conflict began in 1642 and centred on what Charles I considered his divine right to rule without consulting Parliament. It quickly escalated into civil strife and by the autumn Leeds was the setting for skirmishes between Royalist troops, led by Sir William Savile, and Parliamentary forces under the command of Sir Thomas Fairfax – nicknamed 'Black Tom' by his many West Riding supporters.

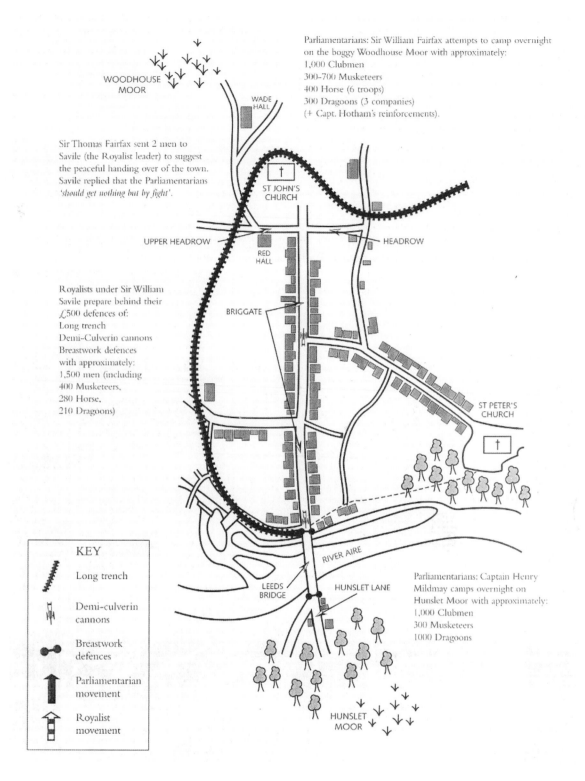

Parliamentarians: Sir William Fairfax attempts to camp overnight on the boggy Woodhouse Moor with approximately:
1,000 Clubmen
300-700 Musketeers
400 Horse (6 troops)
300 Dragoons (3 companies)
(+ Capt. Hotham's reinforcements).

WOODHOUSE MOOR

WADE HALL

Sir Thomas Fairfax sent 2 men to Savile (the Royalist leader) to suggest the peaceful handing over of the town. Savile replied that the Parliamentarians 'should get nothing but by fight'.

ST JOHN'S CHURCH

UPPER HEADROW

HEADROW

RED HALL

Royalists under Sir William Savile prepare behind their £500 defences of:
Long trench
Demi-Culverin cannons
Breastwork defences
with approximately:
1,500 men (including
400 Musketeers,
280 Horse,
210 Dragoons)

BRIGGATE

ST PETER'S CHURCH

KEY

Long trench

Demi-culverin cannons

Breastwork defences

Parliamentarian movement

Royalist movement

RIVER AIRE

LEEDS BRIDGE

HUNSLET LANE

Parliamentarians: Captain Henry Mildmay camps overnight on Hunslet Moor with approximately:
1,000 Clubmen
300 Musketeers
1000 Dragoons

HUNSLET MOOR

**Plan of the Battle of Leeds – January 23rd, 1643. It shows not only how the Royalist and Parliamentary forces were assembled but also gives a good impression of medieval Leeds at the time. Briggate, the broad market street heading due north from the bridge over the River Aire, formed the axis of Maurice Paynel's new settlement of 1207. The earlier Anglo-Scandinavian village of Leodis was centred on Kirkgate, which heads east from Briggate to St Peter's Church. (courtesy Royal Armouries)**

The Royalists gained control of Leeds in December 1642, their position being secured by digging trenches round the town. It did not take long for the Parliamentary forces to regroup and on January 23rd, 1643, Fairfax headed through a howling blizzard with three thousand musketeers and fearsome local volunteers, known not without good reason as 'clubmen'. 'Black Tom' divided his forces, sending around a thousand men to attack the town from the south by taking the bridge over the River Aire. The remainder approached Leeds over Woodhouse Moor to a point now close to the University, from where two men were dispatched to suggest surrender. The Royalists refused. Charging the earthworks to an accompaniment of mighty cheering and a great deal of hand-to-hand fighting, Fairfax stormed the northern end of the town and was soon able to head down Briggate. His other forces captured the bridge and Royalist troops found themselves trapped in a pincer movement, from which escape was only possible by cutting across to St Peter's Church and attempting to swim the river. Several were drowned and some five hundred soldiers were taken prisoner, along with two cannon, fourteen barrels of powder and four hundred muskets. The Battle of Leeds was over in just two hours.

The town was now too important for that to be the end of the matter. Royalists soon planned to recapture Leeds and, after several skirmishes and strategic manoeuvres, the Parliamentarians were forced to flee after their defeat at the nearby Battle of Adwalton Moor on June 30th, 1643. Six months later they were back on the offensive and, reinforced by Scottish sympathisers, decisively took the town once and for all on April 7th, 1644. Within three months the cause of King Charles ended for ever in blood and gore on the field of Marston Moor.

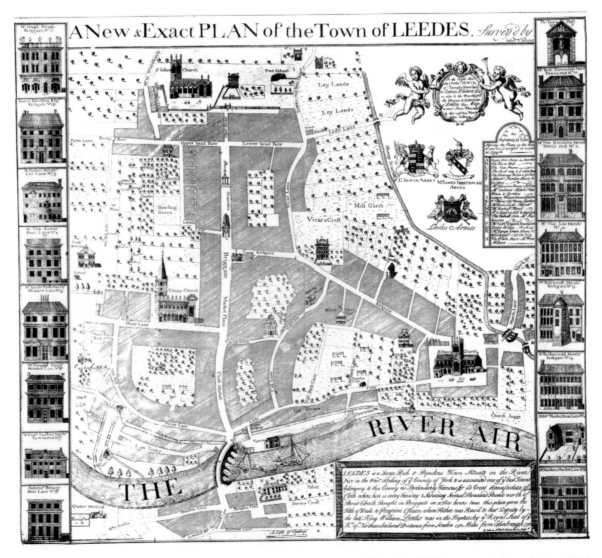

**This map, by John Cossins, was originally thought to have been published in 1725 but now believed to be 1726. (Leeds Library and Information Service.)**

No sooner was Leeds at peace than an outbreak of the Plague in 1645 killed a fifth of its inhabitants. Nevertheless, the population was approaching the 10,000 mark by the end of the century. The corporation's jurisdiction now extended over 21,000 acres of land that included the burgeoning industrial villages of Holbeck, Hunslet, Armley and Bramley to the south and west. Cloth manufacture was especially dense on the eastern side of the town from Mabgate to Marsh Lane, where labourers' dwellings mixed unhealthily with the fumes of the dyeing and fulling mills. The woollen industry ceased abruptly a mile to the north of the town centre in the well-wooded surroundings of Headingley and Potter Newton, creating a social distinction that has lasted into the twenty-first century.

In the centre there had clearly been much rebuilding as the houses noted in the earlier survey to be 'generally all of timber' had by the turn of the century given way to something much more substantial. The diarist Celia Fiennes came this way in 1698 and her views (again more or less expressed in today's English) were enthusiastic:

*Leeds is a large town, with several large streets clean and well pitched and good houses all built of stone. Some have good gardens, steps up to them and walls in front of them. This is esteemed the wealthiest town of its bigness in the country – they have provision so plentiful that they may live with very little expense and get much variety.*

Yet this was still only the beginning. Just one year later, Leeds cloth merchants initiated a venture that was to take the town to even greater heights.

**Leeds was described as 'an ancient market town' as early as the reign of Charles I. A century later its markets were 'a prodigy not to be equalled in the world' Today the city has its Kirkgate Market, the entrance to which is on the left side of this photograph. In the background is the parish church of St Peter, which replaced a medieval structure in 1838.**

# The canal age

In 1699 an Act of Parliament was obtained to create the Aire & Calder Navigation. Completed five years later, the scheme meant that it was possible for sizeable boats to proceed beyond the tidal limit of the Aire at Knottingley right into the heart of Leeds. It was the start of a steady transformation in transport links as hitherto cloth and other products had had to be taken on a tedious land journey to reach the River Ouse at Selby. This involved trains of packhorses proceeding slowly along what was described as 'a narrow hollow way little wider than a ditch, barely allowing the passage of a vehicle drawn in a single line'.

Leeds merchants were now able to tap into markets, especially in southern Europe and the Americas, which had previously been the preserve of their competitors in London, Norwich and Exeter. It was a two-way traffic, the cost of transport being sufficiently reduced to allow long wools to be brought in from Lincolnshire and thus paving the way for expansion of the all-conquering worsted industry. Leeds became the gateway for much of the West Riding, with production of broad cloths almost quadrupling in the fifty years from 1727.

In his celebrated *Tour through the Whole Island of Great Britain*, published in 1725, Daniel Defoe noted that the Tuesday and Saturday cloth markets at Leeds were 'a prodigy not to be equalled in the world'. Clothiers set off in the early hours to be in Briggate for 6.0am in summer and 7.0am in winter in time for an event that had similar temporary tables to a car boot sale but was clearly in a different league. It was not uncommon for cloth to the value of £20,000 – over £1.5 million at today's prices – to be bought and sold in little more than an hour. When it was all over the traders adjourned to the nearby inns for 'Brigg-shot' – traditional refreshment comprising a pot of ale, a noggin of porridge and a trencher of boiled or roast beef.

Increasing prosperity went hand-in-hand with the more roistering facets of eighteenth-century life. The *Leeds Intelligencer*, founded in 1754 and the forerunner of today's *Yorkshire Post*, reported a continuing saga of cockfighting, bull baiting and highway robbery. In one of its first issues it noted that a cloth maker returning from market was stopped by 'two men on horseback, one of which brandishing a sword before his face and demanding his money, took from him two guineas in gold and two shillings and sixpence in silver'.

Money that was not stolen could easily be lost in gambling. In desperation, Leeds magistrates attempted in 1757 to reign in a multitude of temptations by what amounted to bribery:

*Publicans permitting journeymen, labourers, servants or apprentices to play cards, dice, draughts, shuffle- board, Mississippi, billiard tables, skittles, ninepins or any other instrument of gaming in their houses, alehouses or grounds shall forfeit 40 shillings for the first offence, for every subsequent offence £10 to be levied by distress and sale, a quarter to the informer, the rest to the poor.*

Despite such strictures the town continued to enjoy times of plenty, in large measure due to what Defoe described as 'inexhaustible stores' of coal. Soon after the Aire was made navigable, small collieries were established near its banks with the coal being transported from pit to barge by horse and cart. Revolution was in the air when Charles Brandling of Gosforth Hall on Tyneside inherited estates and collieries at Middleton on the south side of Leeds. He came from an area that had pioneered the transport of coal by waggonways, primitive wooden railways using horse power, and lost no time in bringing this system to Leeds. The Middleton Railway was duly opened from his collieries to Casson Close, near Leeds Bridge, on September 20th, 1758, when church bells were rung, cannons fired and 'a general joy appeared in every face'.

Brandling immediately gained a monopoly of the town's supply of coal, although he did not retain this position without a struggle and in 1781 was party to an aggrieved whinge in the *Leeds Intelligencer*: 'Great impositions have been put on the public as well as Charles Brandling Esq by the vendors of coals in the neighbourhood of Leeds, several of whom have sold an inferior sort to their customers as and for Mr Brandling's coals.' It probably cut little ice, and no doubt Brandling's income was increased when the Leeds Pottery was built alongside the waggonway and became a national institution in the four decades from 1780 to 1820.

Improvements in transport links with other centres were hindered by the hilly terrain, although in 1741 a comprehensive scheme provided for the creation of turnpikes – the equivalent of today's toll

**Completion of the Aire & Calder Navigation in 1704 enabled Leeds to become the economic gateway for much of the West Riding, increasing trade to such an extent that it ultimately struggled to cope with what was on offer. *Jane*, a restored 1880 sailing barge, recalls a past era at Thwaite Mills.**

motorways – that would connect Leeds with Wakefield, Barnsley and Sheffield to the south and Halifax and Manchester to the west. Stagecoach services were now ambitiously advertised as 'flying machines on steel springs' that linked Leeds with London in three days, although in reality it often took much longer and the journey was typically dirty, tedious and bone shaking. The twenty-five miles from Leeds to York could take eight hours to cover by coach and it was often quicker to walk.

More remarkable than any of the turnpikes was one of the great engineering feats of its age, the Leeds & Liverpool Canal, commenced in the mid-1770s but not completed across the challenging Pennine watershed for another forty years. It was a development that fostered continuing expansion, epitomised in 1791 when John Marshall built the largest flax-spinning mill in England close to the canal at Water Lane, Holbeck. Establishing Leeds as an important centre of the linen trade, it boasted some 4,000 spindles. The mill was extended five times before its final vast addition in an extraordinary Egyptian style, with a façade modelled on the Temple of Horus at Edfu and a chimney designed as a replica of Cleopatra's Needle.

More massive still was Bean Ing woollen mill, erected in 1792 at a cost of £17,000 in what were then open fields close to the banks of the Aire. Its builder was a thirty-year-old cloth merchant, Benjamin Gott, who was determined to include under one roof all the processes of woollen manufacture from washing the raw wool to dyeing the finished product (the building's length was such that the offices of Yorkshire Post Newspapers, a multi-storey  k, the Crowne Plaza Hotel and a large modern office block all now extend along its former fron became the first mill in the West Riding to have a steam engine constructed by the famous firn lton & Watt. Gott was fortunate to open his new mill at a time when the woollen trade was booming. By 1797 its 12,000 workers were making 4,000 broad cloths per annum, demonstrating the old adage that it is 'an ill wind that blows no good' as they were mainly cheap clothing and blankets for armed forces engaged in the Napoleonic wars.

Industrialisation had come to Leeds with a vengeance and Gott was now one of the world's largest factory employers. He became a great patron of the arts and a philanthropist, helping the poorer members of the community living in houses that had grown up around his factory. Gott and Marshall, along with Edward Baines, proprietor of the *Leeds Mercury*, came to dominate the social and political life of the town. Baines, a colourful figure dismissed by William Cobbett as the 'Great Liar of the North', played a leading role in establishing the first Yorkshire Mechanics' Institute. He later wrote in his paper that its objects were 'to promote the intellectual and moral improvement of young men of the industrial classes, to counteract the temptation to sensual indulgences by which they are beset, to supplement an imperfect education, and to introduce to the study of science and art those whose talents or vocations especially led them to such pursuits'.

The population of Leeds reached an estimated 16,380 in 1771 and then almost doubled to 30,669 in the first official census thirty years later. It was now an industrial powerhouse and the seventh largest town in England, far outstripping York, which had hitherto been considered 'a northern metropolis'. Symbolic of the age was Richard Paley, an entrepreneur combining the considerable talents of soap-boiler, ironfounder, potash manufacturer and property developer, who built two steam-powered cotton mills in 1790. Ultimately he went bankrupt and the embryo Leeds cotton industry failed, but other trades that took root and flourished ranged from dressmaking to sugar refining and shoemaking to printing. By the beginning of the nineteenth century Leeds had overtaken Wakefield as the West Riding's leading centre of leather production and soon had the largest leather market outside London.

[ 1 ]      N° 22

*An* ACT *for Eſtabliſhing Agreements made between* Charles Brandling, *Eſquire, and other Perſons, Proprietors of Lands, for laying down a Waggon-Way, in order for the better ſupplying the* Town *and Neighbourhood of* Leeds, *in the County of* York, *with Coals.*

**Dereas** *Charles Brandling,* Eſquire, Lord of the Manor of *Middleton,* in the County of *York,* is Owner and Proprietor of divers Coal-works, Mines, Veins, and Seams of Coals, lying and being within the ſaid Manor of *Middleton,* and Places adjacent ; and hath propoſed, and is willing to engage and undertake, to furniſh and ſupply the Inhabitants of the Town of *Leeds* with Coals for their neceſſary Uſe and Conſumption, at the Rate or Price of Four Pence Three Farthings a Corf, containing in Weight about Two hundred and Ten Pounds, and in Meaſure Seven thouſand Six hundred and Eighty cubical Inches, for the Term of Sixty Years, to commence from the Second Day of *January* One thouſand Seven hundred and Fifty-eight, and for ſuch further Term, or longer Time, as the ſaid Mines, or any of them, ſhall continue to be uſed and wrought ; and, at his own Charge and Expence, to carry and convey, or cauſe to be carried and conveyed, from

A                                    his

Title page of the Act of Parliament that allowed Charles Brandling to build a waggonway from his collieries at Middleton to the centre of Leeds. It gave him a monopoly of the town's supply of coal and was also used to transport the products of the famous Leeds Pottery. (David Joy collection)

Leeds had become the centre of the West Riding leather industry by the beginning of the nineteenth century. It spawned many related trades, such as these premises of John Tullis & Son, leather belt makers, at the junction of Mill Hill and Bishopgate Street.

Continuing to play a dominant role were the affluent cloth merchants, mainly descended from substantial yeomen or smaller landed families and having close business and social links with neighbouring gentry. They in turn prospered in an environment that had much to do with the foresight of their ancestors in turning the town into a borough back in 1626. David Hey sums it up neatly in his book *Yorkshire from AD 1000*: 'The town's corporate status gave it a dignity that was rarely matched by other West Riding towns. Leeds was as fashionable a social centre as many a county town, with attractions ranging from horse-racing on Chapeltown moor and cockfighting to a theatre which brought performers from London, dancing, card assemblies and musical concerts.'

# The railway age

The Napoleonic wars did more than just create boom conditions at Benjamin Gott's Bean Ing mill. They also meant that Leeds was ushered into the railway age at a much earlier date than any comparable towns. The price of horses and fodder increased to such an extent that John Blenkinsop, appointed agent at Middleton Colliery in 1808, forthwith started to experiment with the then embryo steam locomotive.

He was fortunate in that among the men of genius attracted to Leeds was Matthew Murray, who as an out-of-work blacksmith walked the sixty miles from Stockton with nothing more than a bag of tools on his back. He soon became the leading partner in the engineering firm of Fenton, Murray & Wood at the Round Foundry, Water Lane. Here he consolidated the Leeds tradition for mill engines, machinery and plant that had been fostered by John Smeaton, best remembered for the Eddystone lighthouse. Murray built his own home, Holbeck Lodge, reputedly the first dwelling in Britain to incorporate underfloor steam central heating and thus always known as 'Steam Hall'.

Remembered as the 'father of Leeds engineering', Murray was one of the few men capable of putting Blenkinsop's ideas into practice. He did so triumphantly, with his proud creation *Prince Regent* being tested in June 1812. When it went into daily service two months later it was the first locomotive in the world to be used commercially on rails. Replacing fourteen horses and able to draw twenty-seven wagons at almost four miles per hour, the 'Prince' helped the colliery to achieve a record output of 100,000 tons in 1814.

Disaster struck four years later in an incident described by George Stephenson: "The driver had been in liquor and had put a considerable load on the safety valve, so that upon going forward the engine blew up and the man was killed."

Throughout this period Leeds continued to experience scarcely controllable growth. The town had become the acknowledged woollen capital of England and its trade with Europe was still expanding. Existing roads were utterly inadequate and the Aire & Calder Navigation was struggling to cope with the traffic on offer.

With the proven success of the Stockton & Darlington Railway, the decision was taken in 1830 to build a line from Leeds to Selby, where trains would connect with fast steam packets running down the Ouse and Humber to Hull. The Leeds terminus was on the north side of the Aire at Marsh Lane, then

The Stockton & Darlington Railway is often acclaimed as the first in the world, but in fact Leeds was there thirteen years earlier in 1812 when Matthew Murray put his pioneer locomotive into service on the Middleton Railway. It is seen here at the line's terminus alongside the River Aire and close to Leeds parish church. (David Joy collection)

Railways in Leeds expanded at a prodigious rate in the mid-nineteenth century with passenger facilities becoming focused on two separate termini. Leeds Central handled express services to London, as seen here with The White Rose about to depart for King's Cross. On the left are the luxurious coaches of the Queen of Scots Pullman, which linked London and Glasgow via Leeds. Central station closed in 1967 when services were transferred to nearby Leeds City. (Eric Treacy)

described as 'one of the most unpleasant and dirty parts of the town'. It was here that a crowd of over 40,000 greeted the first return train on the line's ceremonial opening on September 22nd, 1834.

The journey from Leeds to Selby was shortened from thirty miles by waterways to twenty miles by rail, the immediate upshot being that the Aire & Calder Navigation reduced its tolls by almost half. The railway had as its most notable feature the 640-metre long Richmond Tunnel, just outside Marsh Lane, the first in the world through which passengers were drawn by a locomotive. Many of the early travellers were terror-stricken at the thought of a 'steam monster' in such stygian depths, and so the interior was whitewashed and copper plates installed at the foot of the air shafts in order to reflect light. It was claimed that a newspaper could be read inside the tunnel!

Leeds went on to play a pivotal role in the railway age with George Stephenson building its initial main lines south towards London and west to Manchester, their basic outline and function being remarkably similar to that of today's M1 and M62 motorways. The first main-line terminus was at Hunslet Lane, far removed from the town centre as a result of continuing opposition from the still powerful canal interests.

The surrounding parish of Hunslet soon became one of the most concentrated centres of locomotive building in the world, with such famous firms as John Fowler, Hudswell Clarke and the Hunslet Engine Company forming a near continuous sprawl of workshops destined to produce over ten thousand steam locomotives for home and export.

Among the many noted engineers who worked there was David Joy (1825 – 1903), who kept some racy and well-informed diaries of his experiences that provide one of the few eyewitness accounts of this extraordinary era. An innovator in the best traditions of the age, he is remembered for perfecting a new form of locomotive valve gear but his many other inventions included an organ blower, a steam hammer, a revolving gun and an improved earth closet!

A huge area south of the river became one of the world's largest centres of locomotive manufacture. The last of the major builders to survive was the Hunslet Engine Company, which produced its final steam locomotive in 1971. Press photographers assembled to record the scene before the narrow-gauge saddle tank left for Indonesia. (David Joy collection)

Boar Lane was one of the central streets widened in the late Victorian era to create a new shopping area. Here it is seen in a transitional phase after the first motor cars had made their appearance but had yet to swamp the city. A Headingley-bound tram is heading towards the camera and, on its right, goods are still being delivered by horse and cart.

# High noon

Leeds was by now a town of many talents and trades. A plentiful supply of cheap coal, a large labour force, entrepreneurial endeavour and constant attention to improved transport meant that it could do little wrong. When the Whig politician Lord Brougham spoke at a Reform dinner in 1830 he effusively commented: 'Leeds is the seat of the greatest commercial community in Yorkshire. Whether we regard its population, its wealth, its intelligence or its ingenuity, the skill or the industry of its inhabitants, it is among the most important of all the towns which stud the British Empire.'

By mid-century the town was home to thirty-seven flax mills employing 9,500 people, mainly women and children, but there were twice as many workers in the woollen and worsted industries. There was also considerable trade in carpets, cotton yarn and silk, all of which created an important market for machines produced in the local engineering works. Casting of wrought iron in local foundries became part of a great metalworking tradition, which only began to slip away as local reserves of iron ore were exhausted.

Brewing came to prominence when Joshua Tetley, head of an established family of malsters in Armley, bought a small brewery in Salem Place, Hunslet. After a shaky start, the business expanded rapidly and eventually in 1890 acquired its first public house, The Duke William, which still stands in the brewery yard. Consumption of ale was by this time so enormous that the company had some thirty coopers engaged in the ancient craft of making and repairing wooden beer barrels.

Cloth manufacture decreased from the 1850s with flax production almost ceasing in the face of foreign competition. Leeds took it all in its stride and became known as the town of ninety-nine trades, with decline in one sector being replaced by expansion in many other fields. One activity would soon spawn another as instanced in the leather trade. By mid-century there were not only some twenty tanneries employing almost two thousand people but manufacture of footwear was flourishing to the extent that Leeds would ultimately produce 100,000 pairs of boots a week.

Similarly, chemical companies rapidly expanded to supply dyestuffs for woollen and leather manufactures as well as oils and lubricants for the engineering industries. Epitomising the new era of diversity was the firm of Smith Dixon & Lodge at Harper Street Chemical Works, which managed to combine the production of blackcurrant and glycerin cough medicine, soap, metal and furniture polish, baking powder and children's teething powders!

Handsome arcades appeared in Leeds at the close of the nineteenth century, many of them replacing dingy ginnels and yards going back to the medieval origins of the city. This is the County Arcade, off Briggate, completed in 1898. Happily, its magnificent roof was replaced after destruction by fire in the 1970s.

As might be expected in a town destined to go down in history as the birthplace of such disparate inventions as Portland cement, moving pictures and traffic lights, there was no shortage of innovation and enterprise. The long-established wire works of Procter Brothers prospered through making the Little Nipper Mouse Trap, brainchild by one Herbert Atkinson. Two brothers, Thomas and James Braine, perfected the oilcan, which they began to produce in a building in Hunslet Road rented for 7s 6d a week. Running short of capital they advertised in the *Yorkshire Post* for a loan, duly answered by a clergyman who provided his life savings of £500 and happily had them repaid many times over.

A development destined to have massive consequences occurred in 1851 when Isaac Singer patented his revolutionary sewing machine. Five years later John Barran installed some examples in his Leeds factory, thus pioneering the local clothing trade that was to become more dominant here than in any other town in Britain. Its rise to pre-eminence was helped by a rapid growth of the railway network, which not only took lines into new stations in the heart of Leeds but also enabled cheap cloths such as shoddy and mungo to be readily transported from other manufacturing areas.

The clothing trade reached its zenith with establishment of the famous business of Montague Burton & Co, 'the largest tailors in the world', founded in Sheffield with a capital of £100 but soon transferring to Leeds. Here it eventually built a huge complex in Hudson Road with a canteen that accommodated 8,000 employees at one sitting, the *Leeds Mercury* noting that they could have 'a mid-day meal of meat, potatoes, vegetables, bread and pudding for ten pence'.

The town also played a pivotal role in the early days of retail stores, with Thomas Lipton, pioneer of the multiple grocery trade in Scotland, opening his first English shop here in 1881. He was followed by a penniless Polish refugee, Michael Marks, who borrowed £5 and in 1884 opened a Penny Bazaar in Kirkgate market. Success was such that he soon teamed up with a Leeds cashier. His name was Thomas Spencer and the rest, as they say, is history.

Leeds created a central shopping area by widening Briggate and Boar Lane and building a number of handsome arcades. It was in Boar Lane that the Grand Pygmalion, the town's first departmental store, opened its doors in 1888. Setting a new trend in the sense that merchandise could be physically handled, it was at the same time highly traditional in devoting the whole of one floor to dining and living rooms as well as mostly separate bedrooms for fifty of the one hundred staff employed.

Expansion of industry and trade went hand in hand with a growth in cultural activities. The reference and central libraries were opened in 1871-72 followed by the Yorkshire College, forerunner of the university, in 1874. Members of wealthy families, and especially the descendants of Benjamin Gott, were now touring the Continent to collect art treasures that formed the basis of the new Art Gallery opened in 1888.

The necessity of private patronage was clearly demonstrated in 1875 when both the existing theatres in Leeds were destroyed by fire. The upshot was a meeting of 'influential gentlemen' determined to build a theatre worthy of the town and of 'the support of the very best people'. The occupations of the first ten directors clearly showed that it was to be largely financed by 'new' money from the city's burgeoning industry. There were three merchants, a machine maker, a machinist and engineer, an ironmaster, a flax spinner, a maltster, and a card, comb and pin manufacturer. The tenth – and the only member of the professions – was a surgeon. Meetings were reputedly convivial affairs, the directors having their own personal bottles of whisky. With true Yorkshire thrift, they were stored away after each meeting, suitably marked with a line showing the amount that had been consumed! It may have all helped to ensure that the magnificent Grand Theatre in Upper Briggate was duly opened in November 1878.

Leeds became a city in 1893, a move that reflected pride in its past achievements. Fiercely independent, it may already have realised that the days of unlimited growth were on the wane. It had for many glorious years been one of the great trading centres of the greatest country in the world, supplying a myriad of goods to all corners of the globe, but now foreign competition and ultimately war lay round the corner. For the moment it could at least look back on the high noon of the Victorian age and arguably its greatest achievement of all.

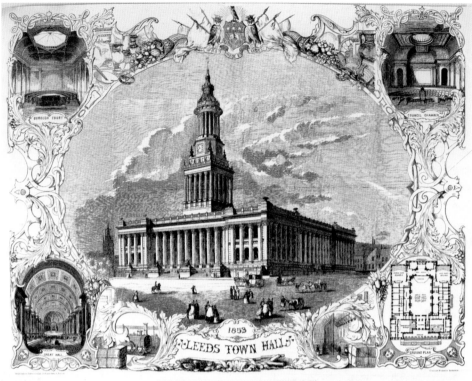

The populace of Leeds had its appetite for the new Town Hall whetted by this splendid example of Victorian illustration, presented with the *Leeds Mercury* in September 1853 a month after the foundation stone had been laid with immense pomp and ceremony. The tower, already the subject of much wrangling over cost, was never completed in the form shown.

# Brodrick's grand project

There has long been intense rivalry between Leeds and Bradford. Close geographically but never part of one great whole in the sense of Manchester and Salford, they spent much of the nineteenth century eyeing each other with mutual mistrust and suspicion. When in 1849 a public meeting was called in Bradford to initiate what became the imposing St George's Hall, it was inevitable that Leeds would take steps to go one better. It set up a Town Hall Committee, which consulted Joseph Paxton, designer of the Crystal Palace, and sent deputations to look at similar trail-blazing ventures in Manchester and Liverpool. It then decided to hold an open competition for designs for a new Town Hall. Sir Charles Barry, then supervising construction of the new House of Commons, was brought in as the project's distinguished advisor.

The results of the competition must have caused some surprise. Relegated to second place were Lockwood and Mawson, noted architects who would logically have been the obvious choice. In an age when pride and prejudice went hand in hand, they may not entirely have helped their cause by being Bradford based and the designers of St George's Hall. There was also a lingering suspicion that the winner was chosen simply because he would be cheaper. Cuthbert Brodrick, a young Hull architect, was only twenty-nine when he prepared the plans and his previous experience was limited to little more than a railway station at Withernsea. His mother reputedly tried to dissuade him from entering the competition on the grounds that he was bound to fail.

No sooner had the architect been chosen in February 1853, and a contract let for the Town Hall's

**The completed Town Hall in all its magnificence. Like virtually every aspect of the building, the modified design for the tower cost considerably more than estimated. The lions, fashioned from Portland stone from Dorset, were created by sending a carver to the Regents Park Zoological Gardens to model the real thing!**

construction at a cost of £41,835, than a bitter and protracted argument broke out over whether it should or should not have a tower. It turned into a dispute between the more economically minded inhabitants of the town and what were termed the 'cultural classes' led by prominent Leeds doctor, J D Heaton, who nailed his colours firmly to the mast: "If a noble municipal palace that might fairly vie with some of the best Town Halls of the Continent were to be erected in the middle of their hitherto squalid and unbeautiful town, it would become a practical admonition to the populace of the value of beauty and art, and in course of time men would learn live up to it."

Verging on arrogance, this lofty statement nevertheless carried the day and a great 225ft high tower was added to the initial designs. This was the first of many issues that were to dog the project from the outset. Labour problems and difficulties in obtaining suitable stone from quarries at Rawdon were

The Victoria Hall at the centre of the Town Hall was deliberately designed to be bigger than anything comparable inside St George's Hall in Bradford. It is dominated by the organ, installed at a cost of £6,000 and described at the time as a 'gigantic instrument that excited considerable interest amongst organists and amateurs throughout Europe'.

factors that culminated in the contractor going bankrupt in March 1857, fourteen months after the work should have been completed. Parts of the building, including the controversial tower, were still unfinished in the summer of 1858 when Queen Victoria and the Prince Consort agreed to open the Town Hall on September 7th. Quite what the worthies of Bradford thought of the official invitation referring to Leeds as 'the real capital of the West Riding' is open to question.

The two-day royal visit, which attracted crowds estimated at over 150,000, was both a great occasion and the cause of considerable expenditure. Over 32,000 children from Sunday Schools were somehow mustered on Woodhouse Moor, flags and triumphal arches were everywhere, a statue of the Queen completed at a cost of a thousand guineas dominated the Town Hall vestibule and there was a great luncheon for nearly four hundred guests.

It was not until 1859 that the Town Hall was finally finished in all its glory with striking internal decoration, cut-glass chandeliers and a magnificent organ that was then the largest in Europe. One writer commented that it was 'the best place in Britain to see what it looked like on the inside of a wedding cake'. Outside, a vast terrace created to increase the commanding position, a flight of twenty steps and the imposing black lions completed the picture.

Now it was time to tot up the total cost. It came to £122,000, almost three times the original estimate. Pride and a latent desire to outshine anything that Bradford could offer had proved horrendously expensive. Leeds was forced to come down to earth and cost cutting became a watchword in the council's affairs for many a year.

Brodrick's creation endures as an impressive monument to his age. By the time it was completed he had finished work on the distinctive Wells House hydro in Ilkley and in 1860 went on to complete the unorthodox Leeds Corn Exchange with its magnificent glass roof reminiscent of the hull of a ship.

**Cuthbert Brodrick emerged relatively unscathed from the financial controversy surrounding Leeds Town Hall and moved on to design the fascinating Corn Exchange. The semi-elliptical ribs of the roof have been described as creating 'a curious, somewhat giddy effect'.**

# Slums and squalor

There is nothing unusual in great public projects running wildly over budget. Today it inevitably creates an outcry that the money could have been better spent easing the plight of the disadvantaged. Such should also have been the case in Victorian Leeds, but social and health problems existed on so great a scale that it was easier to brush them under the carpet. In the fifty years from 1801 the population had trebled to 101,343, creating such vast deprivation that there was neither the organisation, the power or, more importantly, the will to remedy matters.

Many inhabitants were densely packed into cramped quarters, as instanced by the infamous Boot and Shoe Yard that in the late 1830s housed 341 people in 57 tiny rooms. An official report in 1842 noted that in a typical weaver's dwelling 'the kitchen is not only appropriated to culinary purposes, but is the house, the sleeping room, the hen-house and the piggery; whilst upstairs are three or four looms, all but touching each other; and perhaps, in a corner, a bed on the floor for one of the owners of these looms'. South of the river, terraces of back-to-back houses were crowded among the mills, foundries and railway workshops. By 1850 there were 360 streets of back-to-backs and the great social gulf between the 'haves' and 'have nots' was widening, In the first half of the nineteenth century three times more houses were built in Holbeck and Hunslet than in the more affluent northern suburbs such as Headingley and Chapel Allerton.

Overcrowding was made worse by primitive sanitation. The Health of Towns Committee did not mince its words when it described the streets in the Calls area of Leeds as 'more or less deficient in sewerage, unpaved, full of holes, sometimes untenantable by the overflowing of sewers and other more offensive drains, with ash holes, etc, exposed to public view and never emptied'.

Water supplies were equally inadequate. 'The Aire below is doubly dyed and dammed, the air above with lurid smoke is crammed' quipped the poet William Osburn. Yet this did not stop some two thousand homes taking water from the river, with most of the rest relying on wells and supplies carted round the streets. It is scarcely surprising that dysentery and typhus were among the major killers of the age, with cholera claiming over 700 victims in Leeds in 1832 and over two thousand in a more serious outbreak in 1848-49. Slum dwellers were always the first victims and their life expectancy was truly appalling. In the 1840s the average age of death for mill operatives and labourers in Leeds was nineteen, compared with twenty-seven for tradesmen and shopkeepers and forty-four for the gentry and captains of industry.

There was no lack of condemnation. Charles Dickens, a fine journalist as well as a noted writer, dismissed Leeds as 'a beastly place, one of the nastiest places I know'. As Richard Hoggart later related in his classic work *Uses of Literacy*, conditions in Hunslet and Holbeck represented the most dire aspects of privation and segregation. Hunslet was 'meanly built, consisting of narrow and dirty lanes', while Holbeck was 'one of the most crowded, one of the most filthy and one of the most unhealthy villages in the county of York'.

Leeds was fortunate in having some outstanding medical visionaries, who as early as 1833 took part in an indignant meeting that demanded drainage, proper sewage disposal and street paving. Yet little progress was made until 1852 when the council bought out the Leeds Waterworks company and brought supplies under its own control. In the same year work began on a long overdue project to construct sewers for the main streets. Another landmark in health terms was the opening in 1869 of the famous

**Red House Inn Yard, Quarry Hill, epitomised the squalid living conditions that existed in much of Leeds throughout the nineteenth and early twentieth centuries. Fresh air there was little; green grass there was none. (Leeds Central Library)**

Shuttered windows were no doubt a necessary feature of the dreary-looking Tunstall's Fold, also in the Quarry Hill district. Today it seems strange that a country then leading the world should tolerate such conditions, but truth to tell there had never before been anything like the Victorian economic miracle and no one knew how to cope with its down side. (Leeds Central Library)

LEEDS FROM HOLBECK JUNCTION.

**Leeds in 1868 from a contemporary engraving. Factory chimneys belch forth smoke everywhere but the Town Hall rises above it all on the skyline. Although conditions gradually began to improve, J.D. Kohl writing sixteen years later still found it 'a dirty, smoky disagreeable town – perhaps the ugliest and least attractive town in all England'.**

Leeds General Infirmary, successor to an earlier establishment stipulating in its rules that 'patients be supplied with a pair of clean bed sheets once in three weeks'.

It took until the 1870s before conditions improved to the extent that deaths from cholera and typhus were virtually eliminated. At the same time, wounds over the cost of the Town Hall had healed and there was a new civic pride in the elimination of slums and the creation of broad thoroughfares, spacious squares and new public buildings. In 1872 the Council acquired the 689-acre Roundhay Park for £139,000 and provided Leeds with what was hailed as the finest open space of its kind in England, complete with Waterloo Lake dug by French prisoners after the Napoleonic wars. It was a development only eclipsed many years later when the great Tudor mansion of Temple Newsam and almost a thousand acres of grounds were acquired for a bargain £35,000.

Despite such initiatives, the earlier spirit of improvement was not maintained and on the eve of the First World War around half of the houses in Leeds were more than seventy years old. Two-thirds of these were back-to-backs, some 75,000 of which still existed in the 1930s. Often they were infested with bugs and it was common for council workers to be sprayed with disinfectant before entering them. Social worker Brenda Hall recalled that they were 'terrible houses, one up, one down, long streets of them, and every so often two knocked down and a row of filthy lavatories in their place'.

It was not until 1933, when a Labour council was returned by a narrow majority, that Leeds appointed its first city architect, R A H Livett, and embarked on a massive programme of slum clearance and the creation of suburban estates. Then seen as the jewel in the crown and hailed as 'Europe's most progressive housing scheme', Quarry Hill was developed between 1935 and 1941 to become the largest council estate in England with 938 high-rise flats providing accommodation for 3,280 people. Reminiscent in scale of municipal housing in Berlin and Vienna, it was described by Nikolaus Pevsner as 'somewhat forbidding though undeniably impressive'. Six years after it was completed the Leeds Medical Officer of Health proudly announced that infant mortality at Quarry Hill was only 10.9 per thousand compared with 13.4 in the remainder of the city. This massive development undoubtedly solved a problem of its time but housing of this kind ultimately proved deeply unpopular and the flats were demolished in 1978 after a life of less than forty years.

Roundhay Park, purchased by Leeds Council in 1872, has proved invaluable both for recreation and major events. This aerial view was taken during the Michael Jackson concert on August 29th, 1988.

Revolutionary at the time but ultimately flawed, the world-famous Quarry Hill Flats are seen here under construction in 1936. Stretching into the distance are row upon row of back-to-backs, many of which would be demolished once the flats were completed five years later. Some have already gone as indicated by the open space at top right with the parallel lines of the former streets still visible.

Leeds in the golden age of the tramcar, with three efficient and pollution-free trams working their way along Duncan Street, the eastwards extension of Boar Lane. Alan Bennett has pointed out that Leeds trams had 'a song to sing' and were 'a cheap and sensible way of getting from point A to point B, and with a bit of poetry thrown in'.

# The age of the tram

Most of the occupants of the leafy northern suburbs of Leeds probably never got to Quarry Hill, just as they had no desire to visit Holbeck and Hunslet in the nineteenth century. Helping the middle classes to move away from the smoke and noise were the horse-drawn omnibuses that linked the centre of Leeds with Headingley and Roundhay from 1858 onwards. They gave way to horse trams and then steam trams, but a key date was January 8th, 1892, when Leeds became the first town in England to operate electric tramcars.

The initial service was from Sheepscar to Roundhay, the private operators opting to serve the more affluent areas of Leeds where the most profit could be made. It was not until the corporation took over running rights that a deliberate policy was implemented to build routes into underdeveloped and working-class areas. Leeds came to have a superb tramway system, which by the 1930s was carrying 170 million passengers a year, in large measure due to a maximum fare of just two pence. Many of the routes had their own 'reserved tracks' segregated from road traffic, while others headed directly across country to appease ungrateful slum dwellers re-housed in new estates on the windy heights of Middleton.

In the post-war years the city centre started a remorseless march towards traffic congestion. An innovative scheme to put the trams underground was way ahead of its time and was shelved. Instead, they became the subject of years of political infighting over whether or not the system should be retained and modernised. In the end the last, sad services ran on November 7th, 1959, and a great opportunity was lost. Trams have triumphantly returned to the streets of Manchester, and with less success to those of Sheffield, but proposals for a light railway system in Leeds reached an advanced stage only to be defeated by a government putting cost considerations before environmental benefits.

Traditional tramcars have engendered extraordinary affection. Devotees of the writings of Alan Bennett can be forgiven for not putting a modest paperback *Leeds in the age of the tram* on their list of required reading, but in fact it opens with a three-page foreword that vividly portrays his memories of tram travel during the war – complete with father's 'huge and threatening' double bass. After the war the family moved to Far Headingley and lived with the sounds of 'trams getting up speed for the hill before Weetwood Lane, trams spinning down from West Park, trams shunted around in the sheds in the middle of the night, the scraping of wheels, the clanging of the bell'.

To Bennett, trams were 'bare and bony, transport reduced to its basic elements, and they had a song to sing'. And he is in no doubt about later developments: 'I was away at university when they started to phase them out, Leeds as always in too much of a hurry to get to the future, and so doing the wrong thing. If trams ever come back, though, they should come back not as curiosities nor, God help us, as part of the heritage, but as a cheap and sensible way of getting from point A to point B, and with a bit of poetry thrown in.'

**Next page: Horse trams still held sway in Briggate in the 1890s. This view looks up the busy street from the junction with Boar Lane. Beyond the gaslamp standard in the foreground is one of the earlier horse-drawn omnibuses.**

# Transformation

Leeds in the heyday of its trams was an utterly different city to that of today. Most of its buildings were soot-blackened, with factory chimneys dominating the skyline and fires burning in countless household grates. Leisure activities looked to the big screen on a scale that now seems inconceivable, with the city having no less than seventy-one licensed cinemas in 1938. Engineering and clothing were still the dominant industries, but printing was also now a major employer, with the Crown Point works of Alf Cooke boasting that it was the largest in the world. Equally famous was John Waddington Ltd, not just for printing but for devising games of many kinds including the all-conquering Monopoly.

It was possible to lose everything in reality as well as on a board game, the depression of the 1930s meaning that pawnshops flourished as never before.. Yet despite the difficult times, civic pride continued to be evident in a complete rebuilding of the old Headrow to create both an 80ft wide shopping street and a more spacious feel to the city centre. Round the corner in Calverley Street, the Civic Hall was opened by King George V in 1933 but could not hope to match the Town Hall in grandeur. Pevsner later tactfully commented that its towers 'impress from a distance'. Three years later came the opening of the University's Brotherton Library, a vast circular building with green marble pillars that was designed to hold a million volumes.

**Prior to the Second World War there was an amazing total of over seventy cinemas in Leeds of all shapes and sizes. Often the frontage was quite modest, as suggested in this 1939 view of the Rialto in Briggate where patrons were being urged to enjoy the last week of *Woman Tamer*.**

The almost triangular Civic Hall, completed in 1933. Architecturally it has been summed up as being 'as ambitious as the Town Hall but not quite as self-confident'. In the post-war era it formed a key link in 'a vision of twentieth century utopia' with a series of spacious buildings stretching past new Central Colleges right up to the University.

In 1935 the LMS Railway boldly decided to build a new Queens Hotel at Leeds City station. Designed by W Hamlyn, the company's architect, and W Curtis Green, who had been responsible for the interior of London's Dorchester, it was in many respects revolutionary. With each of the 206 bedrooms having its own bathroom, fitted wardrobe and telephone, it was also the first new hotel in Britain to have air conditioning and central heating in all its rooms. Rich decorations that included goatskin wall linings and walnut furnishings may have been part of the brief to create a 'cosmopolitan classic with decided transatlantic bias', but proved too much for the average Yorkshire customer and were received with far from universal acclaim.

Leeds emerged from the Second World War relatively unscathed compared with other Yorkshire cities such as Hull and Sheffield, suffering only nine bombing raids and the loss of seventy-seven of its inhabitants. In a post-war boom that has never been equalled, it was soon able to embark on the construction of new housing estates spread over a wide area. Nevertheless, much of old Leeds remained with shops at almost every street corner and such household names as the Co-op, Thrift Stores, the Maypole and Home & Colonial Stores still holding sway. Horse-drawn delivery vehicles were a common sight and small boys were on hand to deliver groceries on large shop bikes complete with tailor-made basket.

It was at times a drab and dismal era, epitomised by the spluttering yellow glow of the twenty thousand gas lamps that still dimly lit the streets. This was especially so south of the river. Writing her outstanding book *Yorkshire West Riding* in 1950, Lettice Cooper was brutally honest:

*Here in this workshop of the city, the prevailing colour is black, and the sky, even on a sunny day, is obscured by a pall of smoke. Here are the inevitable terraces of brick houses, the yards and side streets draped on Mondays with lines of washing that begin to gather soot again before they are dry. Here are the dingy pubs that yet look like home to their regular clients.*

The twenty thousand gas lamps that still existed in Leeds at the start of the 1950s were gradually whittled away or converted to electricity. A surviving example in Sweet Street, Holbeck, receives a last polish in 1979 before being sent to Germany. Carrying out the work is Eddie Mullan, a lift engineer with the City of Leeds Public Works Department.

Little expense was spared in 1935 when the LMS Railway completely rebuilt the 72-year old Queens Hotel facing City Square. The white Portland stone cladding of the façade contrasted with a colourful interior, with the French restaurant decorated in cream, silver and gold, enlivened by red doors and a green carpet! Measures to reduce noise extended to rubber cushioning in door rebates, sound-resistant floors and even rubber paving bricks on the adjacent station approach.

A classic study of washday in Watless Street, in the Burley district of Leeds. Although dating from 1968, it still accords exactly with Lettice Cooper's earlier description of 'terraces of brick houses, the yards and side streets draped on Mondays with lines of washing that begin to gather soot again before they are dry'. Watless Street no longer features on present-day maps of Leeds.

**Help was hopefully at hand following a tour of the city's worst slums in 1962 by the then Minister of Housing & Local Government, Dr Charles Hill. He was a household name in another capacity as the 'Radio Doctor' making a daily broadcast on the BBC Home Service.**

The 1950s brought more optimism and saw the start of a grand plan to create a true civic centre with groups of spacious buildings in the middle of the city. By virtue of sinking a much-needed Inner Ring Road in cuttings and tunnels, it was possible to embark on a vision of twentieth-century utopia stretching from the Town Hall past the Civic Hall and new Central Colleges right up to the University.

The next two decades saw shopping malls and precincts becoming commonplace. Many buildings were cleaned, although sadly others were demolished to make way for so-called modern architecture that was not always of the best. Some of the high-rise offices proved to have the briefest of lives, as instanced by the Royal Mail Building in Wellington Street, erected in 1976 and lasting only until 2003. Yet aided by key road-building schemes, Leeds undoubtedly felt that it was going places and went as far as boasting on its franked mail that it was the 'Motorway City of the Seventies'.

Development continued ceaselessly through the 1980s, a milestone occurring in 1989 when Judi Dench laid the foundation stone of the West Yorkshire Playhouse. Completed at a cost of £13 million, it was opened by another Yorkshire lass, Diana Rigg, and has become widely acclaimed for its versatile features, youth participation and diverse range of productions.

Some felt that the Playhouse was the most exciting development in Leeds since the building of the Town Hall well over a century earlier. It may say something for the age in which we live that others pointed to the decision of up-market store Harvey Nichols to open premises in Briggate that won a Civic Trust Award in 1998. In a manner akin to the nineteenth century industrialisation, it was just one link in a chain reaction. New 'big name' stores formed part of a more widespread relocation from the 'Deep South', with Leeds entering the twenty-first century as Britain's leading financial centre outside London. As befits the city that invented Freeserve, it could also claim to be the UK's Internet hub. A third of the country's Internet traffic was at one stage routed through Leeds, which continues to handle a significant share of the nation's megabytes.

A development boom has seen an estimated £2.5 billion investment in large-scale commercial, retail and residential property in Leeds during the last decade. Land values have been pushed so high that buildings are tending to move ever upwards rather than outwards. The city's skyline is changing out of all recognition as instanced by the thirty-two storeys of Bridgewater Place, hailed in marketing jargon as 'Yorkshire's latest iconic structure' and undoubtedly one of the tallest buildings of northern England.

Expansion on this scale has brought a large influx of key management and skilled staff from the London area, with incomers happily ensconced in what to them are inexpensive high-rise flats. The bonus that many of these have the luxury of waterside views would have been unimaginable to previous generations, but Leeds has finally been able to reveal a river that has for so long been hidden away as a polluted embarrassment. Instead it is now the fashionable focal point of revival on a heroic scale.

If a city is judged by the number of cranes dotting the skyline then Leeds is certainly in the big league. Many of them are very close to where the Norman lord Maurice Paynel founded his 'planned' settlement. Quite what he would have made of Harvey Nichols or high-rise flats is an interesting question, but hopefully he might have seen them as continuing the visionary progress that he started close to the banks of the Aire eight hundred years ago.

**Left: By 1968 high-rise flats were symbolically dwarfing the old terrace houses as dramatically portrayed at Holborn Towers, off Woodhouse Street. Which would have the longer life was in some cases an open question.**

**Right: Lampooned in the TV series *Absolutely Fabulous*, the prestigious store Harvey Nichols nevertheless represented a considerable coup for Leeds when it opened premises in Briggate. Looking stunning at night, they stand close to the point where Maurice Paynel built his 'wattle and daub' houses eight hundred years ago. Both have set trends – in very different ways.**

It was once said that no city was less 'on its river' than Leeds, which for almost two centuries regarded the Aire as something to hide away and not mention in polite company. By the date of this photograph in 1992 matters were at last changing, with the demise of industrial effluent enabling the waterside to be developed into an area of smart apartments, restaurants and many other good things in life.

# 2: Pride of Place

## Briggate

The changing face of Leeds has rapidly increased in tempo with one confident prediction that it will eventually become one of the top ten cities in Europe.

Take a stroll in Briggate's pedestrian precinct where vans, cars, buses and bone-rattling trams once made crossing the road a hazardous experience. You will find that the years have been kind to a mixture of ancient and modern buildings – some still sporting the grime of soot-blackened Yorkshire stone but the majority gleaming examples of architectural brilliance.

Briggate is a prime example of the transformation, although old-timers will miss certain characters who made this section of city life their own preserve. Bob Hooker was a familiar sight. He was the uncrowned King of Briggate –a tall figure, invariably wearing a heavy overcoat, even when temperatures soared. He also wore a trilby tilted in the style reminiscent of film star gangsters and he rarely smiled.

Bob rocked from side to side – like a galleon in choppy water – and the unusual gait carried him up and down Briggate hour upon hour. His tour of the area started at daybreak and finished late at night. Popular belief was that he 'opened and shut' Briggate and would have gladly accepted keys to the city had they been available.

Bob rarely spoke. He occasionally took time from his marathon to enjoy a coffee in the well-patronised Kardomah. This popular meeting place served regular customers from 1908 to 1965 when Leeds lost one of its many prime cafés regarded as a rendezvous by shoppers and city centre workers.

Another Briggate regular was Joe Field, a dapper chap, clad in a well-pressed dark grey suit, with brown trilby and brown suede shoes. In winter he donned the inevitable camel-coloured Crombie beloved by city slickers. Joe's job was to stand at the bar in Whitelocks pub from opening to closing. He claimed he was put on earth to drink halves of bitter and he certainly fulfilled that mission.

Joe was an authority on most things. He settled many alcohol-fuelled arguments. He was the original fount of knowledge and a character in the same vein as Jonas Bletherbottom. Jonas was a colourful gentleman with spotted bow tie round his expensive shirt, bespoke-tailored suit, and expensive trilby. He sometimes wore spats in addition to the top-of-the-range rolled brolly that dangled from his arm.

Jonas Bletherbottom was not his real name. He claimed it was and I never learned his true identity. But he was a swell from the tip of his titfer down to the soles of his shining shoes. He drank half-pints because he insisted that 'gentlemen of breeding did not sup pints'.

He was proud of his Yorkshire heritage and he spoke in dialect with a unique difference. The letter 'I' always became 'Y'. For instance if he mentioned his great friend – the late sportsman and bookmaker Jim Windsor – he referred to him as 'Jym Wyndsor'. It was a strange habit. I never really came to terms with it and he used to address me as 'Myster Morgan' and probably added that he would be 'taking a walk down Brygate to have a drynk at his favouryte pub'.

Jonas was a vision of sartorial elegance and so was Little Leslie, the best- known window cleaner in Leeds city centre. His round included Briggate and adjoining streets. He dressed in a blue cotton jacket, with pockets big enough to hold his leather, and he had matching trousers, ladders, and all the accoutrements for his labours.

But when his duties were done there was a transformation. He dressed to kill. He sported a hand-tied bow and finished off his ensemble with a silver-topped cane. He was better dressed than a tailor's dummy.

Leeds city centre was rich with eccentric folk and arguably the most famous was Alice Porter who became known as 'Woodbine Lizzie'. When it was my job to produce a weekly nostalgia column in the *Yorkshire Evening Post* there were occasions when inspiration was lacking. 'Woodbine Lizzie' often came to the rescue. The mere mention of her name resulted in a flood of letters, cards, and telephone memories of Lizzie who, in modern jargon, was simply 'a bag lady'.

Several legends almost became 'factual' and referred to 'Woodbine Lizzie' being the unwanted daughter of a lord of the realm; the illegitimate child of a nobleman who disowned her at birth. Others talked of her wealthy background and how she refused to marry a man of her father's choice and she eloped with her lover only to be left in the lurch. It was all untrue.

She was born in Stanningley and, at eighteen, she moved with her parents to Pudsey. In the same year she married Joe Hartley. They produced six children in twelve years including five boys. The marriage was over during the First World War and Lizzie reverted to her maiden name of Alice Porter. In a rare interview Lizzie said: "Joe and me simply did not hit it off. I was thirty-eight when I abandoned my home and became a vagabond – a lady tramp to you."

Lizzie claimed that the open air helped her to survive because she was a weakling from the day she was born and weighed under nine stone during her pregnancies. She said: "I was always able to look after myself and I had more guts than most folk. I've never been unhappy, although I was sad when I had to leave the kids. I love to sing and have a good voice even though I say so myself."

That opinion was not shared by those who teased her about the lifestyle she had chosen or her appearance. She embarked on a walk to London but only covered a few miles and returned to Leeds where she became a very unkempt lady, dressed in several coats, with a basket over one arm, a bag and raincoat over the other, and a tram conductor's hat perched on her straggly hair. Her regular haunt was the passage leading to The Ship public house on Duncan Street, where she puffed on the Woodbine cigarettes she cadged from generous pedestrians.

Lizzie was 'warned off' many stores but often gained entrance to Lipton's store in Kirkgate. She invariably fingered food which assistants could not put on sale and they would bark at Lizzie: "Take them and clear off. And don't come in again." But she did and shoppers either hurried from the premises or cleared a passage for the untidy figure.

She was often taken to the Bridewell in Leeds Town Hall where she was bathed and fed before she returned to her principal occupation of asking for 'Woodies'. She did become famous overseas in the Second World War. Soldiers in the Eighth Army, serving in the Middle East, named a transporter 'Woodbine Lizzie From Leeds'. When she was acquainted of the honour she growled: "My name should be on a tank."

'Woodbine Lizzie' died in Stanley Royd Hospital, Wakefield, in 1947. But thousands of Leeds folk, who either exchanged the time of day or skirted round the lady, will remember her with varying degrees of affection.

When you walk down Briggate spare a thought for the citizens who left an indelible mark on this busy thoroughfare. This all happened before the arrival of Harvey Nichols and other fashion houses of international repute.

**Left: Woodbine Lizzie is pictured in her working gear, peaked cap, three raincoats, well-filled basket, and cigarette clamped in the corner of her mouth. Lizzie – or Alice Porter – was a street beggar and many citizens had affection for the lady who was regularly taken in charge by friendly policemen and escorted to a place where she would be given a 'wash and brush up'. She did not appreciate remarks from passing children or grown-ups and often retaliated with phrases not becoming a lady.**

**Right: In this picture Woodbine Lizzie is seen in her Sunday best with a fashionable hat, gloves, and possibly contemplating whether or not she should attend morning worship.**

**Horse-drawn cabs await their next fares in nineteenth-century Briggate, opposite the entrance to the Queen's Arcade on the right. Cars are mercifully absent – and in that sense the wheel has come full circle as Briggate is now a pedestrian precinct.**

When the sun invades the long passageway fronting historic Whitelocks there is no better place to enjoy a chat, a pint and a thick beef sandwich. Customers have sampled this facility for well over a century and one can mentally turn the clock back and dwell on days and nights when the gentry patronised the pub and hailed a horse-drawn carriage to take them to their respective abodes. Whitelocks is hidden from Briggate. It nestles at least twenty yards from the main thoroughfare unlike pubs and hotels in Lower Briggate,

The Golden Lion was originally built on the site of a coaching inn with stables. In more recent times it was the home of Gosney's News Agency which provided stories and sports reports and statistics for papers throughout the country.

Mr Gosney was related to a fiery-tempered *Yorkshire Evening Post* news editor Archie Glover. Tales about Archie are legendary and my favourite concerns the day he had a bad round of golf at Roundhay Park. He proceeded to lean his clubs on the wall surrounding the Mansion Hotel and drove his car over them.

Archie and many of his reporters enjoyed drinks at Whitelocks as they did at the Viaduct, which is near to the Golden Lion. It was believed that an underground passage led from the Viaduct cellars to Leeds Parish Church and was used by Catholic priests on the run during the time of the reformation. One of my colleagues, Brian Cowell, and me put the claim to the test. We had crawled for quite a distance when the battery in our single torch expired (thank God). Our mission was aborted and we returned to daylight and a walk back to Whitelocks for sustenance.

# Whitelocks

There was a time when I took pride in my knowledge of Leeds and the city centre in particular. It was my domain. I boasted that I knew every nook and cranny and every crook and granny. Those were the days when the *Yorkshire Evening Post* offices were based in Albion Street and we were at the hub of the town action.

I felt that my finger was on the pulse. I believed that I knew everyone worth knowing and even legions of those who were not. My daily beat included major streets and backyard ginnels and there was not a hostelry in which I had not supped at least a half of best bitter.

But times and the face of Leeds have changed. Visits to my old stomping ground have become infrequent. I often feel a stranger when I walk down once familiar thoroughfares like Briggate, Duncan Street, The Headrow and Bond Street.

Pubs which once echoed to my happy chatter are foreign to my presence. But one hallowed hostelry resists change. It has served Leeds citizens since 1715 and it claims three names – Turks Head, First City Luncheon Bar and its more familiar Whitelocks.

The late Poet Laureate Sir John Betjeman was impressed when he visited arguably the city's most famous and dare I add 'most popular' pub. Sir John compared it to Fleet Street's Old Cheshire Cheese and he added: 'Whitelocks is the very heart of Leeds city.'

The comparison with London's haunt for media folk is justified in as much as Whitelocks has for decades been a 'watering hole' for journalists, thespians, gamblers, members of the legal profession, insurance salesmen, university students and those who stumble on the delights of this pub by chance or design.

It was originally called The Turks Head and became Whitelocks when Percy Whitelock bought the premises in 1880. The family held the licence for ninety years and it was John Lupton Whitelock who altered the bar and restaurant into what it is today. He was the last member of the family to run the pub. He sold the licence to Youngers Brewery in 1944 to concentrate on his career as a renowned flautist.

If you push open the main door you turn back the clock with menus mirrored on pillars: 'Cheese and biscuits one penny; sausages and potatoes threepence; and pies twopence'. Little seems to have altered in two hundred years. But the secret is sympathetic adaptation and restoration. It retains a Dickensian image with a glass and brass interior. One feels that if you stepped outside a horse-drawn cab would be waiting.

Giants of the Press – like *Yorkshire Post* editor the late Ted Crossley, bowler-hatted writer ...n Greenwell, Jimmy Stanford, Alan Weir, Dennis Haywood, Alan Thompson and others were regular drinkers of Youngers Number 3 or double rums.

During their patronage Alan Bentley and his wife Anastasia were mine hosts for ten years. They were in charge when miscreants brought crimson embarrassment to the faces of senior members of the Leeds police force. It was September 12th, 1965, when plain-clothes police gathered for a goodbye drink and beef sandwich with one of their departing colleagues. High-ranking sleuths mingled with lesser lights. It was a jovial and relaxed affair. Stories were swapped and drinks were ordered by the dozen as the bobbies settled down for a good evening.

Whitelocks is famous for its beef and a huge joint, still warm from the hostelry oven, nestled on a silver salver at the end of the bar. It was a succulent roast, ready for carving, and it suddenly disappeared as if by a miraculous conjuring trick. Now you see it. Then you didn't. Newspaper reports implied that the number of bobbies on the premises was no more than three. Don't believe it. The pub police presence was plentiful and bordered on 'enormous',

The revellers thought it was some kind of prank and the beef would quickly return. But it was never seen again. The beef weighed 37lb and so did the tray. One person could not have carried both away. Alan Bentley was summoned to the end of the bar where he told us that the beef was worth about 'ten guineas' and the tray's value was 'seven pounds and ten shillings'.

It was a long time before the police lived down the fact that the pub was barren of the Baron of Beef. Hopefully it went to a hungry family. The culprit was never caught.

Towsands Maloney was an occasional patron of Whitelocks. He was a racecourse gambler. He was Irish and he his nickname was gained because he often told listeners: "I had a towsand pounds on this horse and a towsand pounds on another..."

Maloney was in the bar one night when he turned to a Brian Cowell, a colleague of mine, and said: "I believe you are a bit handy with your fists. If I give you £50 will you take that chap down yonder outside and give him a going over?"

Cowell agreed. He motioned the victim to follow him out of the pub where he told him the story, gave him £25, and told him to scram. He then pocketed the other £25 and ten minutes later returned to the pub, rubbing his knuckles and winking to Towsands that the job had been done. Towsands was highly satisfied.

There was one character synonymous with Whitelocks. His name was Alec and he was a former Polish cavalry officer. No one could pronounce his surname even if they rehearsed it. Alec arrived at Whitelocks after the war. He feared a return to Poland for some unknown reason. He worked behind the bar and appeared to commit regular orders to memory. He usually served customers before they actually asked for their drink.

Alec's English was his own variety and at times puzzling in the extreme. For instance 'Packerdyorse' was the local Pack Horse and 'Ze oppy Enkie' referred to the Hope and Anchor. He was a gentleman, smart, industrious and highly suitable for a public house which reigns supreme in the affection of countless patrons. It is of course – as Sir John declared – 'the very heart of Leeds'.

# McConnell's

McConnell's was a famed watering hole and it enjoyed a unique position in Leeds city centre. It was the only pub from Boar Lane to the Headrow with its entrance opening on to that particular stretch of Briggate. There was a byelaw – instituted and implemented by an anti-drink religious body – which prevented pubs facing out on to the main thoroughfare. That is why such historic hostelries as the Pack Horse, Whitelocks and The Ship are hidden in back streets.

McConnell's has long been gone. It called time on drinking in 1959 and the cavernous, dimly lit, gathering place for shawled ladies, and particularly the city's Irish population, was demolished for shop development. But the memory of the pub – opened in 1859 by Alexander McConnell under its official name The Alliance Hotel – will never fade because it had atmosphere.

The ceiling was stained a deep brown hue by years of nicotine-packed smoke from pipes and fags. There was sawdust on the floor. Barrels lined the walls and hard, highly-polished and jolly uncomfortable seats at the bar, were fashioned for drinkers not loungers.

Nowadays pubs seem to sell more food than beer. The plastic emporiums are ideal for young love birds to kiss and canoodle to the point of turning real topers off their liquid sunshine.

Such behaviour would not have been tolerated in McConnell's where the principal pastime was supping whisky, with a drop of hot or cold water, sampling a glass of 1927 port at two bob (10 pence) a nip, and gazing at a picture of King Teddy pulling a pint of the beer brewed in his honour in 1927.

Ladies of high and low repute enjoyed a drop of Mother's Ruin in McConnell's in the knowledge that they were in respectable company. And old men gathered at the longest bar in town and jawed and jarred to their heart's content. The beer flowed and the blarney billowed on all sides. It was a haven for many and a pub second. One felt safe and comfortable in McConnell's and the prices were right.

I thought of McConnell's, and other town pubs which sadly disappeared, when I heard the story of a landlord who decided to turn the clock back sixty years and treat his patrons. He termed it the appropriate thing to do to mark the anniversary of the end of the Second World War hostilities.

A chap walked into the bar and ordered: "Two pints of bitter, a large scotch, a gin and tonic, and a sweet sherry."

The benevolent publican placed the order on a tray and smiled: "That will be 65 pence sir."

Sir exclaimed: "My goodness! Surely you are wrong – it must be more than that."

The landlord polished a few glasses and explained: "Just for tonight I am charging the prices of sixty years ago."

The delighted drinker expressed gratitude and pointed to a group of men at the bottom of the bar. They were not drinking and the customer asked: "Why haven't they ordered?"

The man behind the bar said: "They will do shortly. They are waiting for Happy Hour."

McConnell's was only a short walk from Albert Cowling's Wine Lodge – a splendid pub – which stood for years in Boar Lane. There was a placard outside the ornate building which carried the tempting offer: "A glass of beer, corned beef sandwich, cigarette and a match. And change out of a two bob piece."

A disbelieving chap murmured: "There must be a catch. What beer is it?"

However the offer was thoroughly genuine. You could actually drink half of Heys, Worthington or Bass, eat the well-filled sandwich and enjoy a smoke. You were given a halfpenny change from your florin (10 pence).

The Wine Lodge was built like a concrete and plaster circus tent with a high roof and a circular bar. Adjoining this huge cavern was a room reserved 'For Gentlemen Only', where the main topic of conversation was the quality of bottled Bass, India Pale Ale, Hey's Gold Cup and what was Mick's Double in the city's racing daily *The Sporting Pink*.

It was Lord help any misguided female who had the temerity, or sudden rush of blood to the brain, and entered the forbidden quarters. In fact I never saw a member of the opposite gender even try to place a dainty toe over the threshold. Believe it or not ladies but many pubs in those fairly recent days had rooms reserved for the exclusive use of the gentry. This state of affairs would certainly not apply today.

The round bar at Cowling's was popular because of its Mighty Wurlitzer, which used to swing into foot-tapping rhythm to entertain lunchtime diners. The usual repertoire included marches and nostalgic melodies from the shows like the *Desert Song* and *Maid of the Mountains*. The organist was a talented musician but not in the same league as Henry Croudson who delighted patrons of the Paramount Cinema, which became the Odeon Cinema and is now a huge shop called Primark.

But back to McConnell's. I often bought a carrier bag brimming with fruit and vegetables from Harry, a market man who used McConnell's for sale of his goods. We didn't ask questions about the source of the supply but simply paid one shilling and sixpence for sufficient goodies to feed two families for a week. Harry was proud of the produce and rightly so. He claimed every tiny orange was a Jaffa.

One day a woman asked him for a pound of tomatoes. Harry sipped his whisky and murmured: "You had better make it a couple of pounds lady. I'm not cutting one in half just for you."

**McConnell's unique interior had sawdust on the floor and huge vats behind the bar. It has been described as a cross between a Wild West saloon and something out of Dickens. But it had warmth, a loyal clientele and top quality beer served in half-pints.**
**Barrels provided seating for customers – many of them Irish – and there was a busy out sale department with bottles of whisky and gin the best sellers. There were pubs with 'men only rooms' but McConnell's welcomed ladies who ordered 'Mother's Ruin' at the long bar. Although it was one of the oldest pubs in Leeds City Centre, the Pack Horse Inn, off Briggate, was catering for thirsty Leeds topers long before McConnell's came into existence. (John Morgan collection)**

The Odeon Cinema, originally the Paramount, was noted for its cinema organ, which was considered to be in a different league to a similar 'Mighty Wurlitzer' at Cowling's Wine Lodge in Boar Lane. The cinema has now given way to a huge Primark store.

# The King Charles

The King Charles pub was demolished to make space for Schofields Centre and so was Sherwins Restaurant – both popular with the Leeds theatre-going public. Hedrick Tyson – known as 'Ed' – was landlord at this haunt for journalists, market traders, villains, ladies of leisure and honest to goodness shoppers in need of sustenance and a refreshing glass of beer. From the *Yorkshire Evening Post* in Albion Street to the pub in King Charles Croft we strolled by Steve Emmott's betting shop and passed the Doll's Hospital.

Mr O'Toole – father of Peter – studied *The Sporting Pink* in the Oak Room and another ever-present 'Buck', from Mac Fisheries in the Headrow, invariably propped up the lounge bar. This was run by bubbly Marian, mother of the Radio Leeds broadcaster John Boyd.

Writer, poet and racehorse punter R C Scriven – known in the literary world as 'Ratz' - frequented Emmott's and the King Charles where he drowned his losses or celebrated his winnings.

'Monty' with pink face and long silver hair was always in evidence. He cadged drinks with dignified aplomb, patting his overcoat pockets and murmuring: "Excuse me old boy but I happen to have left my shekels at home."

The upstairs restaurant was the preserve of headwaiter Bill Olbison, who bowed and scraped when a toff with a potential monetary tip hove into view.

I recall a diner complaining: "Waiter, these chips are hard."

Bill picked one from the chap's plate and chewed it.

He agreed: "You are correct Sir. The customer is always right. They are indeed very hard chips. I hope you enjoy them."

Unflappable Bill once asked my wife Maureen if she fancied a boiled egg with her ham salad. She nodded and Bill produced one from the back his hand with the magical dexterity of Paul Daniels.

When Bill signed off duty at 3pm he stepped into Lands Lane with the swagger of a city gent. He wore a bowler, winged collar, and a bow tie. But he usually spoiled the sartorial effect with his paper carrier bag – packed with a few goodies from the pub kitchen.

Sherwins adjoined the King Charles. It was managed by Angus Grantham and he usually exhibited a joint of beef or a cooked chicken in the window. I can't remember eating there. It was probably outside an impoverished reporter's price range, although many assured me that the fare was value for money and the premises were scrupulously clean.

Hagenbachs was just across the road and it was another popular café, if not as endearing to 'townies' as Collinsons or the Kardoma. We also had 'Fields' and the Lonsdale never lacked patronage. It was in Commercial Street and eventually became one of the first Chinese restaurants in the city. Woolworth's had a huge cafeteria and Marks and Spencer - when it was further up Briggate - also had an excellent restaurant.

I often went there but somehow I was never tempted to enter Sherwins' portals. I'm only sorry I didn't. However the real attraction in that area was the King Charles manager Ed Tyson, who often took a short cut to Briggate by driving his car down Thornton Arcade, much to the horror of shoppers. One lady reported the fact to a policeman but Ed convinced the constable that the poor woman had a reputation for 'seeing things'. He asked the bobby: "What man in his right senses would attempt such a stupid prank?" The policeman agreed.

There was an occasion when Ed was out on the town and he returned to the pub after midnight. The front door was closed and Ed had forgotten his keys. He shinned up a drainpipe and squeezed his bulky frame through a window only to be stuck there. He was eventually released and, when he pushed the front door, he discovered it was not locked.

We look back on the King Charles with many memories. Mr Tyson is now living in France.

# Fish and Chips

The mere mention of Youngman's restaurant has me smacking my lips with memories galore of the fish and chips many considered the best in Leeds. Youngman's enjoyed a prime position in Upper Briggate and was a must for those who felt hungry after visiting the Grand Theatre or the Paramount picture house. Alas, Youngman's is long gone and, although the refurbished Grand Theatre remains a strong attraction, the Paramount as already noted is now a huge Primark.

One of my first recollections is running errands to the local chippie for neighbours who ordered 'a ha'porth of each'. It was at that time a cheap and convenient meal for a harassed housewife to place before her husband on his return from a shift down the pit.

Chips were better in those days. They were thick, soft and fried to a golden hue, unlike the anaemic or matchstick 'French fries' we now often buy with equally insipid fish. Good old Yorkshire chips, fried in sizzling beef dripping, were on the go long before Napoleon chipped his spuds with a guillotine.

I blame our politicians for giving the French credit for the humble fried chip. Mind you I attribute a worse disaster to Maggie Thatcher. She had the infernal gall to slap VAT on fish and chips within a month or two of eating a free portion of haddock at Harry Ramsden's Guiseley emporium.

Do you remember the first Harry Ramsden's in the original wooden building? Customers travelled from far and wide for Harry's fish and chips with Leeds folk catching a Sammy Ledgard bus or taking a train ride to the shop. Harry's secret was in the batter. It was crisp and crumbly, a meal in itself, and it was almost a Yorkshire disaster when he served his final customer and succumbed to a takeover bid.

Harry Ramsden junior opened a chippie a couple of miles further down Otley Road. He exhibited a sign, 'The Original Harry Ramsden's', but the buyer of Harry senior's business quickly quashed young Harry's enterprise.

TV and radio will never replace newspapers because you can't eat fish and chips from a television and a wireless. Newspapers were invented simply to hold fish and chips because they taste better in newsprint than they do on a plate. Renowned author Keith Waterhouse, a former *Yorkshire Evening Post* reporter, is known to drink champagne with fish and chips eaten from a newspaper.

The late cricket correspondent John Arlott was a regular at Brett's, Headingley, during Test matches. He drank nothing but claret at Jack Brett's café and takeaway. But the proper beverage for fish and chips as every true Yorkshire gourmet knows is dandelion & burdock.

A liberal sprinkling of salt and a good dousing of vinegar is essential and best eaten when you are courting and strolling on a moonlit street with a girl on your arm. But be careful with the dandelion & burdock because it tends to bring on the burps. Such indelicate noises have been known to nip a blossoming romance in the bud.

We had a mobile fish and chip man on the Gipton estate. He also served mushy peas from a huge jug. Our local chippie was owned by Mr Woodhead and our childish game was to stand at the door and shout: "Have you any left?"

When Mr Woodhead nodded the usual response from the kids was: "You shouldn't have fried so many."

Scraps were a must with fish and chips. You were given them even if you didn't ask for the same. God knows how many calories they contained but we ate them by the thousand and we are still here to tell the tale.

My great pal the late Jim Moran, a boxing champion, usually had a couple of Yorkshire puddings with his pile of 'fish and dirks'.

However my favourite tale concerns a fish and chip cafe in Leeds where a loud youth threatened to spoil the meal with his verbal antics. An elderly gentleman – returning from the toilet – put him in his place.

"You are wanted outside," he told the noisy customer.

"Who wants me outside?" asked the lad.

"Everyone inside," replied the veteran.

The teenager heeded the message and we proceeded to enjoy the rest of our 'meal of a lifetime' in Nash's in Merrion Street. See you there!

# Leeds Market

Decades have elapsed since proud citizens of Leeds pointed Quarry Hill Flats out to visitors and smugly claimed: "They're the biggest in Europe." Alas, general decay, structural faults, dampness, plus rat infestation, resulted in the 1978 demolition – a mere thirty-eight years after more than three thousand people filled the flats. Closure of the once greatly admired housing estate had an immediate affect on the adjoining Leeds Market.

Peter Madden recalls life as a market trader with a mixture of nostalgic affection, lingering memories and a degree of sadness. He said: "The death of Quarry Hill was a blow to us. We were the 'corner shop' to those people. The loss of their custom was a financial shock and we never really recovered from the setback. We also missed regular and familiar faces – people who moved to other parts of Leeds. However, market people are a resilient breed. Many of us soldiered on in spite of a drop in turnover and the ever-increasing rents. When I first moved into the market I paid £70 a week. When I retired it was £800 a week."

Leeds Market or Kirkgate Covered Market, as it was originally known when it opened in May 1857, was periodically extended to cope with the demands of traders and a faithful population of shoppers. The new wholesale fish market was completed in 1894 and the rebuilding of the entire structure and layout was accomplished at a cost of £80,000 in 1904.

March 1941 saw damage from an air raid and the market hall was almost destroyed by a huge blaze that broke out on the evening of December 13, 1975.

Peter said: "We will never forget that scene of devastation. Many lost their business and the will to start again. With Christmas approaching we were keen to resume trading and we made the most of a huge marquee erected to encourage us to holler 'business as usual'. Of course it wasn't but it gave our morale a fillip. We managed to tick over and three months later the site was cleared and a start made on erecting a new hall. Another building was completed in 1981 and in 1993 to 1995 another refurbishment scheme was finished at a cost of £10 million."

But the market is not simply about buildings, produce and stalls – indoor and outdoor. It is not confined to the scene of my youth when the decision had to be made whether to buy a ham sandwich from Big Nan or Cliff at Birbecks, a milk shake at Granelli's, or plump for a plateful of pie and mash at Jack Cuthbert's or Rhodes cafe.

The market is about people and colourful characters like the late 'Clicky' Hoban who sold handkerchiefs (often called wipes), tablecloths and other linen goods. 'Clicky' was so-called because of a speech impediment, which resulted in his 'clicky clix' for 'sixty six'. He not only worked in the market; he often packed a suitcase with goodies to sell on the front at Blackpool and other seaside gaffs.

The story is told of how he hawked toy airships and was apprehended by a policeman who marched him to the local station apparently to charge him with illegal trading. 'Clicky' returned to his pitch an hour later with an empty case. He had sold one airship to the desk sergeant, two to the duty inspector, another to the chap who arrested him –and so on. There wasn't any evidence left to charge him!

**Peter Madden, one of the many famous names associated with Leeds Market. He recalls both the loss of trade following the demolition of nearby Quarry Hill Flats and the havoc wrought by a devastating fire in 1975. (John Morgan)**

Leeds Market has survived many threats of demolition and take-over, once instance occurring in 1985 when strong protests greeted plans by Dutch interests to build a shopping mall on the site. Fronting this demonstration are, left to right, Mrs H. Higgins, Joan Hilton, Ronnie Hilton, Fr Michael Buckley, Henry Higgins and Eddie Cornell.

Bernard was his proper name and his fame spread beyond the confines of the market and the seaside. Also famous were Big Nan's pal Ann; Johnny Summers, a great professional boxer; flower seller Kenny Dobson; Jimmy Hayes, who had 149 bouts; Tubber Whitfield, his wife Anne and son Brian; Louis Pope; Dan Pascoe; Fred Best, who responded to the nickname Linnett; Archie Scarr; Eddie Madden; Harry, Kenny, and Ronnie Higgins; Vic Fuller; Len Scott and countless others.

We remember Welhams, Bethells, Naylors, Hodgsons, Hayes, Busy B, Wildblood, Jack Fulton and Stringers, where you bought a book to read and then sold it back to the proprietor. We used to gaze on mountains of apples, oranges and pomegranates, and often buy crab claws, whelks, mussels and periwinkles at Hayes, waiting until near closing time to take part in the 'burglars' sale of meat and fish offered at greatly reduced prices. Shoppers with the patience to wait secured amazing bargains. Housewives called this sale of perishable produce 'milking time' – especially on Saturday evenings – and they could feed a family for a couple of shillings.

The banter was entertaining and the whole scene was exciting and colourful, especially at the covered bird market where canaries and budgies twittered, linnets sang, parrots squawked, ducks quacked, cocks crowed and dogs barked. Not far away there was a machine that told us 'Electricity Is Life'. If you paid a penny and grabbed two brass handles, you were given an electric shock. It was supposed to improve your health and this was also the intention of the 'quack doctors' who sold pills, ointments, cough cures, and concoctions guaranteed to give you a muscular and powerful physique.

The market has survived threats from hostile aircraft, fire and attempts by outside forces to take-over the site and premises. Long may it continue!

Finally, there is one law that has not been repealed. Swearing and smoking are not allowed in the covered market. Dogs are also banned, which puzzles me because we had a mongrel Flossie many years ago. She was the daughter of a champion market ratter who was not unknown in Quarry Hill Flats.

**Left: The redeveloped Market, photographed in May 1994 following a £10 million refurbishment scheme.**

# The Town Hall

When the war ended we had a Victory parade in Leeds. The King's Own Yorkshire Light Infantry marched with fixed bayonets past the Town Hall steps. The salute was taken by the Princess Royal – Princess Mary – and the *Yorkshire Evening Post* photographer Charles Bowrey hit on the idea of a bird's-eye photograph from the clock tower. Charlie used plates not film, and I was his runner. We stood on the flat roof below the clock, sharing the vantage point with the remains of dead pigeons, as Charlie prepared for the next stage of the climb.

It was then he realised that he did not have his slides with him. I raced back to the *Yorkshire Evening Post* to pick them up. When I returned after pushing through crowds the parade was over. We were scooped by the *Yorkshire Evening News*.

It was at the Town Hall where Charlie committed another painful error. Thomas Beecham was conducting an orchestra when Charlie fired off two photographic flashes at the stage just as the musicians had reached a quiet musical movement.

Beecham turned and shouted: "Throw that man out!"

Within two minutes Charlie and his camera were standing next to one of the stone lions outside the building.

The Town Hall, designed by Cuthbert Brodrick and opened in 1858, has been the scene of numerous activities with highlights including all-in wrestling, boxing and even snooker championships. It is now a concert hall and base for many functions, not least the Lord Mayor's annual dinner on the night of 'Mayor Making'. It is also a fine conference centre but is no longer used for Assize Courts and the prosecution and defence of lesser criminals.

It was here the infamous murderer Charlie Peace was sentenced to death and hanged at Armley Gaol. Charlie was held prisoner in the Bridewell in the bowels of the Town Hall building. When a judge says "send him down" the guilty person descends to one or another of the cells established years ago.

Charlie's cell is now open to the public. It is supposed to be haunted. The dark, dank, cell was built to accommodate four prisoners but surely Charlie had it to himself? The original cell has a wooden bench with shackle rings for the wrist and ankle, whitewashed walls and gas lighting. The Bridewell Charter of 1858 held that 'each prisoner should have half-a-loaf of bread and a pint of ale, together with sufficient straw for bedding'.

Perhaps the ghost of Charlie stalks the premises? You can ask him if you visit the Bridewell because 'Cuthbert', the Town Hall designer, will be present to show visitors round the building. 'Cuthbert' will introduce you to 'Charlie' who will probably ask you for a glass of whisky for his sickness. But 'PC Bonney' will also be present to take part in the dialogue and make sure you do not treat or patronise the wicked 'Charlie'.

Groups are welcome. You will even see Charlie's toilet. He last used it on February 25, 1879 when he was sent to Armley. His final request was "Do they have whisky in heaven?"

**Jubilant Leeds people in front of the Town Hall during the VJ Day (Victory in Japan) celebrations on August 16th, 1945. In spite of heavy rain the crowd appear to be in high Spirits. Women are wearing head scarfs in turban fashion and tied round the head. (Leodis Collection / Yorkshire Post)**

# 3: That's Entertainment!

## Jimmy Savile

When a colourful character with king-size cigar greets you with "Now then, now then, how's about that then" it can only be the unique Jimmy Savile. This walking bundle of joyous energy has accomplished so much it required two appearances on *This is Your Life* to even scratch the surface of the human dynamo's existence.

Jimmy is the only owner of two of the famous 'Red Books' – one from the late Eamon Andrews and the other from Michael Aspel . It was quite a shock for compilers of the long-running television saga because planners are under orders never to duplicate recipients of the surprise award. But Jimmy's name somehow escaped the stringent precautions and he duly accepted the double honour with typical Savile gratitude and perhaps a semblance of mock surprise and innocence.

Jimmy is Leeds from the tip of his once tartan coloured hair to the soles of his sandals. He has five dwellings – an apartment in London, a flat in Scarborough, quarters on the front at Bournemouth, a majestic cottage in the mountain region of Glencoe and an elegant penthouse suite overlooking the verdant charms of Roundhay Park.

Jimmy said: "They have individual attractions – especially Glencoe. But Leeds is not only my local habitat, it is my true home. I will never leave Leeds and I am proud to have been born here. I was brought up in the Woodhouse area where the population was a mixture of Catholics, Protestants and Jewish neighbours. We lived in harmony. Now the city has hundreds of different creeds and all are welcome. But I feel that Leeds is mine. I was here first and I am proud of my birthright."

Jimmy's pride in his home town is reflected in his lifestyle which includes a regular spell of 'portering' and a stint of 'patient visiting' at Leeds General Infirmary. He explains: "When I am in Leeds I like to do two days a week at the LGI. It is not that I am a goody-goody, virtuous or sanctimonious. I just love people."

This affection for others and a passionate concern for the elderly is genuine and not for publicity or self-esteem. His love for his mother is reflected in the ornate gravestone he commissioned for her plot in Killingbeck Cemetery, Leeds. It is engraved 'The Duchess', the name he gave to the lady he loved so much.

Her funeral was held at Scarborough and coincided with a promise Jimmy had made to open an extension at St Georges's Hospital, Rothwell. Although heartbroken he kept faith with people he 'didn't want to let down' and he drove from the service to perform the opening ceremony. He said: "I felt duty bound to honour the promise I made to the staff and visitors."

This concern for others was fostered from day one at the Savile's humble but happy home. It was a close and loving family. Jimmy was the youngest of seven and is the only survivor. His much-loved sister died in 2005.
Jimmy attended St Anne's School, where he was taught right from wrong, and he still follows the Catholic faith imbued in pupils at that place of learning.

He comments: "I enjoyed school days but didn't fancy further education. Come to think of it I was never offered the choice. I watched lads from St Michael's College with satchels filled with homework and didn't envy them at all. I spent most evenings reading my comics or listening to the radio with occasional visits to Leeds where my dad and mum organised tea dances at the Arcadian, which was the upper floor of the Mecca Locarno Ballroom. It was old-time dancing and when I was eleven I could dance the Military Two-Step, Waltz, Square Tango – the lot. My dad raised money for charity and the income from the dances helped poor people including many in Malta."

The dances were Jimmy's introduction to the world of entertainment, which was destined to give him a flamboyant image and earn him worldwide recognition.

Jimmy is not a paragon. He can produce an earthy turn of phrase and humour when the occasion demands and he has the knack of frustrating reporters who interrogate and attempt to strip any veneer from this private individual.

My favourite story of this son of Leeds concerns an auction of a case of moderate wine with proceeds going to St Gemma's Hospice, Leeds. I was the auctioneer and expected the modest wine to bring about £20. Jimmy bid £500 and no one was going to top that generous amount.

I asked why he – a teetotaller – wanted it so badly and he explained: "I have a little old Jewish pal who is down on

It may sound a trifle ostentatious but Sir Jimmy Savile bought a flat in Park Crescent, London W1, simply for somewhere to park his Rolls Royce. But the deal was not flash or flamboyant. It was 'just practical' claims the man who owns five places he can call home.

It was the garage space that influenced his decision to clinch the London purchase. At the height of his television career Sir Jimmy spent so much time in the capital it was essential he had a London address.

When he was a youth he dreamed of owning a Rolls. His number plate has been on nineteen – not that he does a lot of driving. When he is back at base – his home in Leeds – he drives a nifty little van.

Life is fun for the enigmatic man who is as recognisable to teenagers as he is to those who remember him presenting the first *Top of the Pops* in 1964. This was followed by the smash hit programme *Jim'll Fix It* which was a television must for young and old alike. When he recently introduced the last of *Top of the Pops* he received countless calls from broadcasting stations and newspaper offices. Some of them came from even the most remote places in the world.

He is as familiar to generations as the proverbial Bellman. But does anyone truly know the real Jimmy who is a happy chap in tracksuit, string vest and trainers? He has simple tastes and keeps himself fit with regular sessions on exercise machines he stores in each of his five abodes. He smokes cigars and claims every time he lights one it is akin to a celebration.

Jimmy lives alone but he is never lonely. In fact he claims to be 'boring' because he 'doesn't do drugs or booze'. He greets every day as one to enjoy with a bit of fun, never losing his temper, and no slagging off people'.

"That's not my scene," assures Britain's oldest teenager whose concern for his fellow men and women is reflected in excess of the £40million he has raised for charities.

Jimmy has one special friend. He knows that God is his pal and he is regularly on his knees to 'talk to Him' and intercede for those who need help, comfort and guidance.

his luck. He loves 'plonk' but can't afford to buy it. Tomorrow morning he will open the front door of his flat in Meanwood to collect his daily milk. There will also be twelve bottles of wine standing on the step and he will never know from where they came. My only regret is that I will not be able to see his face when he discovers the bottles."

Little wonder Jimmy is Sir James Savile OBE, knighted by the Queen; knighted by the late Pope, John Paul; and knighted by the Governor of Malta. He is a Freeman of Scarborough and has plaques and trophies listing fifty years of radio work as well as a Golden Heart presented by the Variety Club with their award to the Show Business Personality of the Year.

Jim's latest acquisition was the award for being a true legend. He is now among the country's top ten National Treasures. He shares this distinction with fish and chips, Wimbledon Tennis Championships, red telephone boxes, cream cheese and such outstanding males as Sir David Jason, David Beckham, Sir Trevor McDonald, Michael Parkinson, Prince William, Prince Charles, Cliff Richard and Freddie Flintoff. Isn't it about time Sir James Savile was given the Freedom of the city he loves?

Jimmy has back problems – a legacy of his wartime days as a Bevin Boy. When he was summoned for military duty he volunteered for service in the Royal Navy. He reasoned: "At least I would have a clean bed at night if only the bed of the ocean."

But he was drafted into the coalmines and his meagre pay was hardly more than the amount he earned as a twelve-year-old drummer at the Leeds Mecca Locarno tea dances.

Jimmy was involved in a serious pit accident. There was a fear that he would never walk again and this makes more remarkable the fact that he has run 218 marathons. He has ridden his bike from Land's End to John O' Groats and also competed in the Tour of Britain. He fought in the all-in wrestling ring and climbed mountains, including Ben Nevis, on which he was once lost for a couple of days.

Jimmy is delighted that the decision was made recently to honour the unsung heroes who laboured at the coalface or did other work in the pits. He still has problems with his back. He has to be careful how he perches on any seat but he still has his Bevin Boy equipment, helmet, overalls, the lot, just in case he is called up for war service again.

Perhaps it was his painful back that urged him to raise £10 million to ensure the continuation of the essential National Spinal Injuries Centre at Stoke Mandeville Hospital, where he is a familiar figure with staff and patients.

The question is posed: "Does anyone really know what makes Jimmy Savile tick?" Interviewer Louis Theroux failed in his quest to pierce the Leeds man's privacy and strip the veneer from this enigmatic character. But Louis did concede that he was surprisingly sorry when he had to say goodbye to the Yorkshireman.

## Chris Moyles

**YOU can't imagine that the good priests who represent the Oblates of Mary Immaculate would countenance the occasional language employed by Britain's number one DJ and pop-presenter Chris Moyles. The religious order founded Mount St Mary's – the school where Leeds-born Chris was educated.**

**Chris is a loyal Leeds United supporter and follows the team in spite of their fluctuating football fortunes. He rarely misses a game home or away and he is friendly with the past players as well as the present team members.**

**Chris is a record breaker with more listeners to his early morning Radio One show than any previous presenter. His chatter has earned him cult-like status and he is never reluctant to sings the praises of his native city.**

**By the way he is a brilliant singer and if his present profession ever comes to an end he could always earn a good living as a vocalist. The Moyles family members are entitled to be proud of the young man's progress and achievements. He has talent to match his ambition.**

**Richard Whiteley, who was helped by a ferret to gain international fame, was talented, friendly and easygoing but also very shy. In addition, he had a brilliant sense of humour. This photograph featured on the Order of Service for his memorial service at York Minster.**

# Richard Whiteley

It is a little known fact that the late Richard Whiteley asked for the recording of his painful episode with a ferret to be scrapped. Richard didn't realise that the oft-repeated scene would gain him worldwide recognition and sympathy. But I can understand his reticence because he was not only talented, friendly and easygoing. He was also basically very shy.

This modest and almost bashful disposition is not usually associated with those who front programmes for millions of viewers. But Richard once confided that he occasionally felt like 'doing a runner' when asked to address an audience.

A few of us once discussed this trait when we gathered in the Yorkshire Television bar. Fred Dinage admitted that he was often physically sick before a programme. Keith Macklin had to allay his nerves with a large Scotch and Richard survived with a few deep breaths and his ability to portray a non-existent calm exterior. Even veteran broadcaster Michael Parkinson has had his share of collywobbles. He is convinced that only a masochist would agree to make a public speech or submit to the glare of TV cameras.

Richard had a brilliant sense of humour and we shared a private joke that had its origin at a trades union meeting held in the YTV canteen. We were not involved in the political discussions. We simply enjoyed a cup of tea and listened to the lighting and electrical workers discussing possible strike action.

The late Geoff Buckle was spokesman and he hollered: "The situation is this brothers! We are engaged in what can only be termed a game of chess and we are simply the PRAWNS and the management have got us in a snooker!"

Richard almost choked on his cuppa and for months all I had to do was whisper 'prawns' to have him in hysterics.

We often shared social evenings and occasions – not the least trips to the racecourse to enjoy our mutual passion for the Sport of Kings. He was not a gambler but he once bet me that his horse would finish nearer first than last. When it came in a remote little figure nearly a furlong behind the rest he cheerfully paid his losing stake of a bottle of bubbly – albeit the cheapest on offer at the time.

I once secured his services to open a new betting shop in The Calls, Leeds. Richard brought his *Countdown* partner Carol Vorderman with him and we challenged her to match her mathematics against the seasoned staff of bet settlers. Doubles, trebles and other multiple bets at odds stretching from 11 to 10 to 85 to 40 were no problem to Carol and she managed to draw with the experienced employees who were able to use computerised calculators. Richard and me were suitably impressed by her prowess.

We were also lost in admiration of a YTV floor manager who gave us a huge laugh when we watched rehearsals for a comedy show. Ventriloquist Ray Allan and his dummy Lord Charles were in full flight but there was a problem with an overhead microphone. It kept dropping into vision, much to the annoyance of the director. He decided that the solution was to dispense with the boom mike and replace it with one clipped to the artiste's lapel. The floor man was despatched to the stores for the clip mike. He returned and attached it to Lord Charles's lapel at which the noble dummy said: "It is him what ruddy talks not me!"

Once again Richard dissolved into gales of merriment. He was always a good laugher.

The last time we were together was at the funeral of John Meade, the first producer of *Countdown*, and Richard spoke with typical eloquence and humour in a tribute to a man we admired as a fellow journalist.

John's passing was premature. Richard's departure from this mortal coil was even more so. He was at the zenith of his career and shock waves travelled worldwide. There was neither a vacant seat nor a dry eye at Richard's memorial service where stories were told in abundance. But only Richard, and you and me, know about the 'prawns'.


# Have a Go!

It was that bubbling broadcaster Kathryn Apanovicz who turned my thoughts to the late Wilfred Pickles when she asked me to take part in her Radio Leeds show *Have a Go*. No doubt she wanted me to recall the days of Wilfred and his wife Mabel and trot out one or two anecdotes about the Yorkshireman who enjoyed a career as shop assistant, newsreader, actor, quizmaster, pantomime star and poet.

But no! I arrived in the studio for the live interview and perched before the effervescent Kathryn with my favourite collection of Wilfred stories ready to burst on the unsuspecting listeners. At times like this I try to portray a cool exterior, although the mere presence of a microphone is sufficient to send the collywobbles churning, hence the torrent of words which gush and gain momentum as my contribution hits the airwaves.

So you can imagine the inner panic when Kathryn told me she was asking me to *Have a Go* and answer such soul-searching questions as 'when did you have your first kiss' followed by 'name your favourite schoolteacher'. I had to confess to the adorable Kathryn, a gal with an infectious giggle, that to my eternal shame I was not aware of the content of her programme and that we had got our wireless wires crossed.

But at least I was able to tell her of the original *Have a Go* programme, which lasted for two decades, travelled the length and breadth of the British Isles and had a regular audience of more than twenty million listeners. It was broadcast from Leeds. It was unscripted and off the cuff. It was homespun fun and visited hamlets, villages, towns and cities, where inhabitants were invited on stage in front of family and friends to answer innocent questions. It was mostly predictable but we all waited for the moment which drew crimson blushes from embarrassed and probably spotty teenagers.

Wilfred asked: "Are you courting?"

This was sufficient to stir the locals into gales of laughter as the 'victim' shuffled and stumbled.

But there was one other question that I will never forget because it resulted in a major change to *Have a Go's* format. Wilfred was on stage with a genteel old lady of four score years and she faithfully answered his queries about the neighbourhood, local customs and the rest. He finally produced his poser: "If you could make the world a happier place in which to live what would you do?"

The pert pensioner replied: "I would buy everyone a bicycle and we would ride round the streets – smiling at each other."

Wilfred, with due solemnity, murmured: "What a beautiful thought!" And the audience erupted into a burst of applause.

Wilfred then turned to producer Barney Colehan and whispered: "Have you ever heard such bloody nonsense?"

Unfortunately this sotto voce aside was heard by millions and the expletive shocked the nation. Wilfred was summoned to appear before the broadcasting hierarchy and he was censured and warned about his future conduct.

*Have a Go* had been a live programme up to Wilfred's slip of the tongue. After that it was recorded and subjected to editing before it was allowed to burst into our living room from the domed Cossor radio.

Barney Colehan was a good friend. We enjoyed many happy chats and his flying officer handlebar moustache fairly bristled when he talked of his triumphs with the universally acclaimed *Good Old Days*. His pink features always creased into a smile when he reflected on *Have a Go* and he estimated that he must have travelled at least half a million miles to mount the broadcast.

One of the ever presents on the show was Violet Carson who played the piano as volunteers walked on and off the stage. She also thumped out the signature tune which the audience sang with gusto: "Have a go Joe, come on and have a go..." Violet progressed to play Ena Sharples in *Coronation Street*.

Wilfred was born in Halifax and was always proud of his Yorkshire roots. He worked in the family business with his father who was a builder and he dabbled in amateur dramatics. He secured a job with the BBC reading the news from the Leeds studio, although his northern accents did not suit every listener. Wilfred first hit the headlines when he ended one news summary with "Good night and to all Northerners, wherever you may be, good neet." This caused a furore of objections but Wilfred was allowed to repeat his 'neet' on a few occasions.

I first met him when he was in pantomime at the Theatre Royal, Leeds, and remember another long conversation with him and wife Mabel in the General Wade Bar at the Merrion Hotel, Leeds. I recall that with clarity because thrifty Wilfred did not pay for a drink all night but kept us entertained with stories, true and otherwise. He certainly had the gift of the gab and he enjoyed a giggle just like Kathryn Apanovicz.

# Alan Bennett

When Alan Bennett was granted the Freedom of the City of Leeds he realised that he would have to make a speech at the ceremony staged with due solemnity at the ornate Civic Hall. The versatile playwright, author and actor is accustomed to the limelight. He is no stranger to 'treading the boards' and as a professional thespian he knows the value of rehearsal. Alan was at the Civic Hall hours before the function because he wanted to ensure the word-perfect delivery of his speech and no doubt he made a sound check of the in-house sound system.

Alan has travelled to the four corners of the earth. But he has never lost touch with his roots and he was visibly touched by the civic approval of his works and the gratitude of Leeds citizens for his diverse talents. He told the audience: "I am moved and humbled by this honour but I think I was given the freedom of the city more than fifty years ago. I was given a free education that set me up for life. I am a great believer that students' education should be free and I hope that situation returns one day."

Alan was a pupil at Leeds Modern School before winning entrance to Exeter College, Oxford University. He was also a junior lecturer at Magdalene College and he paid tribute to author Richard Hoggart for influencing him to turn to writing.

He recalled: "I read Richard's *The Uses of Literacy* when I was in New York with *Beyond the Fringe* and it made me realise that life and growing up in Leeds could be turned into writing. I had been of the opinion that my life had been rather dull. But Richard's book showed me that if you got close enough to any life it was worth writing about."

Councillor Andrew Carter moved the motion to grant the Freedom to Alan and describi him as 'the greatest literary figure this city has produced'. He commented: "His Yorkshireness and his Leedsness has endeared him to the world. Alan Bennett's works have always touched the hearts of those, like myself, who count themselves among his many admirers. I am delighted that the city is able to honour him. This honour is long overdue."

Alan came to prominence with the comedy review *Beyond the Fringe* in which he appeared with Peter

Cook, Dudley Moore and Jonathan Miller. He has written numerous books and scripts for film, stage, TV and radio. He has received the Tony Award (1963), the Royal Television Society Award (1984 and 1986) and the Olivier Award (1990).

He will cherish the Freedom of his native city but is unlikely to follow the dictates of the award to the letter. The ancient title of Freeman gives Alan permission to drive any sheep he may have across Leeds Bridge!

Alan joins an elite band of Freeman including Dame Fanny Waterman, founder and chairman of the Leeds International Piano Competition; Jane Tomlinson, who has defied cancer to raise over a million pounds for various charities; and Nelson Mandela.

# Liz Dawn

If you were introduced to Sylvia Butterworth it is odds on that you would instantly recognise a lady who is as bubbly as the hairstyle which identifies her as one of the nation's most loveable television characters.

'Vera Duckworth' is the uncrowned queen of *Coronation Street* and long may she and her screen husband Jack continue to entertain viewers who voted them the most popular couple in Britain's soaps.

Sylvia was born in Torre Mount, Burmantofts, Leeds. Her family moved to Halton Moor when she was nine and was as adventurous and athletic as any girl of that age.

She recalls: "I jumped over a privet hedge and hit a brick wall. My top lip was badly damaged and I had to have plastic surgery at St James's Hospital. The skin to do the repair was taken from my bum so I've been able to make plenty of jokes about people kissing my bottom."

Sylvia was educated at Corpus Christi Roman Catholic School, Halton Moor, and little did she know in those formative days that St James's would once again figure prominently in her later years.

Life in Leeds was a struggle for her family as it was for many families. Her dad was in the army and her mum worked at a clothing factory but the girl destined to become Vera Duckworth was a happy and contented youngster.

She said: "It's not what you have in life in material gifts but how much love one had. And I had a lot. All I remember from my earliest days was family love and laughter."

There was even a trace of fun and a giggle or two when she made what she describes as her 'disastrous' entrance into the world of entertainment. She was seventeen and was booked to appear at a working men's club and remembers: "I wore my cousin's old wedding dress and walked on in front of an audience of flat-capped fellows. They were probably too puzzled and amazed to laugh. However I earned nearly thirty bob for singing 'The Nun's Chorus'."

Eventually her engagements increased and she gained a loyal following with songs like 'The Birth of the Blues'. Sylvia married and gave birth to Graham. Her daughters are Dawn Elizabeth, Ann, and Julie. And when it became essential that Sylvia should have a stage name she turned to her eldest daughter and became Liz Dawn.

Liz made her initial appearance on *Coronation Street* in July 1974. It was a small part compared to her present exposure. She played the role of a factory union girl demanding a better deal for the workers. She maintained her links with the clubs because she did not expect the TV work to be regular. But it was and the role of Vera Duckworth was made for the Leeds lass.

Liz said: "Vera is a bit like me really. That's why I feel so at home in *Coronation Street*. I love it."

The family left Leeds to live in Manchester but Liz concedes that her heart was still in her home city. She said: "It doesn't matter where you go – you never forget your roots."

That is probably why she and husband Don now have a house in the quiet village of Thorner, a matter of about twelve miles from Leeds city centre. Their home is also a short drive to St James's Hospital where the governors, surgeons, doctors, nurses and most of all patients have reason to bless the name of a lady who helped to raise a million pounds for the Liz Dawn Breast Cancer Appeal.

She said: "St James's is special to me. My son Graham was born there and I decided that I wanted to give something back to the city. Every man, woman and child in Leeds has a mother wife, partner,

Allan Bennett – dramatist, actor, writer and born in Leeds. He has accomplished so much but little is known about this man who prefers to leave the limelight to others. Although he is associated with countless plays, many Yorkshire people still rave about his compelling series *Talking Heads*. The man is a genius.

Ask any dedicated Yorkshireman or woman to name their favourite *Coronation Street* character and it is odds on they will yell in unison 'Vera Duckworth'. This is not out of sheer loyalty to Liz Dawn who was born in Leeds. It is recognition of the fact that Vera is a regular scene-stealer. The record-breaking series would not be the same without Vera and her long-suffering husband Jack. The character was tailor-made for Liz Dawn. None could play it better.

sister, aunt or daughter who could be affected. The money donated will help the diagnosis and treatment of breast cancer. Each year there are 15,000 deaths. I wanted to get involved in this appeal because I believe women in Leeds deserve the very best possible treatment."

Liz is a former Lady Mayoress of Leeds. When her great unmarried and unattached friend Councillor Bernard Atha became Lord Mayor he required a Mayoress to help with his many duties. Bernard recruited twelve ladies to take office in turn and Liz carried out her civic duties with grace and dignity. Vera Duckworth would have been proud of her.

# Frankie Vaughan

The dark-haired boy with rather more talent for drawing than singing secured his first professional booking when he was a curly-haired nine-year-old. He was at school in Liverpool. His classmates were doing typical injustice to a song and the schoolmaster decided he would sort out 'the larks from the languid'.

The teacher recalled years later: "One little boy had the voice of an angel. It was deeper than the others. It was most impressive, rare and distinctly tuneful."

The impromptu audition gained young Frankie Abelson a place in the local Synagogue choir. He sang with the other choristers for three months and earned twelve shillings and sixpence for his burgeoning talent. Frankie's voice did become deeper and his first real fan was his Russian-born grandmother, who years later told everyone prepared to listen that she was the first to recognise his beautiful voice, and predicted that he would one day become a big star.

Her judgment was based on the fact that she saw the singer Eddie Cantor in a film and knew that her 'Frankie' would one day match the American film star's vocal achievements. The family story is that Grandma – with her curious Russian accent – murmured: "Vorn day you vill be a star on the screen. Make sure you are a good vorn."

Frankie did not take his loving granny seriously. But legend has it that when he decided to make singing his full-time career he remembered her 'Vorn' and adopted the surname Vaughan. The name became known throughout the world of entertainment. He was a truly international star, a heart-throb with good looks and a firm commitment to his loving Leeds-born wife Stella and their three children

Frankie was a gentleman and one of my treasures is a note he dropped me to say "Thanks for the kind words written about me in the *Yorkshire Evening Post*." Would any other idol take the trouble to say thanks?

Leeds was dear to his heart. He was a student at Leeds University, studying art, when he was persuaded to take part in the Rag Revue at Leeds Empire. He not only wowed the audience but was given a letter of introduction to the London impresario Bernard Delfont. With a mere £3 in his pocket he left Leeds to sing for free – at the Kingston Empire. He was an overnight success and, from that humble beginning, he soared to the forefront of the entertainment world. He quickly forgot his ambition to become a professional footballer having briefly played for Sheffield Wednesday and West Bromwich Albion.

Frankie was handsome with a perfect torso. His high kicks and occasional giggles sent girls into raptures. He had forty-nine handkerchiefs pinched by fans and in a matter of days he had requests for over three thousand signed photographs.

Frankie's wife Stella Shock was a Leeds girl and his love for her never faltered. Stardom in films – one with Marylyn Monroe – left him cold and he was more at home fronting his backing group 'The Vee Men' and singing to his adoring audiences.

His work for charity gained him the OBE, and then the CBE, and he was Deputy Lieutenant for Buckinghamshire in 1993. 'Give Me The Moonlight' was his signature tune and he never tired of the song he made his own. Frankie was voted Show Business Personality of the Year by the Variety Club in 1957 and in that year he made the first of his many shows on American TV.

Frankie recalled his early days in Liverpool and often said he might have gone astray but for joining a local boys' club. He had strong links with the Association of Boys' Clubs and encouraged youths to take advantage of this facility. He was a show business great for four decades and will never be forgotten by young and old alike. He was an adopted son of Leeds.

When Al Jolson told adoring audiences "You ain't heard nothing yet" he probably had future singers like Frankie Vaughan in mind. Frankie was the new 'Jolson'. He entertained fans throughout the world and, like Shirley Bassey, he was one of Britain's truly international performers. He was loved from Hunslet to Hollywood and the fact that he married a Leeds girl, Stella Shock, also endeared him to those who attended his concerts, watched him on TV, and bought his records.

Frankie oozed sex appeal with good looks, high kicks and 'naughty' giggles, rocking the ladies. He sang: "Give me the moonlight. Give me the girl. And leave the rest to me."

We should also have given him the Freedom of Leeds.

Frankie ties the knot and swings into action.

Frankie and Stella were sweethearts and loving husband and wife too!

# The Grand

The Grand Theatre is aptly named in view of its imposing grandeur and newly refurbished monumental eminence. It remains the largest theatre in Leeds with a 1,550 seating capacity, which is reduced by 99 seats when the orchestra pit is extended to accommodate huge productions. One claim is that the stage is the country's second in size and apart from its ultra-varied programme it is also home to the much feted Opera North.

The Grand Theatre was opened on November 18, 1878. The site was owned by designers George Corson and James Watson, who bought and developed the project at a cost of £21,102. Leeds City Council secured ownership in 1973 and the existence and future of the magnificent edifice is secure for years to come.

The late Desmond Pratt was *Yorkshire Post* theatre critic for years and like many journalists with this calling he was rather eccentric. He was invariably fair and accurate with his judgment of a production but there was one unforgettable review in which he castigated the theatre-going Leeds public for their apparent apathy to a production at Leeds University.

Desmond was impressed by the acting of the students in a truly ambitious show with the talented actors near to professional standard. He wrote: "This was a truly memorable performance spoiled by the obvious disinterest of the public. There was a mere handful of people in the audience."

His praise for the participants was graciously accepted by the producer but he felt he had to point out to Desmond that the performance he saw was simply a dress rehearsal to which the public were not invited! Perhaps it was Desmond's acknowledged partiality to pints of beer that affected judgment of the sparse attendance. But the saga went down in *Yorkshire Post* internal history with Desmond joining in the laughter of his colleagues.

Desmond frequented The Wrens public house opposite the Grand Theatre and there were occasions when he was in two minds about trusting his unsteady gait to cross the busy highway in safety. He often secured his well being by ringing for a taxi to transport him from The Wrens to the front entrance of the theatre – a matter of twenty yards and a one pound fee.

However there was no disguising the regard and affection Desmond had for the theatrical pride of Leeds. It was a sincere feeling of admiration he shared with the late *Yorkshire Evening Post* critic Ronald Wilkinson who gave Desmond the name 'Dame Daphne' – not that there was anything effete about his colleague.

The love and admiration for the Grand Theatre has not been confined to critics. It is shared by theatre-going citizens, who express mutual fondness for the Victorian proscenium, stalls, balcony, boxes, chandeliers and the versatility of productions. These range from touring musicals to dramas, not forgetting ballet and the magnificent contribution of Opera North, established at the Grand Theatre in 1978 as English National Opera North and changing its name in 1981.

Audiences increased rapidly and popularity soared over the intervening years with 'home' performances, lucrative tours throughout the county and overseas visits to Europe. There is a standing chorus of thirty-six backed by a strong permanent staff. Principal singers are often drawn from an international pool of acclaimed operatic greats. There is also an on-going scheme to discover, recruit and assist home-grown young talent to guarantee the excellence of the well-established operation.

My own memories of the Grand Theatre stretch back to childhood when pantomime was a regular Christmas feature. The annual treats were superior in cast and production to those at the City Varieties but equal to the Theatre Royal where Bunny Doyle was the regular lead.

The last pantomime I saw at the Grand starred singer Ronnie Hilton. He was born in Hull but lived most of his adult life in Shadwell, Leeds, with his wife Joan and family. He achieved everlasting fame with 'The Windmill in Old Amsterdam'. It has remained a favourite with children and Ronnie often said: "If I could find another song about a mouse I would make enough money to retire."

Ronnie had a number of hit songs he sang in the pantomime, which also starred the late comic Ted Rogers of *Dusty Bin* television fame. Ted was one of the most nervous entertainers – anxious about his material and even troubled after a successful performance. I was with him before he went on stage at the Grand Theatre and he paced the room for half-an-hour.

Another chap I visited at the Grand Theatre was Peter O'Toole who was appearing as a detective in a mystery play. Unfortunately for me someone had shown Peter an article in which I cast doubts about his

**The Victorian Gothic façade of Leeds Grand, which survived a threat of demolition in 1969. It remains the city's largest theatre and has recently undergone a massive 'Transformation' project to bring it up to modern standards.**
**(courtesy Leeds Grand Theatre)**

ability to play rugby. He was a member of a Leeds club before he found fame as a thespian and moved to London.

Peter was obviously proud of his rugby prowess and I was greeted in his room with a green flash which almost removed my head from my shoulders. Peter always wore green socks and the kick – playful I hoped – was intended to at least prove his kicking skill. He was quite serious and a quick departure on my part was a prudent action. The following day we met for lunch with another journalist Arthur Haddock and the incident of the night before was not mentioned.

Another memory is of a *Desert Song* production starring John Hanson. It was noticeable that the cast was small and actors took more than one role with Legionnaires doubling as Riffs. It was impossible for one cross-eyed huge figure to convince us that there were two of his ilk. He appeared as a goodie and a baddie and he joined in the giggles emanating from the audience when he walked on stage.

Leeds theatre fans are blessed not only with the Grand but the award-winning West Yorkshire Playhouse, which has prospered and progressed in popularity ever since its opening in 1990. Long may it continue to succeed where several West End theatres are struggling.

The future of theatre and the arts in Leeds is in safe hands.

# Lost Theatres

There was a time when the future of the West Yorkshire Playhouse in Leeds was as dark as a badly illuminated auditorium. But a campaign to rescue the financially troubled centre of elegance and culture succeeded in saving and protecting this theatrical treasure for posterity. It is a pity that similar salvage action was not launched to maintain the existence of the Leeds Theatre Royal, Leeds Empire and other beloved edifices of entertainment.

The Theatre Royal closed its portals on April 1, 1957, and it was a significant date because it was a foolish decision to rob the city of a familiar landmark. The final performance was watched by a capacity audience of 1,600 and at the end of the show, *The Queen of Hearts*, the curtain descended slowly to the beat of a muted drum roll. It was an evening charged with emotion and a farewell address, written by Mrs Gladys Laidler, was read by Wilfred Pickles.

Comedian Eddie Henderson made a brave but feeble attempt to lift the gloom. "Don't be sad," he quipped, "They've pulled down every place I have worked in."

The following day 1,600 seats were removed and many were bought by amateur theatrical companies. Fittings and fixtures followed and eventually bulldozers moved in to clear a site for new owners Schofields – now replaced and renamed the Schofields Centre.

The Leeds Empire opened on August 29, 1898, with a seating capacity of two thousand. The first managing director was Edward Moss, who was later knighted for services to the theatrical world. Edward suffered from first night nerves and started with an unintentional Spoonerism that had the audience in hysterics. He said: "Ladies and gentlemen I won't occutime your pie."

The patrons were described by top-of-the-bill comedian Harry Tate as 'magnificent and distinguished'. They greatly approved of the ornate structure and gasped with amazement at the latest innovation, a sliding roof that opened to allow smoke out, the moon to be seen and the odd dicky bird to enter.

The Empire ceased to function on February 25, 1961, with Six Royal Welshmen singing 'God Save the Queen' and the cast of *Babes in the Wood* joining in. Among those saying goodbye to the 'Lost Empire' were manager Leo Lion, a dapper executive; musical director Ronnie Roberts, who was also landlord at the Woodman Inn, Selby Road; barmaid Helen Wheatly, who was Nellie to thousands of her regulars; and probably the best-known employee Charles McConomy.

Leo started life in the theatre as a callboy and shared these duties with Val Parnell, a chap destined to become a national impresario. Nellie worked in the dress circle bar for forty-five years when Bass was fourpence a bottle, whisky fourpence a tot and liqueurs sixpence.

Charles McConomy was Charlie to regulars and he wore a blue uniform with the job description 'Foreman' picked out in gold letters. He was a master of all theatre trades but he loved to mingle with the Briggate crowds shouting 'Seats in all parts!' Charlie was the last to leave the Empire. He stayed to help clear the demolished area. He was not too dispirited because – like many of us – he truly believed that another music hall would rise from the debris. But now only memories remain of the era when laughter and applause echoed in these icons of varied entertainment.

# Stars of Empire

The passing of the Empire was a tragedy for those who patronised the much-loved music hall on a regular basis. Couples met under the famous Dyson's clock in Lower Briggate and walked to the 'palace of variety' to enjoy two-and-a-half hours of vaudeville.

The Empire's final show – the pantomime *Babes in the Wood* – starred the rubber-necked comic Nat Jackley and the the baritone Ian Wallace. Nat started his theatrical life as a straight man to a comic. But audiences found him funnier than his partner and roles were reversed. Nat's eccentric dancing appealed to old and young. He starred in over fifty pantomimes and appeared in three Royal Command performances.

But if there was a more popular 'turn' than Nat – especially in Leeds – it was Issy Bonn who sang to packed houses. The Leeds jewish population and gentiles alike appreciated his comedy based on the imaginary Mrs Finglefeffer. When he sang 'My Yiddisher Momma' there wasn't a dry eye in the stalls, circle or gods.

The story is told of one pantomime when Cinderella was offered three wishes by the Fairy Godmother.

Cinders said: "I want a lovely dress for the ball."

"Granted," said the Fairy.

Cinders asked: "May I have a coach with ponies to take me to the ball?"

"Granted," said the Fairy.

Cinders paused and murmured: "I would like to hear Issy Bonn singing 'When that Old Gang of Mine Get Together' followed by 'Mr Yiddisher Momma' please!"

The benevolent Godmother of course granted the wish. The stage blacked out leaving one spotlight to pick out the figure of Issy in smart white suit with matching trilby worn at a jaunty angle. Issy knocked them cold for twenty minutes and Cinderella reappeared to return to the pantomine script.

When music halls closed, Issy's career – like many others – slumped. But he had taken precautions for his future. He bought props, scenery and costumes. He got them for a song, stored them in London warehouses and loaned them to producers of professional and amateur productions at a generous price. Issy was shrewd and financially secure, unlike many in the entertainment sphere.

My most precious memory of the Empire started with a visit to the King Edward pub which stood a few yards from the stage door. The hostelry is no longer there but the sign depicting 'Empire Palace' is still visible to folk who visit the Victorian Centre. The King Edward was a haunt for journalists, police, racecourse gamblers, diners, drinkers, ladies of the night, members of the Empire orchestra and, of course, artistes who appeared at the music hall.

Josef Locke was in great form. He had sampled the Guinness and one or two drops of whisky. He warmed up his act with a few bursts of high notes when a page boy arrived to say: "Mr Locke – your music is being played. You are due on stage!"

Josef invited his new-found journalist friends to accompany him and we watched his swaggering entrance from the wings as he caught up the band with a resounding chorus of "I'll Join the Legion That's What I'll Do..." He hit the challenging high notes with aplomb. He took 'Kathleen' home a couple of times and twenty minutes later he had the audience waving handkerchiefs to the tune of 'Goodbye...'

Then it was back to the King Edward with the second house at the Empire still to come. He was in even better voice then if just a little unsteady as he marched up and down the stage.

Josef was even more 'unsteady' when he sang in a charity concert at Leeds Town Hall a few years later. He was singing his final number – 'Goodbye from the White Horse Inn' – when he fell off the stage. At least half a dozen ladies tended to the fallen idol. They loved him, his voice and his blarney.

The night was one of his last in Leeds. He had tax problems and he returned to Ireland. Rumour had it that he made occasional visits under an assumed name to sing and earn a few bob at clandestine promotions. I like to think that was true. He had a magnificent voice.

Possibily the most famous Leeds man to play at the Empire was Ernie Wise who appeared several times with his partner Eric Morecambe. Their act usually saw Ernie on stage with Eric heckling from a box before joining him in a song and dance. Years later Eric spent time in Leeds Infirmary after a heart-attack. He was helped by a passerby Mr Butterfield who sat by Eric's bed and – according to Eric – asked the star: "May I have your autograph before you go?"

Eric couldn't stop laughing even though he was seriously ill. He died in 1984. Tears were also shed when Ernie followed his faithful partner to the place reserved for funny men.

Johnny Riscoe was another Leeeds-born comic who worked at the Empire. His partner at one stage of his career was Archie Leach who became film star Cary Grant.

Peter Wallis, now 80, was also born in Leeds. He worked at Bellows' Machine Company before turning full-time professional comic. Opposite him at the work bench was Adrian Hill who won a singing contest at the Shaftesbury Cinema, Leeds. He sang 'With These Hands'. Adrian became Ronnie Hilton and I am sure that Peter and Ronnie were great losses to 'Bellows'. Peter is still cracking gags with the speed that earned him the nickname 'Machine Gun'.

Many performers at the Empire enjoyed a drink or several at the King Edward where singers Harry and Archie Bendon provided cabaret with other local acts like the Johnson Brothers – Terry and Geoff – and Tony 'Ascot' Heath, Jack Platts and many others. But few booked accommodation in the city centre. They preferred the cheaper theatrical digs in Headingley or Spencer Place.

Roy Hudd recalls the time he spent in Leeds rehearsing for pantomime. Every night he and his mates returned from rehearsals to the damp digs where the landlady served them a supper of baked beans. The night of the dress rehearsal was Christmas Eve. It was after midnight when they returned and Roy vowed: "If she serves me baked beans again I'll throttle her!"

She walked in the dining room with beans and a sausage on top. Roy shouted: "I think you've made a mistake. I've found a sausage."

She shouted: "I know – Merrry Christmas."

Bill Pertwee, who played the ARP warden Mr Hodges in Dad's Army, has fond memories of Leeds. We shared a platform at a Pudsey cricket dinner where he recalled that he and his wife Marion were in panto at Leeds just before the closure of the Empire.

Bill said: "It was nothing new to us. We closed more theatres than any other act. It was just coincidence. But we were on the road when many variety theatres were putting up the shutters. Television killed music hall."

But many of us still have memories. See you under Dyson's clock.

# The City Varieties

If you stroll up the Headrow to a pub officially named The Horse and Trumpet and unkindly tagged by some 'The Whore and Strumpet' you will see a gap in the adjoining wall. The untidy fenced-off little passage is grimy and strewn with litter. But it once was an illuminated front entry to the time-honoured City Varieties – the oldest music hall in Britain and a theatrical edifice that has survived countless threats to its survival.

It was my privilege to stand on the hallowed stage and introduce an amateur edition of The Good Old Days. Having 'sung for my supper' at many a function, stage fright did not even enter my build up to this charity production.

I spent the hour before 'curtain up' building the confidence of a singer who insisted he could not perform because his nerves were shattered. It was little short of hypnotism on my part but I finally convinced him that he would charm the audience and bring the house down.

With the tenor now brimming with self-belief the minutes ticked away to the opening and I asked the orchestra leader (a keyboard player and drummer) for details of my role.

He said: "You will stand in the middle of the stage like the professional Leonard Sachs used to do. The band will play 'There's No Business Like Show Business', the curtains will fly open, the spotlight will hit you and you are on!"

With two minutes to go I took my place. And suddenly panic and frenzied fright, coupled with almost hysterical terror, struck simply because I reasoned: "Charlie Chaplin stood on this spot. So did Roy Hudd, Max Miller, Jimmy James, Mike and Bernie Winters, Florrie Forde, Gertie Gitana and countless others. What on earth was I doing standing on this hallowed platform?"

All I could do was pray and I murmured two Hail Marys and an impassioned "Oh dear God I place all my trust in thee". There was a drum roll and suddenly the velvet drapery between me and the audience flew open with a swish. I mentally cursed the singer who had denied me a rehearsal. I stared into a blinding light. There wasn't even a shadow visible from the auditorium and I managed to stutter a rather pathetic: "It's only me...."

The audience laughed bless 'em. It reached out to me. I walked to the side box often used by the great Mr Sachs and we were in show business for real. The rest of the night is still a blur but I know that I used every joke in my repertoire before the calm and collected singer 'paralysed' the patrons.

I love the City Varieties. We have been friends for over sixty years. My first visit was in 1945 when my duties as a cub reporter decreed that I would cover the 'Verts' first performance on Monday evenings and then cross Briggate to do the second house of the Empire production. Our chief sub-editor John Bolton was also a theatre critic. He attended the Grand Theatre and expected me to produce sixty words on the City Varieties show and one hundred and twenty on the Empire production.

In fact I stayed up until midnight producing yards of copy only for Mr Bolton to slash and often rewrite my reports without a word of praise or criticism. It was good training but I dare not tell my religious mother where I was spending Monday evenings. She was under the impression that I was learning Pitman's shorthand and typing at Osmondthorpe Night School.

The reason for my presence at the 'Verts' was that the majority of senior newspapermen were away at war and it was given to pimply-faced youths, wearing their first pair of 'longies', to represent the newspaper at all manner of adult promotions.

The City Varieties welcomed reporters and provided two tickets for admission and two passes for a free drink at the bar. I was not old enough to visit the licensed part of the building and saved my free drink dockets until the arrival of Christmas. I then presented the manager Mr Pip Pawson with a fistful of tickets and asked: "Can I have a bottle of gin and a bottle of whisky please?"

Mr Pawson conferred with the theatre owner Harry Josephs. The drink dockets were confiscated and I was presented with a bar of chocolate. It was small, dark and edible, but not bad when you consider that sweets were on ration.

I covered the Varieties and Empire for three years and laughed at the jokes of such comedians as Harold Behrens, Yeadon-born Joe Black, Doctor Crock and his Crackpots, Hylda Baker, Jimmy Gaye and others. We marvelled at the magic of Jasper Maskeylin and applauded the inevitable acrobats and juggling acts, and the antics of Leeds-born Morton Fraser and his Harmonica Gang.

My favourite story of Harold Behrens was told by himself in the bar. It concerned a lady who rang him to ask if he would perform at her daughter's wedding reception. They agreed a fee and later in the week she rang again to cancel the arrangement. She said: "I've had a long talk with my daughter and we were unable to choose between you and a fish course. We thought about it a lot and the fish won."

Another of my favourites was Talbot O'Farrell who was billed as 'The Voice that stopped the roar of Dublin's Traffic'. In actual fact Talbot started his career as a singer of Scottish ballads. He flopped so he switched to being Irish and he could bring tears to a glass eye with his speciality 'That Old Fashioned Mother of Mine'.

Another 'Irish' singer was the 'strolling vagabond' Cavan O'Connor, who was born in Nottingham. Cavan was booked by the Leeds Ex-Boxers' Association to sing at their annual dinner held at the Queens Hotel. He was accompanied by his wife on the piano and, after one hour and twenty minutes, he was still singing. We left him half an hour after that and he was still churning out his ditties in a sort of musical marathon.

Terry 'Toby Jug' Cantor ruled the pantomime roost for generations at the Varieties. He was originally an entertainer and turned producer to stage the longest running pantomime in the country. His son Kenny – a comedian and producer – succeeded him.

But it was the ladies who pulled in the male public at the 'Verts' with Phyllis Dixey, who was married to Jack 'Snuffy' Tracey, a real favourite with patrons who enjoyed a little bare glamour. 'Snuffy' packed in his comic act to become his wife's manager. She had her own show 'Peek-A-Boo' with girls who stripped as she talked to the audience. Finally she posed in the 'all together' with nothing at all showing.

She once held court in the City Varieties ' famed Victorian Bar and told us that a woman's greatest asset was a man's imagination. And this imagination seemed to run riot when she was posing on the Leeds stage.

Phyllis was quite a lady and beautifully spoken. 'Snuffy' was a duff as a manager. He eventually went bankrupt and Phyllis ended her theatrical career. She returned to her proper name of Selina and dropped the title 'The Girl the Lord Chamberlain Banned'. She finished her working days as a cook and,

I believe, a happy one.

'Jane of the Daily Mirror' was Chrystabel Leighton-Porter and she appeared with her dachshund Fritz who also starred in the newspaper cartoons. She was the darling of the RAF bomber crews. Her portrait with the dog was painted on the side of planes with the number of hits they made against German aircraft and cities.

Jane sang: "I'm Jane, Jane, the model that's plain. I can't sing. I can't even croon. And the dog that I fondle is also a model that you've seen in a daily cartoon."

"Gerrem Off" was usually the ribald shout from the gallery.

Miss Leighton-Porter was also a lady, educated and, like others, she posed in picture frames. They were not allowed to move. They were pin-up girls and posed inside ornate frames. They were perfectly still and didn't even shiver with goose pimples as the curtains opened, paused, then closed again.

Members of the Watch Committee attended the first night to keep an eye on the girls. Even a flutter of the eyebrows would have resulted in the show being closed. 'Peaches Page' was chosen for an historic challenge to the law. It was my assignment to see the first moving stripper. Police were in evidence. We waited with pencil poised to record every detail of the sensational act. There was a roll on the drums. The drapes parted and Peaches, with a few sequins dotted on her curves, sat astride a bike. This was propelled from one side of the stage to the other as the orchestra played 'A Pretty Girl is like a Melody'.

We roared our appreciation. The explanation to the police and members of the Watch Committee was that Peaches was motionless and it was the bike that moved. Shortly afterwards the law was changed and the girls were allowed to dance with fans and feathers strategically placed.

My story appeared in the *Yorkshire Evening Post* under my name. My mother read the story and realised that her curly-haired little paragon was not attending night school but reporting from what she described as a 'den of iniquity'. It took a rise in my wartime wages from twelve shillings and sixpence a week to twice as much to placate my dear old mum.

The City Varieties stands as a monument to entertainment and the golden era of music hall. Hopefully it has the brightest of futures. Perhaps we will see you at one or another of the forthcoming shows. I can recommend *The Good Old Days* with a truly professional 'Mr Sachs' of course.


# 'The Good Old Days'

Elland Road Greyhound Stadium was an unlikely venue for my first meeting with the late Barney Colehan, a BBC producer, impresario and inspired originator of *The Good Old Days*. But Barney was more than a show business genius. He was a gentleman – in every sense of the word – and kind, charitable, modest about his achievements and easily recognisable.

Barney was as well-known in remote parts of Europe – where he recruited star acts – as he was in his native Yorkshire, which he toured with Wilfred Pickles to record the radio hit *Have a Go*. That show spawned an everlasting catchphrase "Give him the money Barney" and 'Give Him The Money' and 'Good Old Days' were the names given by Barney and his late wife Monica to greyhounds they had at the popular Leeds Stadium.

They enjoyed an occasional relaxing few hours in the track restaurant, from where they could watch their canine athletes hurtling round the circuit. But Barney could never hide from The Good Old Days because people – and reporters like yours truly – never hesitated to steer the conversation in that direction.

It was a show loved by millions. It ran for thirty years, from 1953 to 1983, and Barney produced 244 editions of the programme, which was watched throughout its lifespan by 2,000 million viewers. It was at the "dogs" where Barney invited me and my wife Maureen to attend Sunday night recordings of The Good Old Days – an offer gratefully received much to the envy of thousands.

When the BBC closed the show there was an eight-year waiting list of ten thousand people prepared to dress in appropriate costumes simply to sit in the audience. Folk searched the attics and even

**Barney Colehan was easily recognisable by his handlebars moustache and his ever-ready smile. But there were a few occasions when the 'tash' bristled and he was not too happy with the world. This demeanour was only in evidence when he had a poor round at golf. If he hit good form at Sand Moor Golf Club, Leeds, he bought sandwiches and drinks at The Jester Pub for people like me. If his driver and putter were not in tune the clubs were slammed into the car boot and we had to pay for our own 'sarnies' and pints.**

**Barney was a loveable man and a great pioneer for Northern radio and television.**

patronised theatrical costumiers to dress for the occasion and I am ashamed to say that we failed in this direction. We always perched on seats out of camera shot in the dress circle and surveyed the City Varieties music hall and the colourful creations worn by the audience.

Barney had other acclaimed productions like *It's A Knockout* with Stuart Hall and the late Eddie Warring, which hit the TV screen in 1966 and ran for sixteen years. One of Eddie's last appearances in public was with Barney at a sportsmen's dinner at the Queens Hotel, Leeds. It was an enjoyable function but there was a sad note and Barney rang me the following morning to report that Eddie's famous titfer – his grey trilby – had been stolen from the hotel cloakroom.

Eddie was understandably upset and Barney was perhaps even more distressed because of his friend's loss. He asked me to offer a reward for the return of the hat but not to divulge who was putting up the money. Unfortunately the person who deprived Eddie of his celebrated hat failed to return the property. The story is typical of Barney's sincere regard for other people – not only his friends, but also and sometimes lonely people at Meanwood Park Hospital, Leeds.

Barney will never be forgotten and neither will *The Good Old Days*, which many who appeared in the show, like Roy Hudd, Norman Collier, Ken Dodd, Danny Le Rue and others, agreed should never have finished. Barney left us a theatrical legacy in a dozen sheets entitled: 'Historical Information on Leeds City Varieties – compiled by Barney Colehan'.

The City Varieties battles on and still produces a version of *The Good Old Days* without the TV exposure. There is an association called the Friends of the City Varieties with members dedicated to preserving the perpetuity of this famous Yorkshire landmark. Long may their efforts continue.

Barney Colehan would certainly have joined their ranks and I must do that myself, if only in memory of the man who arguably saved this fine old theatre from possible extinction. May we never forget Barney's slim figure, immaculate suits, curly handlebar moustache, ready wit and dedication to *The Good Old Days*. He never missed a single programme.

# Fanny Waterman

The Leeds Triennial International Pianoforte Competition was founded in 1961 and continues to attract worldwide acclaim and patronage. It owes its existence to Dame Fanny Waterman and Marion Countess of Harewood, who persuaded Jack Lyons to chair a committee and back the enterprise with a substantial donation.

Fanny was born in Leeds. She was educated at Allerton High School and Leeds University and studied the piano at London Royal College of Music. Fame as a concert pianist came early in life with appearances at the annual Promenade Concerts. But Fanny always claimed that teaching was her vocation with pupils Michael Roll, Allan Schiller, Paul Crossley and many others testimony to her enthusiasm, encouragement and sheer professionalism.

The fact that the Leeds competition matches the one promoted in Moscow is a living tribute to the lady who spent sleepless nights deciding whether or not she should sacrifice the concert stage for teaching. The competition was an overwhelming success from the first day with Fanny grateful for the help she was given at the outset by 'so many true friends who sadly are not with us today'.

She recalls Benjamin Britten composing a special piece for the initial competition and often reflects on the distinguished musicians who 'surrendered lucrative engagements to join the jury at Leeds Town Hall'.

When Leeds-born Michael Roll emerged triumphant from the competition beating rivals drawn from all parts of the compass, he stressed the role Fanny had played in his education. He was gracious and modest when he bowed to the acclaim of jury members and those who filled Leeds Town Hall. And Fanny must have had a sense of satisfaction having played such a major part in Michael's burgeoning career. His success made the sleepless nights worth worthwhile.

# All that Jazz!

The mere mention of the White Eagles Jazz Band is sufficient for afficionados of traditional Dixieland rhythm and blues to stomp down a musical Memory Lane. Martin Bowland helped to found the band forty-eight years ago and he is still playing clarinet and soprano saxophone in a style reminiscent of Sidney Bechet.

Martin recalls: "When we started we were atrocious. We rehearsed in a rat-infested warehouse on the River Aire quayside near Spiller's Wharfe. It was probably just as well we only had rodents to listen to our pathetic attemps at music making. But the premises – now a posh development – were sufficient for our modest requirements."

Ed O'Donnell, a legend in Leeds jazz circles, was in the original White Eagles line-up and the band's first proper base was at The Royal, Lower Briggate – an historic staging post lost to rebuilding.

Martin remembers: "By the time we played at The Royal we had improved and we later performed at The Peel, in Boar Lane, and enjoyed a spell at The Star and Garter on Kirkstall Road."

He adds: "At the time I was playing Rugby League with Hunslet and studying for accountancy so it was a busy life. Our brand of music enjoyed a boom and our fame spread with monthly bookings at the famous Cavern Club in Liverpool. In fact The Beatles were our support group and played for an hour in between traditional jazz contributions. At the time they had not had a hit number. Things certainly changed and I will never forget Paul, Ringo and George – although it is highly unlikely that they will remember us."

Ed O'Donnell left the White Eagles to demonstrate his brilliance on the trombone with Kenny Colyer's renowned band. Ed has enjoyed a lifelong love affair with trad-jazz but music did not always pay the bills and he supplemented his income with sessions as a model at Leeds Art School.

Martin comments: "All who have played with the White Eagles remain good friends and we often join each other in other bands."

Martin retired from work as a chartered accountant and he is able to concentrate on his hobbies including art, a twelve-month course on the French language and of course music. He says: "After forty years in jazz I think I am just about getting the hang of it!"

Jazz from another age is also remembered by Stan Belwood of Gildersome: "I played at various venues with different bands in the 1940s and 1950s. I remember appearing with Mick Mulligan's Band and George Melley at both Leeds Town Hall and Morley Town Hall."

Similarly, Ronnie Encell recalls: "I remember tales of the Yorkshire Jazz Band enjoying jam sessions on train journeys to London. They made a few records and I believe the first two included 'Big Chief Battleaxe' backed by 'Muskrat Ramble', 'When You Wore a Tulip' and 'Washington and Lee'.
'Big Chief Battleaxe' became the Yorkshire band's signature tune."

Local jazz is also recalled by Jeff Clayton: "I remember in the 1950s happy times at The Adelphi, the Scarborough Taps and later the Dock Green. Those Leeds pubs featured the famous Al Potts, who took his teeth out to play clarinet and put them back when he sang one of his rather rude vocals. Former Member of Parliament Mike Meadcroft was on soprano sax and there were also sessions with the White Eagles and ther Ed O'Donnell band at The Eagle in North Street, Leeds."

# Dance Halls

"Ladies and gentlemen please take your partners for the last waltz...."

The announcement signalled the end of another night of romantic nearness, the scent of Californian Poppy and perhaps a tinge of sadness at the impending finale of the weekly hop. 'Who's Taking You Home Tonight' was one of the more popular melodies as you glided into strict tempo movements and, if you were like me, counted one-two together, one-two together'. My calves always ached at this stage of the evening because it was the in-thing to attempt every dance.

There were unfortunate lads who couldn't get a partner and 'wallflowers' too shy to cross the floor and ask: "May I have this dance please?"

But it was a case of everyone for himself when novelty numbers like the Conga, Ballin' the Jack, Lambeth Walk, Knees Up Mother Brown and the ever popular Hokey Cokey were in full flight. It was the Yanks who introduced us to Ballin' the Jack with the instruction: "First you put your two knees close-up tight, you shake 'em to the left, and you shake 'em to the right."

The Conga often zig-zagged its rhythmic route from the dance hall to the pavement and back. But the Hokey Cokey was even more rumbustious.

It was in 1942 when Canadian songwriter Jimmy Kennedy penned the immortal words: "You put your left arm in..." – and so on. His title was Cokey Cokey but this smacked of cocaine. British decency prevailed and it was Hokey Cokey in our country and remained so throughout my years as a dance-hall patron. The final verse of the Hokey Cokey was akin to a rugby scrum as we 'put our whole self in' and charged into the centre of the circle with the grace of a rampant rhino.

I suppose our forebears were equally knocked out when the Charleston was all the rage and such bandleaders as Harry Rabinowitz, Herman Darewski, George Elrick and Nat Gonella were heartthrobs.

I interviewed trumpet star Nat at the City Varieties in the early 1980s when he made a brave but short-lived attempt to resurrect his career. We had a strange conversation because he blew scales on his trumpet in between questions and sometimes in the middle of a sentence.

Nat was a super player and so was a Leeds hornblower Arnie McBride. Arnie overcame the disadvantage of losing an arm but I suppose the trumpet can be played as well single-handed as it is with two. But something else amazed me about Arnie. He gave me a lift home after visiting a club in Leeds and he drove a vehicle with a manual gear change. It was the next morning when I asked myself: "How on earth did Arnie do this? He must have taken his one hand off the wheel to operate the gear stick."

Yorkshire was rich in all kinds of music in those days with the new wave 'boppers' lessening the popularity of the quickstep, tango, foxtrot and old-time dancing. The first Leeds bopping boys were newly-arrived West Indians who sported long jackets with trousers pegged at the ankles. Did we call them zoot suits? They took over the upstairs room at the Mecca and one of the great movers was David Owale who was destined to meet his death in mysterious circumstances.

The Mecca 'attic' bounced to the music of the Tommy Allen Trio and jazz fans were also catered for with weekly sessions at the Judean Club, Chapletown; Armley Baths; and The Starlight Roof. York Road. The John Dankworth Seven, with a young Cleo Laine, were regular turns in the days of the Tito Burns Sextet and the Latin American bop of Kenny Graham. But that music was not for me.

Bands led by Leeds' own Freddie and Ernie Tomasso, Johnny Adlestone and Roland Powell were more to my musical palate. I still prefer the old-fashioned waltz and a partner in my arms rather than the shaking all over more than a yard away from the girl of your dreams.

# Nightlife

Leeds city centre nightlife blossomed in the 1960s with the opening of Cinderella-Rockerfella catering for those who love to dance the night away. The dual venues were the brainchild of Peter Springfellow, later to make his international mark with dancing clubs in London and New York.

Casinos mushroomed with gamblers prepared to bet until croupiers made the final spin of the roulette wheel or dealt the last hand of cards. It was not unusual for punters still to be chasing the elusive crock of gold at 4.0 am.

The Ace of Clubs, Woodhouse, staged a nightly cabaret before gamblers moved into the Wedgwood Room. It was similar fare at the Windmill Club, North Street, owned by 'Lucky John Lonsdale' who booked top line artistes to attract patrons who stayed to gamble when the entertainment finished. Tony 'Ascot' Heath was resident compere and comedian with a fine singing voice. He still talks about the wonderful nostalgic days of the Windmill. It ruled the gambling roost before the likes of Ladbrokes,

Napoleon and other clubs and betting promoters moved into the city.

Saturday night fever became contagious with dance clubs like the Phonographique in the Merrion Centre. It was a major attraction and popular with footballers, particularly Leeds United's Gary Sprake. I saw Jack Charles in there too on the night the story broke in newspapers about the Leeds United star having 'a little black book' with the names of opposing players with whom he had scores to settle.

Madisons and Digby's were packed to capacity – not that it took many to fill the latter. It was a great era for those who had scant regard for beauty sleep and often went direct from the nightclub scene to their respective places of employment.

Leeds can boast over a hundred café bars and at least two dozen clubbing outlets attracting patronage from as far afield as London and Glasgow. A weekend's clubbing in Leeds, with hotel accommodation, is often cheaper than a night in London's expensive West End. Little wonder that Leeds is a magnet for merry makers and it is estimated that the '24-hour city' is firmly established as one of the country's leading entertainment centres.

Where else would you find more folk on the city centre streets at 3.0 am on Sunday than you would at noon on a weekday? Places like Atrium, Birdcage, The Warehouse and Jongleurs comedy club do roaring business. Clubland is here to stay.

# The Tingalary Man

My aversion to motorway service stations started when I was charged twenty-six pence for a pat of Flora to go with my humble ninety pence scone. Shock waves ran through my wallet when the cashier at an M4 roadside restaurant totted up the bill and added another £2 for a cup of coffee. It was then I decided to shun such establishments, even though the girl at the exit bade me bon voyage and added a sickly parting shot: "Missing you already!"

But I broke my self-imposed rule and popped into the services at Ferrybridge simply to make a telephone call. It was a rewarding move. At the entrance was a chap turning the handle of a tingalary and churning out foot-tapping melodies of my childhood. It was a barrel organ really, but definitely a tingalary, although it lacked the shafts and big wheels, which propelled the unique music-makers through Leeds.

We had our own tingalary man, Mr Tomasso, who was a senior member of an Italian family. He was a quiet gent. He rarely smiled or spoke. But he produced popular tunes for kiddies who danced and skipped round his magical machine.

There was quite a sizeable and welcome influx of Italian people into Leeds between the world wars with the Lusardi, Capitano, Curroto, Maturi, Granelli, Friola and other Latin families contributing much to the scene. They introduced us to 'hokey pokey' ice cream sold from coloured carts. Another regular visitor was the knife-grinder who sharpened the domestic cutlery to razor standard by holding it on a flint as he pedalled a static bike.

Mr Tomasso's family had a shop at the corner of New York Street and Shannon Street, next to Madden's the undertakers and close to the Woodpecker pub. The tiny shop sold ice cream, pop, sweets and confectionary. Customers also bought cups of Oxo and Bovril which they drank on the premises to while away the hours. It was a more leisurely life in those days.

Old Mr Tomasso kept his tingalary at the rear of the shop and – in good weather – he walked miles through the local estates playing tunes and nodding his appreciation of the pennies placed in a cup attached to the organ. The Tomasso family became well known in music circles with Ernie and Freddie playing for jazz bands like Harry Gold and his Pieces of Eight and other swinging outfits of that era.

I suppose the tingalary was really part of the busking scene and Leeds never lacked street entertainers. It still has them and I prefer to drop a few coins in their caps as opposed to dipping in my pocket to support those who simply litter the pavement. At least the singers, musicians and jugglers are doing something constructive about their parlous state and display their various talents for our appraisal and entertainment.

Who will ever forget the soaring tenor voice of Harry Bendon in his heyday or in recent years the musical marathons achieved daily by the later Busker Bill to boost the *Yorkshire Evening Post* 'half-and-half' appeal?

Many old-timers also recall with affection Doug and Mary who played the tin whistle in Kirkgate and often performed to queues waiting outside the much loved Empire Theatre in Briggate.

I often think of another chap who appeared to have rubber bones. He used to delight people waiting for trams at the Corn Exchange and Saturday nights usually saw him at his best. It was my job to go to Elland Road to report on the greyhound scene and I believe the number eight tram was the one we regularly caught. I always arrived at the Corn Exchange traffic island earlier than was necessary just to see the man who would swallow a plate of cockles or prawns at the nearby Hayes fish bar before starting his act.

He was a contortionist and I could never decide whether he was drunk or pretending to be inebriated. He staggered quite a bit but he never failed to achieve the highlight of his show – taking his shirt off without removing his jacket. The shirt was buttoned at the cuffs and only the neck was loose. How he pulled it over his head and shoulders under his jacket will always remain a mystery.

I listened to a young man playing the trumpet outside M & S the other day and swore it was Eddie Calvert reborn. He was so good I almost bought one of his tapes. But I prefer the tingalary and will certainly return to Ferrybridge service station even if it means buying an expensive cuppa with scone and Flora.

# 4: Looking Back

## Years of Hardship

The 1930s were undoubtedly spartan and difficult for many deprived families with careworn mothers – old and grey-haired before their time – struggling to make ends meet. I remember people talking about the Board of Guardians, means tests, slum clearance, bug vans and the promise of a new life on beautiful council house estates springing up miles away from such grimy and ancient sites as The Bank and other impoverished parts of the city of Leeds.

I recall ladies making Monday morning visits to the local 'pop shop' – sometimes known as 'Uncles' – where they would pledge their husband's best suit for a shilling of two and redeem it the following Friday for the man of the house to wear over the weekend. He had to be careful with the suit because it was due to be deposited in the pawnbroker's shop again on the Monday for the pittance that would see the family through the week. Many poor people were never out of debt with 'tick' available at most shops and it was like a credit roundabout with little or no escape. No sooner had one grocery or clothing bill been settled than another was being 'ticked up'.

But it was not all doom and gloom. Many homes were warm and cheerful from home baking and a kettle boiling on the hob. Mums and dads worked miracles to keep their kiddies nourished and, above all, loved, wanted and regularly hugged.

We were blessed with two evening newspapers in those days. There was the *Yorkshire Evening Post*, a little up-market and owned by the Yorkshire Conservative Newspaper Company, which gave an obvious clue to the politics of the publishers and the bulk of its readers.

The other paper was the *Yorkshire Evening News*, which catered for the other end of the political spectrum but had circulation figures well below that of its rival. In an effort to close the gap the *Yorkshire Evening News* printed coupons that readers clipped out and collected until they had sufficient to claim a full tea service with cups, saucers, side plates, teapot, milk jug and sugar basin – the lot! This became the Sunday best in many households and when visitors arrived for tea out would come the prized crockery. It was white with a little flower pattern round the rim of the cups and the edge of the plates.

Every house in our street had a set but it was not everyone who took advantage of another *Yorkshire Evening News* promotion. This was called 'Boots for Bairns' and it provided laced-up footwear for deprived children. It was welcomed by mothers who could ill afford to buy their offspring a pair of stout shoes or boots. A few of my pals wore the boots donated by the newspaper. They also received parcels of toys from the *Yorkshire Evening Post* at Christmas time and they were accepted – much to my envy – for a fortnight at the Leeds Poor Children's Holiday Camp at Silverdale.

In the bad old days there were many totally neglected 'bairns' among the tiny holidaymakers, but as described on the next page Silverdale was not always regarded as a brief panacea for poverty and penury.

## Children's Holiday Camp

In the mid-1930s the four principal railway companies decided to sell off old coaches and many of the renovated, gaily-painted, pieces of rolling stock became holiday homes. They were stationed in sidings on country and seaside branch lines and became quite a hit with families who liked to 'keep themselves'. One of our neighbours swore by this novel base and the kids loved life in the carriages. They played 'puffer trains' from dawn to dusk in between sunshine sorties to nearby beaches and farmyards.

In 1934 a party of eight could rent a coach for a mere £3 a week, which was infinitely cheaper than our first caravan vacation when my wife Maureen – and three sons and a daughter – headed for Thornwick Bay on the East Coast. All I can remember is the nauseating smell of Calor gas, children nursing sunburn and a plague of ants and earwigs that emerged from under a damp mattress. It was not exactly the holiday of a lifetime, although I must admit that a second attempt at caravanning, at Primrose Valley, was more enjoyable. However that sickly odour of Calor gas cured me of any thoughts I might have about repeating the experiment.

I once visited Leeds Children's Holiday Camp at Silverdale and joined thirty-six youngsters in a tour of the spacious living quarters, with playrooms containing computers, electronic games, books, records, table tennis and musical instruments. As stated on the previous page, the original name of the venture was the 'Poor Children's Holiday Camp'. However, a campaign by Leeds golfer Hedley Muscroft and the TV entertainers Bert and Fred Gaunt had the word they regarded as a 'slur' removed from the title.

Silverdale was blessed with an indoor swimming pool and a couple of go-karts. They travelled at a rare old speed round the site, which nestles in a secluded and rather picturesque curve of Morecambe Bay. Food was prepared in modern kitchens with a dedicated staff soothing homesick children and joining in recreational activities as well as singing the time-honoured camp anthem.

Silverdale, which opened in 1904, was never intended to be a children's paradise. But it served the original purpose of bringing fresh air and sunshine into the lives of youngsters who sampled this brief escape to a seaside haven. It gave joy to thousands who recalled their fortnight at Silverdale with lasting appreciation. But for many who failed to settle and enjoy the project it was a disaster and remains a haunting memory.

Historian Sam Wood recalls with graphic detail his childhood sojourn at Silverdale. His father died in June 1912 leaving his mother with four young lads to rear. Sam was eight, George six, Ernest a few years younger and Billy was the baby.

Sam remembers: "There was no welfare state, just a meagre handout from the Board of Guardians and free dinners for me at Prince's Field School. The newly-formed Leeds Poor Children's Holiday Camp had an office in Great George Street and some kind person recommended me and George for a fortnight's holiday at Silverdale.

"I will never forget that exciting day when my brother and me set out from our little back-to-back house in Holbeck for our very first holiday at the seaside. We ran as fast as we could to Isle Lane School where we were told to leave our clothing in a locker. We were then given a pair of light-coloured corduroy shorts, a dark blue jersey, cape, a pair of boots and stockings. There were a lot of other lads – some of them I knew. Others were strangers and we lined-up in pairs and marched along Sweet Street through ginnels in Water Lane towards Leeds Central station. We were happy and we were herded on to the train for Arnside.

"We were happy and excited. We sang all the way to our destination and I can still remember the ditties like 'Knick Knack Paddywhack give a dog a bone' and others. We were met at Arnside railway station and marched through lovely country lanes to the wooden camp buildings. We were seated on forms in front of long trestle tables, feasting our hungry eyes on plates piled high with slices of bread and jam. We were warned not to start eating until we heard a bell ring. We all sat there looking for the thickest slices and when the bell was eventually rung the bread vanished faster than any conjuror could have made it disappear.

"We all slept on little beds in a large dormitory. George slept next to me so that I could look after him. I will always remember the wonder of waking up and looking out of the big windows and seeing the beautiful bay with lots of fishing smacks with red sails. I had never seen anything like it in all my young life."

Sam remembered washing before a breakfast of porridge and treacle, playing in nearby woods and responding to the warning given by the warden Mr Wilson who was very strict.

Sam said: "He told us not to get our light coloured shorts dirty or we would be in trouble. Many boys did get them grubby. But those who had been to the camp before told them to roll about on white pebbles and this covered up the dirty marks. It worked too.

"Mrs Wilson and her lady helpers were very nice and kind to the children. They took us on lovely walks and rambles and gave us sweets. One day we were informed that Mrs Briggs, one of the benevolent founders of the association, would be paying us a visit. When the great lady arrived we sat on the grass and she emerged from an old porch and we scrambled for sweets, which she hurled by the handful. The biggest lads got most of them."

Forty years later Sam returned to Silverdale. This time he drove his own Rover car and he was introduced and escorted round the new modern premises. He signed the visitors' book as an old camper.

Leeds-born journalist, author and playwright Keith Waterhouse never forgot his Silverdale experience or the unofficial camp song:

There is a happy land far, far away,
Where they have jam and bread three times a day.
Eggs and bacon they don't see, they get no sugar in their tea
Miles from the familee, far, far away.

Keith said: "I found this so unbearably poignant that my eyes pricked with tears. But I was not homesick. I was town sick, city sick and street sick. And twenty years on I did get the title of my first novel out of that moment – *There is a Happy Land*."

# Best and Worst Times

In 1937 Britain had an empire and in Germany a lunatic was preparing to plunge the world into mortal conflict. Kiddies played backyard cricket with wickets chalked on walls and mums patronised Bell's Old Pharmacy, where Mr Bentley dispensed 'diddledum' guaranteed to put teething infants to sleep.

Grocer's shops had huge hams hanging from hooks and Leeds boasted the Empire Music Hall with such top-liners as Issy Bonn, George Formby, Ted Ray and Cavan O'Connor. Gramophone records were played on a wind-up machine and the music emerged from an unsightly horn. Arthur Askey and Stinker Murdoch starred in Band Wagon on our Cosser wireless. And the little comic pranced about in pantomime singing: "Buzz, buzz, buzz, busy bee, busy bee, buzz if you like but don't sting me."

The *Yorkshire Evening Post* regularly scooped our opposition paper the *Yorkshire Evening News* and sports enthusiasts were given the latest news and scores in our Saturday edition of 'The Buff'. Will Watch covered the Leeds United scene and Elland Road stalwarts regularly cracked: "We will win the cup when Nelson gets his eye back." Leeds Rugby League supporters and Yorkshire County Cricket followers were kept informed by a prolific writer 'Little John' – the pseudonym for the late John Bapty.

Those were they days when telegrams were delivered by GPO messengers and mums and dads suffered pangs of anxiety as they opened the little yellow envelopes. Such missives usually contained tragic news.

Many homes had an upright piano with youngsters playing scales for hours on end and Gracie Fields warbled about the biggest aspidistra in the world.

No house was complete without one of these leather-leaved plants, which were put outside when the heavens opened. It was reckoned that rainwater helped a healthy growth.

We went to church twice on Sunday. We had Whit walks, Children's Day at Roundhay Park, donkey rides, school trips to Scarborough and Bridlington, police stations with blue lamps, teachers who caned misbehaved laddies, and swings round lamp posts.

Leeds was the clothing capital of the world in 1937 with Burton's, Hepworth's, Sumries and other tailoring establishments providing ample employment. The year 1937 saw Mary Mason of Lombard Street, Leeds 15, start work at Price's Tailors. Mary, whose maiden name was Walker, remembers: "I was fourteen and we made ladies' suits. They were called costumes. The firm was in Harper Street before it moved to Garnet Road in Hunslet. We worked on piece rates and were paid one shilling and nine pence a dozen for a pair of plain sleeves or four shilling a dozen for fancy ones.

"We had our own fine drawers who repaired damaged garments. If we caused the damage, the price of the fine drawing was knocked off our wages. We also had to pay for cotton we used and I started with the princely sum of two pence an hour and eight shillings for a 48-hour week. We worked from 8am to 6pm five-and-a-half days a week. We had a tea break in the morning but not in the afternoon. If work was in short supply we were sent home without wages and at first we did not get paid for holidays. But the National Union of Garment Workers achieved pay for our one-week August break. All in all they were happy times. We were all friendly and chatted and sang as we worked."

Eileen Hall, Kirkwood Lane, Cookridge was Miss Hanlon when she left school at fourteen for employment at Marlbeck House, Leeds. She remembers: "Each new girl was given two green overalls to wear. This kept our own clothes clean but mine touched the floor. We looked like walking tents until one of the older machinists took pity on us and shortened them. New employees were messengers for about two months and then we were taught to use a sewing machine. We had our legs pulled and were sent for 'a card of button holes' or a 'long stand'. The lady behind the counter would keep you waiting quite a time if you asked for the long stand. When we became machinists we played the same tricks on the new-comers."

I remember those japes well. At the *Yorkshire Evening Post* young apprentices were sent for 'a bucket of blue steam' or 'a bubble for a spirit level'.

Kathleen Moran, Rookwood Gardens, Leeds, recalls: "My mum was Gertrude Taylor and she worked at Marlbeck House for a number of years. When she married she was presented with a beautiful silver cake dish by the directors of Thomas Marshall & Company Ltd. She was also given a cut glass vase by her workmates. Seventy-four years later these presents are still in the family. I also have the Military Medal, which my father Thomas Moran won in the 1914-1918 war. He was in the Royal Dublin Fusiliers."

I am sure you are justifiably proud of these keepsakes, Kathleen. They hold such lovely memories of years ago – like 1937 when Yorkshire monopolised the cricket championship, streets were safe at night, we had conductors on trams and buses, and so on.

# The Bank

The Bank in East Leeds was poor and rich. It was poverty-stricken when it came to dwellings and money. But it was also endowed with characters and it had a wealth of charity and community spirit. Irish, Jewish, and Italian people lived in harmony with the majority of residents from the Emerald Isle having arrived in the wake of the famine and other problems.

Relatives on my maternal side hailed from County Sligo and our nearest neighbour Mrs Canale was a long way from her Tipperary birthplace. She had a favourite expression: "We have nothing in our pockets but we have love in our hearts." She derived immense comfort from the claim even though many other impoverished people would rather it had been the other way round.

It is easy to say, "We have nowt but we do see life", when there is no prospect of cash or comfort on the immediate horizon. By the time it came for a mass exodus of Bank people to new estates at Gipton and Seacroft the area had become a seedy slum of gigantic proportions.

Children like me did not know we were poor. We had nothing with which to compare our humble lifestyle and you can imagine that the move to a brand new corporation house, with garden, indoor bath and toilet, was akin to transportation to fairyland.

Memories of The Bank are both sad and joyous. Infant mortality was not unknown and the practice of displaying a coffin on the pavement outside the deceased person's house was one calculated to give youngsters nightmares. Women with black shawls gathered to mourn and moan with discordant hymns sounding as if all the banshees in Hades had been released on the scene.

But there were happy days too, not the least the May Sunday walks from Mount St Mary's Church which dominated the skyline towering above The Bank. The May Sunday affair and the Whit Walks were always rounded off with tea, jam tarts and sticky buns in the parochial hall. Many participating adults preferred the delights of The Cavalier, The Prospect and other pubs of cheerful charm.

My only objection to the Whit Walk was to being 'tarted up' like Little Lord Fauntleroy. Grey short trousers, white shirts and red ties were the norm. Grey stockings were pulled up from black shoes and kneecaps were pink from the extra scrubbing inflicted by doting mums on the big day.

But my ordeal was worse. I had to wear a white satin suit with pearl buttons. It had a top with crimpled collar and the white trousers were long. I wore white running shoes and white socks and I looked like a junior edition of 'The White Tornado'. Lads dressed like me were embarrassed. We had to face the taunts of sensibly clad mates. And we had to turn a deaf ear to the whispering of 'cissy' hissed by boys and girls from rival schools.

I used to have my hair brushed just before departing for the church and adding to my crimson confusion was a combed kiss-curl as a finishing touch. I quickly shook out this last blow to my boyhood pride but dreaded leaving my home in Draper Street to listen to whistles and remarks of tough lads who stood on the pavement and watched the 'pansies' walk by.

Boys tended to drag their feet on the way to church but girls loved dressing for the occasion and there was one May walk I will always remember with sympathy for a delightful little girl who endured a most painful experience.

She was bedecked in a long white dress She was the bees' knees. Her long hair – Alice in Wonderland style – streamed down her back and a coronet of pink blossoms perched on her crowning glory. She carried a basket of multi-coloured blooms. She was as pretty as the proverbial picture and onlookers fairly gushed admiration for a girl who would have put Shirley Temple in the shade.

There was only one problem. Her brand new shoes nipped her tiny toes and before long she felt them rubbing her heels. That May Sunday was blazing hot. Her face was scarlet with pain from her feet. Blisters started to appear. She felt like kicking off her crippling attachments. But such an action would have offended the Sister – a watchful nun – who smiled benignly on the scene and was totally unaware of the penance suffered by her diminutive charge.

The girl was in agony and suddenly sanctuary came into view. The procession approached her house. The front door was open. And she dashed through the welcoming gap to discard her shoes and search for replacements. The little lass was determined to finish the walk. She had on her mind the party in the hall. She was not going to miss the sticky buns because of her new shoes. And she made a dramatic reappearance. She had put on her granddad's size-10, clay-covered, well-worn, hobnailed working boots.

The nun almost collapsed. Her fingers flew over her rosary beads. But our brave heroine shuffled and hobbled the rest of the way and explained afterwards that her granddad was fast asleep from his Sunday lunchtime pint and his boots were the only footwear she could find. If ever a lass earned her May Sunday treat she did. And she still talks about it today.

# Morgan's Pomade

They called it Morgan's Pomade! It was a hairdressing concoction that elderly gentlemen applied to their greying locks and I am toying with the idea of getting some now that my once light brown crowning glory is streaked with silver.

I first spotted Morgan's Pomade when I was a callow youth – earning fifteen shillings a week, including a twenty-five per cent war bonus. In those days I used to scour Leeds for the cheapest haircut and eventually became a regular customer at the barber's shop in the market. It was not exactly a tonsorial emporium. It was not the most salubrious salon. It was, in fact, positioned in a corner of the gentlemen's urinal, and down the steps from Riley's, where one could purchase sheet music, second-hand ukeleles and those push-button melodeons beloved of sea-faring folk.

One of the barbers was a tall, ginger-headed gentleman, who walked with a limp. I recall him recommending Morgan's Pomade to one client and my ears immediately quivered at the mention of my name. It was the same hairdresser who advised me to rub Indian Bay Rum into my scalp to arrest a receding hairline. But I ignored his wise counsel and the threat of teenage baldness disappeared without the application of the potion he assured me had magical properties.

But I did fall for one hairdressing aid – it was green solidified brilliantine. It had the consistency of the kaolin your mother spread on a poultice and slapped on your chest. It used to sting my uncultured nostrils into twitching appreciation of the fragrance. But one sniff was sufficient to send more discerning people dashing for their gas mask.

The tall barber – with the limp – used to spread it on my curls, rub it in until the scalp tingled and then he would get to work with two brushes. Hair was dragged back from the temple and simply plastered down. And this youth – who entered the premises with a mass of soft waving curls – always emerged with glistening straight hair brushed in the style of the film-star gangster George Raft.

If the barber felt like it he would give you a parting as straight as if he had applied a cleaver to your skull. He then brushed the hair down on either side.

And the victim walked from the smelly darkness of the dungeon into Leeds market sunshine looking for all the world like a junior edition of Tommy Lawton or other famous footballers of that era.

An increase in salary saw me switch my hairdressing patronage to Bensons' in Albion Place and my initial visit was not without fright. It was there I first saw singeing taking place and sat with mouth agape as the barber passed a lighted taper over the customer's hair, setting it on fire and immediately combing out the flames. This I learned was a method of sealing the ends of the hair, strengthened the growth and prevented influenza germs from dashing down the roots, into the head, and then into the chest, lungs and wherever such bugs are prone to visit.

It was also where I first saw barbers dig into an aluminium container with tongs and pull out a steaming hot towel, which they wafted from one hand to another before dropping it on the face of a chap in the chair. They sat with only their nostrils visible. Their cheeks turned crimson as the barber patted what looked like a boiling flannel and how they stood it only the good Lord will ever know. I would have hit the roof along with the vapours, which soared to the ceiling.

Lathering, stropping cut-throat razors on leather straps hanging from a specially designed chair, styptic pencils to stop bleeding, and bottles upon bottles of various creams were seen in all the barbers' shops.

And of course grown men used to whisper discreetly in the ear of the chap who had just cut their hair and money would surreptitiously change hands. An equally secretive exchange of goods would be made and quickly rammed into the buyer's pocket. I thought that the barber was selling racing tips but years later I learned that this was not the case.

I had to switch from Bensons' because our general manager started to use the place and one mid-afternoon he found one of the employees having his hair trimmed. The boss growled: "You should have your hair cut in your own hours."

And he did not take kindly to the lad's excuse: "Well it grows in the firm's time, sir."

To avoid similar confrontation I took my custom and regular request to Mick Homburg's – nearly opposite the Corn Exchange and just a few yards down from Hayes shellfish shop where you could buy a bag of crab claws. It was in Mick's I sat next to a man who was known in the area as Gerry Dorsey and eventually found fame as Engelbert Humperdinck. His haircut seemed to take hours and it always looked as long when he left as it was when he entered. It's nice to know that he has done so well.

But ladies in those far-off days also had a different carry-on with the weekly hair-do. They timed it so that they were perfectly coiffured for their Saturday night dates with George Raft or Tommy Lawton look-alikes. And I can still pictures lasses tying rags in their tresses, sleeping in them and when they untied them the hair would drop in ringlets.

Then came the evil-smelling home perms, which had all the odour of bad eggs. One solution was applied and the hair wound tightly round grips. Then the second solution was put on – all in the painful pursuit of vanity. But I suppose they were safer than curling tongs, which used to be heated in coal fires and applied to damp hair, which they crimped with a frightening hiss. They were nearly as lethal as those towels, which turned pale gents into panting examples of purple-faced purity.

Barbers, of course, were once blood-letters and appliers of blood-sucking leeches. Nowadays they are tonsorial artistes with nifty scissor-work, expensive shampoos, costly conditioners and services never even dreamed off in my formative years. But I wonder if they have any Morgan's Pomade? I could do with a ton of the stuff.

# Leeds at War

It was June 8, 1946, when King George VI sent a message to boys and girls throughout Britain. His Majesty expressed gratitude for sharing in the hardship and danger of total war that eventually resulted in triumph for the Allied nations.

He said: "I know you will always feel proud of belonging to a country which was capable of such supreme effort; proud too of parents and elder brothers and sisters, who by their courage, endurance and enterprise brought victory. May these qualities be yours as you grow and join in the common effort to establish among the nations of the world unity and peace."

Surviving recipients of that communication will – like me – be approaching dotage but able to draw on memories of air raids, evacuation, black-outs, rationing and Winston Churchill speeches. We remember sitting round our Cossor radios and listening to the Prime Minister's words: "I see the damage done by the enemy. But I also see side-by-side with devastation, bright and smiling eyes, beaming with conviction that we will defeat the enemy. I can see the spirit of an unquenchable people."

That attitude, character, backbone and courage had to exist for another four years and the spirit was sorely tested before the streets of Leeds were swamped with citizens launching the first of several parties to celebrate the declaration of peace.

On Victory In Europe night we gathered in front of Leeds Town Hall to listen to a patriotic eulogy delivered in almost melodramatic tones by the eminent Shakespearian actor Donald Wolfit. We were ecstatic. We greeted complete strangers like long lost friends. We sang, danced and hugged each other, carried away on waves of relief, unbridled joy and nationalistic pride and loyalty.

The scene was definitely more flamboyant than the coverage by a Dales weekly newspaper that was on the point of going to press when news of Germany's capitulation was released. There was no way that the typical Yorkshire editor was going to the expense of re-jigging the front page. On the back cover he summed up the situation with one sentence and the heading:

HOSTILITIES CEASE

It was akin to the Whitby Gazette's attitude to the Titanic tragedy with the parochial lead story: 'Whitby Man Lost At Sea'.

Other newspapers were more expansive about the end of the war in Europe. Editors dug into valuable reserves of newsprint and doubled the print order for eager readers.

Wartime Leeds contributed much to the all-out effort to defeat the aggressors and restore peace to all men. Local industry made a vital contribution with the Barnbow Factory producing guns for the battlefield, and the Royal Ordinance Factory with over three thousand employees – mostly women – working twelve-hour shifts to supply tanks for the various battle grounds. Millions of shells and gun and mortar barrels rolled off the assembly belts at the Fairburn Lawson Combe Barbour factory and Sir George Cohen & Sons employed 14,500 workers at their Stanningley Engineering works. They built engines for Anson Aircraft and the Avro Works at Yeadon made components for Blackburn aircraft.

Employees at John Fowler's factory worked day and night for nearly six years to make 1,500 armoured fighting vehicles in addition to tanks, diesel locomotives and petrol engines. Hudswell Clarke & Co built locomotives including the 'Austerity' class train for the War Department. Waddington's – famous for board games – manufactured playing cards which were sent to soldiers, sailors and aircrew held in German prison of war camps.

Another massive contribution came from the Montague Burton firm at Hudson Road, Leeds. The clothing factory was the largest in the world with over 20,000 employees at the outbreak of the war. The retail staff at the various Burton branches topped 4,000. It is estimated that over 13 million garments for the armed forces came from Burton's. Towards the end of the strife the Leeds tailoring firm made demob suits for returning troops. If a solider wanted a three-piece suit, jacket, waistcoat and trousers, he asked for the 'Full Monty' – a catchphrase quickly adopted by those in civilian life to describe 'the lot' and not just 'a portion' of anything.

Precautions to protect children started before the first shots were fired and it was estimated that 827,000 schoolboys and girls would leave home for safer dwellings with 103,000 teachers and helpers. Plans were also made to evacuate 12,000 expectant mothers from cities to more sheltered rural areas. Leeds planned to move 60,000 children, mothers and babies, and a mass rehearsal took place on August 28th, 1939. The real thing was an adventure for many and a heartbreaking separation for others.

September 1st, 1939, was the day when 3.5 million people were officially evacuated throughout the

One of the vast workrooms at the Hudson Road premises of Montague Burton, which made millions of garments for the armed forces and then produced demob suits for returning troops. The factory boasted a canteen that could seat eight thousand employees at one sitting.

country and another two million made their own arrangements and stayed with families or friends. In Leeds two hundred schools took part with fifty-one special trains taking 18,250 children, 1,450 teachers and 1,350 voluntary helpers from the city to areas of safety. These were Doncaster, Retford, Lincoln, Worksop, Gainsborough and the Yorkshire Dales.

Many from Cockburn High School travelled to Knaresborough and children from Hunslet Nursery School were transported to Bramham Park. The children were labelled with their name and school. They clutched a gas mask with their belongings in a small case or haversack.

September 2nd saw another 8,167 mothers and very young children leave Leeds with the Yorkshire Evening Post recording: 'Evacuated Leeds Children are Happy'. Another headline read: 'Leeds Youngsters are finding Evacuation One Long Holiday'.

However, in spite of all he preparation and rehearsals, only 30,000 children left their homes and not the 60,000 planned by the Education Department. It became evident that despite warnings some families decided they would rather stay and face the dangers of war together. Many evacuees came home for Christmas and did not go back to their temporary 'mums'. Within months the vast majority had left their host families.

The chairman of Leeds Education Department said: "Parents should bear in mind that bombing is predicted in the spring. I should not like to accept the responsibility if Leeds was hit and children were injured. I shouldn't like to think I had brought a child of mine back to that danger."

Rationing was introduced to prevent food shortages. Each person was allowed twelve ounces of sugar, four ounces of butter and four ounces of bacon or ham each week. Meat was only available to buyers from one of three Group butchers and people were encouraged to eat the all-vegetable Lord Woolton Pie or grow their own produce in the venture called 'Dig For Victory'.

Gloom was descending and the threat of planes and bombs gathered momentum. The Luftwaffe bombed busy ports and industrial cities like London, Hull and Liverpool and almost obliterated Coventry. Leeds was the only major city to escape intensive attacks but the statistics still make awesome reading.

We had plenty of false warnings when sirens sounded. In fact the city only suffered nine air raids resulting in 70 deaths, 327 injuries, 197 buildings destroyed and 7,623 buildings damaged. Four of the raids were free of casualties. The worst was on March 14th, 1941 when sixty civilians were killed and two thousand made temporarily homeless.

There has been speculation about why Leeds luckily escaped the 'Blitzkregg' intensity concentrated on other major areas. Leeds was defended by searchlights and anti-aircraft batteries of big guns. Leeds was probably out of range for planes having to fly from certain German airfields because this meant more fuel than some planes could carry. Another suggestion was that many Germans worked and lived in Leeds and Bradford before the war started. They returned home just before the outbreak and were possibly in a position to persuade others not to attack Leeds. One other theory concerned the possibility of a German in the High Command having an affinity with Leeds and ordering pilots not to include the city in the Blitz bombings. We will never know.

What we did learn was that Leeds Air-Raid Wardens, First Aid personnel, Firewatchers and Civil Defence services were the equal to all the Germans could throw at our fair city. Bombers on August 25th, 1940, damaged many houses, shops and a couple of businesses including the Woodpecker Pub and Barleycorn Inn. Campbell's tailoring factory and Morphett's bakery were also damaged. September 1st, 1940, saw 3,000 to 4,000 incendiaries dropped at Quarry Hill Flats, Marsh Lane railway depot and Easterly Road.

March 14th, 1941, was known as 'a night of terror'. High explosive bombs hit the Kirkstall district but most of the bombing was concentrated on Burley. It was the most devastating raid with damage to the Queen's Hotel, the General Infirmary, Town Hall, Hotel Metropole, Withy Grove Stores, the City Museum, Park Square, Quarry Hill and Leeds Register Office, before switching to Burley village, St Simon's School and targets like Kirkstall Power Station, the Lord Raglan pub and domestic dwellings. Greenwood & Batley's suffered and so did Fairbairn Lawson's and goods yards in the Wellington Street area. The following day it was business as usual at Burley in spite of huge craters and the absence of public transport.

The war was grievous. It was an affront to good people. It was a tragedy for the victims here in Leeds and for those fighting at the front and those locked in the concentration camps. Happily, Leeds residents and the majority of people in this country had the spirit so admired by Churchill.

Left: Sir Winston and Lady Churchill leaving Leeds Civic Hall on June 27th, 1945, shortly after the VE Day (Victory in Europe) celebrations. A vast crowd is giving him a rousing send-off, perhaps little sensing that in less than two weeks he would be defeated in the General Election. (Leodis Collection/Yorkshire Post)

Above: An excited group of merry-makers celebrate VJ Day in Albion Street. The number of people in uniform suggests that they may just gave emerged in happy spirits from the NAAFI Club (Navy, Army and Air Forces Institute) on the left. (Leodis Collection/Yorkshire Post)

Left: One of many street parties held to celebrate VE and VJ Days – this one is thought to be in Beaufort Place off Roundhay Road. Communities pooled their resources to organise these celebrations, with particular attention to the needs of the children. On the tables are a trifle and plates of buns and cake, made with carefully hoarded rations. Music was provided by records played on wind-up gramophones or a piano brought out into the street. Celebration drinks were consumed and in many streets a bonfire would be lit, giving great pleasure after the darkness of the blackout. (Leodis Collection/Yorkshire Post)

# Arthur Aaron

Flight Sergeant Arthur Lewis Aaron was the only Leeds serviceman to be awarded the Victoria Cross during the Second World War. He was twenty-one and a hero who sacrificed personal safety to land his stricken aircraft and save the lives of other crew members.

Arthur was born in Leeds on March 5th, 1922, and he was a pupil at Roundhay High School before studying at Leeds School of Architecture. In March 1941 he became one of the cadets who formed the inaugural Flight of Leeds University Air Squadron. From this early interest in aviation came the decision to apply for training with the Royal Air Force and he was awarded his pilot's wings in 1942 and posted to a bomber-training unit to fly Wellington and Stirling aircraft.

Arthur – like many of his colleagues – was swiftly engaged in wartime operations and in the space of thee months he completed eighteen flights over Dutch and German targets. His plane met with heavy defensive retaliation from German forces but Arthur safely returned his aircraft and colleagues to their home base. His plane was damaged on three occasions and once the Stirling bomber was hit by an incendiary dropped by a bomber flying above. But Arthur, and crew members, managed to return home after this threatening incident.

The brave Leeds pilot was on his twentieth mission – flying above Turin in Italy – when disaster struck. Once again Arthur was captain of a Stirling and one story holds that a British bomber fired at him by mistake, killing his navigator, wounding others and inflicting mortal injuries on the brave pilot.

Two bullets lodged in Arthur's chest. His face was half-destroyed and his right arm disabled. He was bleeding profusely and exhausted. His navigator was gone. Only the engine functioned and the cockpit and windscreen were smashed. Controls were broken and Arthur's five remaining crew members took turns at the damaged controls.

Eventually Arthur returned to the cabin to take control. He made four unsuccessful attempts to land his bomber and ultimately a colleague had to help by force-landing the plane on the runway at Bone in Algeria. Arthur was near death. He was exhausted and nine hours later he died of his injuries. The date was Friday, 13th August 1943.

He is buried in the Commonwealth War Cemetery at Bone, along with the navigator who was not only a crew member but also Arthur's closest friend.

Sir Arthur 'Bomber' Harris, who was Commander In Chief of Bomber Command, described Arthur's bravery as an outstanding show of courage. He added: "Never was the Victoria Cross so richly deserved. Arthur's bravery was far beyond the call of duty. His courage and determination, in the face of the enemy was of the highest order. We salute his memory."

A copy of Arthur's VC was on show in Leeds Civic Hall but now the original medal will be visible to the Leeds public. It will be one of the attractions in the new City Museum being built in the old Civic Theatre. It is there we will be able to view a decoration befitting the bravest of the brave.

Our pictures show flight Sergeant Arthur Lewis Aaron ready to fly and also the sculpted figure at the Eastgate Fountain, Leeds. It was unveiled by Malcolm Mitchem, who was the last surviving member of Flight Sergeant Arthur Lewis Aaron's crew. There is a campaign to move the Aaron sculpture to a more fitting sight in Leeds city centre.

# Humour in Wartime

The early days of the war were not without humour.

One teacher asked the class: "Who said: 'Oh to be in England now that April's here'."

One boy shot up his hand and answered: "Hitler."

My favourite tale concerns a gentleman who lived on Wykebeck Valley Road on the Gipton Estate. His name was Mr Foley and his house was just behind a brick-built air-raid shelter on which we – as kids – chalked a set of cricket wickets. This was our Headingley. It was where we played make-believe Test matches. Our ball was an iron-hard 'corkie'. It was like an Exocet missile in the hands of fast-bowler 'Titch' Rourke. You could see it coming but there was little one could do to avoid it. When the ball struck it raised bumps and bruises in spite of the insulation of copies of the Beano or Dandy stuck down our socks. Our bat was hewed from a piece of wood found on the field called Monkey Bridge.

Courting couples made use of our shelter and Mr Foley often yelled at them: "Clear off!" He was too old to serve in the army but he made a few bob by collecting shrapnel from the roofs of houses after air raids. |He also repaired damaged slates.

We lived within the sound of the army battery stationed at Wellington Hill and often heard the gunners taking pot shots at the German planes arriving or leaving the area. I can't recall a plane being shot down but it was comforting to know of the soldiers' presence.

One night there was a heavy air raid and Mr Foley's daughter-in-law Agnes suggested it would be prudent to leave the house and head for the safety of the much-used shelter.

Bombs were falling. The guns were blazing away and Mr Foley struggled to pull on his trousers in the darkness of the front room. He eventually stuffed the tail of his shirt into the back of his pants and he unwittingly pushed the bottom of the heavy front-window curtains into the same place.

Mr Foley walked forward and the heavy rod from which the curtain was hanging came out of its holder and struck him on the back of the head. He sank to his knees and hollered to Agnes: "Get the kids to safety. I've been hit by the ruddy Germans."

The story became part of Gipton Estate war lore. Mr Foley refused after that incident to leave the safety of his bed when sirens sounded. He said: "If the bomb lands with my name on it then I'm ready for the off."

Once again humour was present with the tale that a bomb dropped on Burley's eyesore, Albert Keeling's scrap yard, did hundreds of improvements and in fact tidied it up.

One lady was seen washing the only window left intact in her house and Mrs Cole, a nurse, discovered that a lump of shrapnel had blown out the bottom of her new galvanised zinc bucket. She cried: "I'll kill that bloody Hitler."

When I think of the raids my thoughts go back to a night in the bar at the Empire Music Hall, Briggate, where I interviewed the famous Liverpool comic Robb Wilton.

Robb said: "I am on tour and when my weekly show ends on a Saturday night I do a spell of ARP work at my home and walk round the area looking for chinks of light in the black-out curtains. It was my ambition to be able to shout: 'Put that light out!'"

Robb continued: "Last week I thought my big moment had come. A house was lit up like a beacon. I went through a gate, climbed up a grassy bank, went round a wall, walked on a path, dodged a huge shrub and tiptoed round an ornamental pool. Then I shouted: 'Put that light out!' And I was immediately plunged into darkness.

I had to shout: "Put it back on again so I can find my way out."

# The Man from Wigfalls

Do you remember the man from Wigfalls? We had one who made a Saturday morning tour of the Gipton Estate collecting instalments on all things electrical and also weekly payments on bikes. But he must have thought he was visiting China judging by the number of times his urgent and futile knocking at doors met with the cry: "Shin Tin."

This conveyed to the frustrated representative that mummy was out ["she isn't in"] and that he would have to call again the following weekend when the arrears would probably be brought up-to-date. Some hope!

I thought of Wigfalls when I attended the Yorkshire Cycling Federation's annual luncheon and became a free-loader instead of a free-wheeler. I nearly bought my first bike at Wigfalls back in 1944. And, if you bear with me, I will tell you how I nearly became saddled with a cycle which had drop handlebars, lamp, trouser clips, red reflector, imitation leather bag, pump and all other essential and much-coveted accessories.

I earned a princely sum of twelve shillings and sixpence for my five-and-a-half-day stint at the *Yorkshire Evening Post*. My wage was ten bob but in those days all employees were given a 25 per cent war bonus. It wasn't exactly a fortune, so I decided to become a racketeer.

Our newspaper files were discarded at the end of every month and I used to take dozens and dozens or, to be more technically correct, quires and quires of them down to the fish and game row in Leeds market. I sold the papers for wrapping-up purposes and my best customer was a Mr Milner who worked for Welhams.

Income from my 'fiddle' doubled and often trebled my earnings and it was then I spotted the bike. I will pretend that it was a gleaming and shiny model because chrome fittings were not available for the war years. The bike was austerity black with a Wigfalls logo, the only colourful relief. But to my youthful and eager eyes it was beautiful. And I was determined to buy it.

The bike was part of a selling promotion. It stood in the firm's window and every day it was on display the price dropped by five shillings. It played havoc with my nerves simply because I had amassed seven pounds. And I watched daily with baited breath and sweaty palms for the bike to come within my range. It dropped from £12 and I prayed that none would buy. I used to tear from the office in Albion Street to the shop in Lower Briggate, with nerves threatening to snap and my hands clutching an assortment of pound and ten shilling notes.

The ticket dangling from the front forks showed £11 and eventually it reached £8. It was almost mine. Only four days to go and I would hand over my cash and take delivery of a bike that would be the envy of impoverished mates. I became complacent. It appeared that I was the only one interested in the machine. It was only a question of time. I almost whooped with delirious anticipation. Then the bike disappeared.

The space was taken by a special offer washer. I almost took root peering in vain through the window for the object of my undying affection. I was distraught. I popped in the shop to learn that a youth had acquired the bicycle for £7 15 shillings. And I almost wept.

I walked from Wigfalls with shoulders slumped murmuring something akin to an 'unchained malady' when my spirits suddenly soared. Directly opposite was the firm Watson Cairns. And standing on the pavement outside their cycle-filled window was a second-hand Coventry Eagle, with chrome bits, racing tryes, lamp and pump. It was priced at £4. It was mine within minutes and I had money to spare.

The purchase of my Coventry Eagle was my introduction to cycling and freedom of the then open roads. It was a treat to escape into the vast and rolling Yorkshire countryside to enjoy the gift of God's good fresh air and share the camaraderie which has always existed in the world of wheelers.

I looked round the Yorkshire Cycling Federation gathering. It was a mixture of ancient and modern. Many arrived on bikes. They came from Clifton Wheels, Barnsley Cycling Club and all points of Yorkshire bound together by their mutual passion for propelling pedals.

Years have elapsed since I last rode a bike. In fact my attempts at any form of physical exercise are sparse and pathetic. Perhaps it is time to shed this life of lethargy. And my wife summed up my indolent streak when she presented me with a little bone idol. It was a hint to get off my behind and start doing something energetic. I wonder if Wigfalls have a sale on?

# Liquid Sunshine

My granddad would have been proud of me. There I was in the seat of honour – perched like a good 'un – on Joshua Tetley's chair. The occasion was a gathering to celebrate the Leeds brewery's 200th birthday and, after a quart of extra special ale, I was floating.

It was pleasant to indulge in idle chatter with our other guests and there was a chuckle at my expense when a sudden flush of recognition replaced the puzzled look on a lady's face. She murmured: "I've got you. I know who you are. I've seen your picture in the paper and I must say that I like your articles Willis."

I blushingly accepted the praise on behalf of Willis Hall who – as a son of Hunslet and a man not unknown to Tetley's renowned products – would have leapt at the chance to sit in Joshua Tetley's chair. It stands in the director's dining room to which a dozen or us repaired and it was there I plonked my ample rump on this outstanding example of fine Yorkshire woodcraft.

Joshua was not a mean man, but Joshua was careful. He did not look kindly on waste. One day he took a leisurely stroll on the banks of the River Aire and he came across a fallen tree stuck in the mud. Joshua summoned men to haul it out of the bog and he commissioned a carpenter to make a dozen superb chairs from the trunk. Two remain and I was accorded the one Joshua invariably occupied when he popped into the brewery dining room for the three-course lunch he enjoyed on most working days.

I felt quite privileged. But I probably earned the honour when I was the uncrowned King of the Tetley Bitter Brigade. It was a golden age for beer drinkers and never a day dawned without my modest intake of the nectar I christened 'liquid sunshine'. Yorkshire and Leeds in particular were rich in brewers and, as I rested in Joshua's chair, I thought back to the period when the city boasted breweries like Hemingway's, Melbourne, Whitbread's, Ramsden's and of course 'Tet's'.

I was a Hemingway's fan. I drank it when the Leeds and Great Britain Rugby League loose forward Frank Gallagher kept The Hampton. Frank was a gentle giant – a loveable man – and he often opined: "There's no such thing as bad beer. But some are better than others."

I was a Melbourne fan too and can still recall the sweet taste of the bitter, which is probably a contradiction in terms. But it is the right description for that unique and often-mourned brew. A gang of us used to congregate in The Courtier, on the Gipton Estate, with the cry: "Friday night is music night but Thursday night is Melbourne night." And by golly it carried a kick, even though dedicated Tetley tipplers scornfully termed it 'Boys' beer',

I remember once such chap declaring: "I wouldn't wesh me feet in Melbourne ale." But he always did justice to Whitbreads Pale Ale, John and Sam Smiths, Heys Gold Cup, Worthington 'E', Bass (blue and red label), Younger's number three and any of the other brews.

But many of us were weaned on Tetley's and I recall a trio of Newcastle United supporters approaching as we sat in the cool back room of the King Charles, which pandered to our lunchtime thirst, before planners demolished the lovely pub which stood in Lands Lane.

The football fans asked: "Which is the strongest beer?"

We echoed: "The bitter."

They were derogatory about the first pint. They labelled it 'cat's perspiration' and told us it didn't compare to Newcastle Brown. After three pints their raucous voices told they were on their way to Blaydon Races and not to Elland Road. After four they were on a journey into space and they never made the game.

I must admit I have given yeoman service to the brewing trade and the firm Joshua founded. This is probably why I was allowed to sit on this throne. My granddad would have been proud of me.

Joshua Tetley's motto was obviously 'waste not want not' because of his reluctance to part with anything that might be useful. He was one of eight children born to William Tetley and his wife Elizabeth Rimmington. Joshua was born in the summer of 1778 and the sun certainly shone on his business dealings. He lived in Albion Street, Leeds, and Joshua – like his father before him – was obviously a family man. His wife Hannah bore him seven children with Francis William the only boy. He was the last of the brood and Joshua was relieved finally to produce a son and heir.

Joshua and Francis William had maltings in Armley before they founded the family brewery at Salem Place in 1864. Joshua and his brood lived on the premises next to the brewery. It is reported that he was a kindly man – good to his employees – and the brewery was an ideal place because of an artesian well, which produced water for the beer. Many believed the water came direct from the adjoining River Aire but the well was the chief producer of the essential liquid. If you ever go on a trip round the brewery ask for a sniff of the well. It is a mixture of sulphur and rotten eggs.

Joshua and Francis William both worked at the brewery under the title Joshua Tetley & Son, which stood for years before the business amalgamated with Carlsberg. Joshua lived for 81 years and he and Hannah are buried near Harrogate. Francis William and family friend and partner Charles Ryder took over the brewery in 1858 and ensured that the prosperity enjoyed under Joshua's guidance was maintained for years to come.

At least one member of the Tetley clan is still going strong. Captain Christopher Tetley left the brewing trade to become a regular soldier. On his departure from the army he moved into horseracing and he is Clerk of the Course at Thirsk and Wetherby. Like Joshua he is a stickler for tradition, like wearing the right clothes at the track. He insists on jackets and ties for men entering the county or members' enclosure at Thirsk.

# A 'Billy Bunter'

When your tummy rumbles with hunger pangs – and your saliva buds drool when you think of juicy steaks – you probably have recourse to the hackneyed and totally impossible expression: "I could eat a horse."

I thought about this when a pal told me of the restaurateur who was fined for serving horsemeat to his customers. I believe it is legal in this country to provide such fare if you inform the diner that he is not eating more acceptable meat of the beef, pork and lamb variety. But if you dish up horse and give it another label, then you are in trouble.

It reminds me of the story of the café owner who was charged with such an offence and appeared in the magistrate's court to listen to the charges. He leaned against the dock as the prosecuting officer told the local 'Solomon' of the accused's transgressions and the magistrate asked the chap: "What exactly was the meat content in your pies?"

The unhappy fellow thought for a while and he said: "They were a sort of horse and rabbit pie."

The magistrate made a note of the evidence and then asked: "What was the proportion of horse meat to rabbit?"

The defendant did a mental calculation and replied: "I would say fifty per cent."

The beak peeped over the half-spectacles, which threatened to fall from his nose, and requested: "Can you be a little more explicit?"

The café owner answered: "One horse to one rabbit!"

We had horsemeat shops in Leeds and people used to buy it for their dogs. But during the days of wartime rationing and austerity it was no secret that many cooks filled their pies with meat straight from the hoof.

There was a café called The Cyprus and they served the most delicious minced-meat pies during the period when the citizens of this country were decidedly slimmer and probably much fitter than they are these days. If you found a place serving meat you did not broadcast the fact but I took pity on an undernourished boss of mine and told him of The Cyprus delicacy.

He went along to sample a pie and returned to the office white with horror. He swore: "That is horse meat they are serving."

I argued that this was impossible. But it was not long before the owners were prosecuted and the pies disappeared from the menu.

I tell you all of this dear readers – or reader – because I must admit that I am partial to a bit of meat. But even I blanched the other night when I called in a local pub and heard a stranger order the house speciality – a 'Billy Bunter'.

It is a pub meal designed to terrify even those with gargantuan appetites. It represents a mountain of meat – with all the trimmings – and I dare bet that a horse could not jump over it. There is sufficient to feed a family. I counted four chops before the outfaced eater even stuck his fork into steaks, liver, kidneys, ham, sausages, black-pudding, beef burger, chips, onions, salad and peas – and all topped off with two fried eggs, sunnyside up.

Little wonder that the proprietors offer 'doggy bags' to clients who take a second breath and do their best to plough through the pile, but admit dietary defeat with enough remaining to feed the biblical five thousand. There is an adage: "Never let it be said that your mother bred a jibber."

But I don't mind admitting that I would 'jib' – and that's not the only thing I might do – if a waitress placed a 'Billy Bunter' in front of me. It was said of me – a useful scoffer – that I am no mug with a knife and fork but I am a non-starter when it comes to tackling such a gigantic repast. I wouldn't know where to start.

But I will always make a brave attempt to eat rabbit. I welcome it in casseroles, pies and stews, and it was on the Morgan menu at least once a week when I was a child. The introduction of myxomatosis scared us all out of our wits and tales were told of people growing long ears, buck teeth and developing an insatiable appetite for lettuce after eating rabbits affected by this disease. Rabbits were scarce for a couple of years. People lost the rabbit habit. But it returned on a small scale and I must say I am still partial to 'a bit of bunny'.

The story is told of a chap who had a couple of brainwaves. He crossed a deaf and dumb dog with a deaf and dumb bitch in an attempt to breed Hush Puppies and he also tried to rear a special hunchback rabbit – wait for it – to keep the pie crust up!

'Run Rabbit Run' was a song warbled during the war years and I used to dash as fast as the furry creatures to a place at the back of Leeds market where they sold scrumptious rabbit pies. I also used to swear by the pork pies produced by Newtons and those made by another firm, the Cardis family.

The best minced-meat pies were made at Jack Cuthberts in Leeds market. I tired of school dinners and regularly ran from Mount St Mary's, near Richmond Hill, to Cuthberts during the lunch break. For a couple of pennies you had the most delightful pies and we never asked whether they were horse, beef, mutton or otherwise. The café part of Cuthberts was invariably full of shoppers and we stood at the front of the wooden building with our plates of pies and mashed potatoes perched on a ledge.

They were happy days, even though there were times when we had rumbling tummies, felt the pangs of hunger and had the feeling that we could have eaten a horse. We might easily have done so too, although I still think a 'Billy Bunter' would have beaten us.

# Lord Mayors

**You cannot hope to bribe or twist.**
**Thank God the British journalist.**
**But knowing what a man might do**
**Unbribed – there is no reason to.**

The adage probably rings as true today as it did when it was first coined many years ago. Unscrupulous scribblers like me love a juicy story and even when sworn to secrecy can't wait to publish the unsavoury facts.

However I have been steadfast for twenty-six years in adherence to a promise not to betray a Leeds Civic Hall secret. But now that the city is approaching its eight-hundredth birthday it would be churlish not to publish a scoop story on this momentous landmark in civic history. I can reveal the names of two eminent citizens and one reprobate who actually played rugby in the ornate Civic Hall banqueting suite.

The late Eric Atkinson was Lord Mayor in 1980 and he took part in the demonstration of the sport he loved as a fervent Bramley Rugby League Club supporter. The late Eddie Joyce, who played football for Yorkshire Amateurs until he was near pensionable age, also took part in the scandalous rugby epic. The third player was me!

Eddie Joyce was a great amateur soccer star. His goal tally reached mammoth proportions and he was certainly over two score years and ten when he played in a Norman Hunter benefit game at Guiseley. It is a fact that whenever Eddie went to Wembley for a Cup Final or International he took his boots in his car just in case one player or another did not turn up. On one occasion he broke his leg playing in a match at Manchester and he drove his vehicle back to Leeds for treatment at the infirmary.

Eddie was a businessman and always on the lookout for novelties. He was the first person I knew with a mobile telephone. It had a range of about fifty yards and it was an illegal import from the Far East. Eddie also developed and marketed many inventions and one was the 'Luma Rugby Ball'. It was an illuminated sphere, designed for the training grounds. Clubs without floodlights could use the ball in pitch darkness with players passing the glowing orb as they ran up and down the field.

Eric expressed an interest in the ball and Eddie and I took one along to the Lord Mayor's chambers. Of course we required a darkened room to demonstrate the brilliance of the idea and we closed the curtains in the banqueting suite, turned of all the lights and proceeded to run and pass the illuminated ball to each other.

Eric was impressed but the game came to a sudden end when the Lord Mayor decided on a drop kick. The ball landed on the miniature Minstrel's Gallery with a resounding crash. Play came to an abrupt end and we scampered to the safety of the Lord Mayor's rooms. We never retrieved the ball. If it is still up there ... can I have it back please? It was the only one of its kind.

The reason I have decided to blow the whistle on our behaviour was simply because I glanced down the list of Lord Mayors and Eric's name fairly leapt from the page.

The first to hold the office was Sir James Kitson in 1897 and we have since had many famous incumbents. Frank O'Donnell was chosen in 1950. He was a pupil at my school, Mount St Mary's, and I was truly proud of him when he kicked off a match for Leeds United. Percy Woodward was a director of Leeds United and he was Lord Mayor in 1961.

Who will ever forget the scene of the 1968 Lord Mayor, John Rafferty, conducting a singsong after Leeds United's civic reception on their return from international success? John didn't have a baton. He conducted with his crutch having lost a leg when he was a schoolboy.

Another of my favourite pictures is one of Eric Atkinson congratulating Paddy Crotty on assuming the post of Lord Mayor in 1981. Paddy was a great friend He was a leading Leeds solicitor and chairman of Leeds Education Committee. He was a kindly man. He kept a pocketful of coppers simply to dole out to beggars who might ask for help. He could never refuse them.

Paddy also had a tremendous sense of humour and I recall a story he told on many occasions.

**Although their politics were different, former Lord Mayor Eric Atkinson counted his successor Lord Mayor Patrick Crotty as one of his greatest friends. Few people could fall out with 'Paddy', and Eric – a wonderful teller of jokes – was one of the legion of Crotty admirers. Eric was Lord Mayor in 1980 and Paddy (right) took office in 1981.**

He said: "A lady was asked to talk to boys and girls on the dangers of alcohol abuse and to help get her message over to the school pupils she produced two glasses – one with gin and one with water. She also had a couple of worms and she placed one in the gin where it shrivelled and died, and she dropped the other in the water. It swam happily round the glass. The lady then turned to the class and asked: 'What is the moral of that demonstration?'

"One little lad put up his hand and replied: 'Please miss the moral is – if you have worms drink gin.'"

Leeds has been fortunate to have so many dedicated Lord Mayors who brought added dignity to the office – chaps like Douglas Gadd, who fulfilled an ambition to ride a racehorse and learned to swim for charity during his term of office.

No doubt I will court trouble by missing out names of great friends but Ronnie Feldman, Les Carter, Keith Parker and of course that man of many talents, Bernard Atha, must also figure in the list of outstanding Lord Mayors. Long may this office continue!

# Reporters Remembered

*Former* Yorkshire Evening Post *news editor Geoffrey Hemingway recalls some of those who started their respective journalistic careers on Leeds newspapers and moved on to achieve considerable notability in other fields. Among them are Mark Knopfler, Nick Clarke, Keith Waterhouse, Barbara Taylor Bradford, Peter O'Toole and Willis Hall.*

Mark Knopfler, who at his best was paid less than ten pounds a week as a trainee reporter, and left to make a cool £65 million as a pop group musician, is possibly the best known in my carefully selected list. Indeed I have a feeling that his huge fan base might claim that 'most notable' is not enough and I should be referring to the Sultan of Swing as a global phenomenon rather than merely notable.

I have an amazing and revealing collection of letters from an Italian-based Knopfler addict who contacted me after seeing a contribution I made to an unauthorised biography of my now famous former editorial trainee. The Italian writes: "I am a sincere fan of Mark, the greatest-ever genius in all of music history. I am twenty-eight years old, a fan since the age of twelve, and during these years have spent most of my time building up the biggest Dire Straits-Knopfler record collection in the world. This includes a thousand different records in vinyl and CD, also some ultra-rare acetates."

"And apart from the deepest of researches I've collected 500 different video recordings of Mark's TV appearances from 1978 up to now," adds this extraordinary fan with a 'Mark Knopfler Museum' situated somewhere in Italy.

This is someone who certainly would say, along with millions of others worldwide, that their favourite banjo player is somewhat more than merely most notable. Nothing derogatory is intended there, as my Italian friend tells me that Mark really does play the banjo – and particularly well in a long-ago released Notting Hillbillies album also involving Steve Phillips and Brendan Croker.

***

This brings me to World at One's Nick Clarke in a sort of joint performance with the occasionally banjo-strumming Mark. I say this because the pair worked together on the *Yorkshire Evening Post*, which was then situated in Albion Street, and they entertained at reporter parties. Knopfler practised the most rarefied of chords and Clarke was an outstanding member of an all-male ballet-dancing troupe.

Clarke is recorded as saying that, as a new boy, he watched in awe as Knopfler, also a comparative newcomer, strolled through the office as if he owned the place, treating it as a drop-in centre, as if there was nothing else to do.

"Late night sessions meant that he kept his own time, prompting the famous Hemingway threat if he wasn't careful he might find himself out on his ear, faced with earning a meagre living from music," added Clarke further developing his theme.

Yet right up to today the two remain friends so much so that when his former colleague was approaching his 50th birthday Clarke suggested that greetings from Leeds might be appropriate. I was diffident. Mark had, after all, been a lot off a loner and contacting everyone wouldn't be easy, but despite these difficulties his sometime workmates responded well with generous messages and some sly humour.

The Nick Clarke 50th also posed the odd problem. Just to be different, what to give him, on behalf of his old friends? And where to find it? Then, in pride of place, on the mantelpiece above the front-room fireplace, I espied an ornate jug, which, carefully wrapped up, I'd received from that extraordinary Italian chap. It was, he said, ultra-rare, one of only a hundred made, and given to celebrities of the music world to promote a Knopfler-led tour of America, a jug crammed to the top with the best of English tea, one of two which he had found and millions would love. It was a most-wanted Mark Knopfler-related item, a highly collectable jug (and I shouldn't take the cork off) that he had sent to me, a friend, who like the above mentioned celebrities was also a VIP.

Now the jug rests on the mantelpiece above a much bigger fireplace in Mr and Mrs Clarke's fashionable residence in London W10 6PT. A reminder of a birthday now long gone, it is there because I know the two of them love and understand Dire Straits and Notting Hillbillies music and lyrics to a much greater extent than me.

Nick later moved to the *Yorkshire Evening Post's* then new building in Wellington Street, Leeds,

When Mark Knopfler was on the reporting staff at the *Yorkshire Evening Post* he shared a musical interest with another journalist Stephen Phillips. The pair often strummed and sang at staff parties, especially at functions arranged to say farewell to colleagues. It was an illustrious backing group for 'singers' like John Morgan whose speciality was the Irish lyric 'The Wild Colonial Boy' with dramatic actions. Stephen usually dressed in a black cloak with red lining to sing Elvis Presley numbers. He left the *Yorkshire Evening Post* to join the team at Look North television

Mark was in two minds about a career in the in the entertainment business until he was asked by the editor if he would make up his mind about whether to continue as a reporter or be a pop star. Mark chose the music sphere and when we heard that he was in 'Dire Straits' Morgan proposed we had a whip found to help him with his financial problems. Mark is now a multi-millionaire. He is world famous and perhaps his greatest fan was the late Princess Diana. He is also still in the thoughts of firm friends he made in the newspaper industry.

Our picture shows Mark receiving a gift from YEP News Editor Geoff Hemingway on the eve of the singer's departure from journalism.

where he recalls I once persuaded the morning editorial conference that a team of reporters should set out to see if the coastguards and police could cope with the every-increasing number of illegal immigrants, mainly Asian, reportedly landing nightly on Yorkshire's East Coast and then making their way to the then Heavy Woollen District and Leeds.

Thus, with the fledgling Clarke in the sixfold group, we left for Bridlington where we had arranged to hire a boat. Following a five-mile trip up the coast, and slightly blacked up with burnt cork, we intended to land in a safe cove and in the dark of night travel by car inland. But just before we were about to set sail the editor said he though it might be best if the various authorities were informed and further recommended that I should meet a top member of the local constabulary, seriously to discuss things. But, although I pointed out that an experienced seaman would be charge, the top cop didn't seem that keen. Moreover I quickly realised that the coastguard were in the know.

Of course the trip was aborted but on the way back to Leeds we called at a posh restaurant. Each of us had a four-course meal at the newspaper's expense and, for the first time in our lives, our entertainment and travelling expenses weren't checked. Overall an exciting day, and a useful exercise in newsdesk brinksmanship, I would say!

Now Nick Clarke, a former Radio Broadcaster of the Year, who has been described as a national treasure, praised for his intelligence and elegance of phrase, and written many books, including a best-selling biography of Alistair Cooke, is suffering serious ill-health. Through radio and television and his first love, print, he is gaining, by sad chance, many more admirers and even greater respect as he describes, sometimes in almost saintly detail, how – not least as a family man – he's busy fighting back. And winning!

***

Long ago and faraway in the extremely early 1950s a most moving missive dropped on the large oak desk of the editor of the now long defunct *Yorkshire Evening News* in Trinity Street. The editor, R. W. Shawcross, the most kindly and charitable of men, was almost in tears as he read its contents and urged that his news editor Bernard G Kaye should drop down one floor and quickly see it. The moving missive, explained the editor, was a letter, written in a spidery hand and signed 'OAP Beeston' which paid great tribute to the *Yorkshire Evening News* 'Christmas Fund for Lonely Old People' and, in particular, the hundreds of lovely Yuletide food parcels which it supplied.

This year each parcel had contained half a pound of lard, a Christmas pudding, a quarter of a pound of Trex, butter, tea, nuts of various kinds, a miniature bottle of rum and other seasonable goodies which, indicated the writer, had made his and his wife's Christmas much less pauperous, if not prosperous. By now Mr Shawcross – for the fund was his idea, his baby – really was in tears.

The letter, which he then handed to Bernard Kaye, went on to say that the couple had been readers of the newspaper for fifty-plus years. In addition to appreciating the annual food parcels, they admired the work of the *Yorkshire Evening News* reporters – "them there lads and lasses wot brings us t'news, piping hot, rain or shine, throughout each succeeding year". The eulogy ended by saying that 'OAP Beeston' and his missis were so grateful, so touched, that they felt duty bound to send a free gift – "a packet of twenty Woodies, for them there reporters".

Soon afterwards, at the behest of their editor, a Leeds establishment of sixteen reporters lined up in the newsroom, each to receive a Wills Wild Woodbine cigarette, whether they were smokers or not. Bernard Kaye added that Mr Shawcross would be very upset if any single one of them failed to light up, and this included those who preferred much posher cigarettes.

Thus sixteen reporters went their separate ways, followed by a series of explosions in many different parts of Leeds. The cigarettes had been sabotaged, via small cigar-shaped pellets, which had been so skilfully pushed into them. The saboteur and letter writer was, of course, Keith Waterhouse, the leg-pull, if that is the word, an indicator of even greater creativity still to come.

The other four cigarettes? They ended up in middle-management areas. So powerful were the explosions that in one case it was thought more than one pellet had been used.

Retribution followed. The victims quietly made Waterhouse a member of the *Yorkshire Evening News* Space Club. Oh, the indignity of it! In newsprint later on, and right across Leeds and further afield, his name was clearly to be seen. Keith Waterhouse, aged 21, was in a club for kids aged six, if not three.

Keith Waterhouse left his native Leeds to find fame and fortune in Fleet Street after working at the *Yorkshire Evening Post* and his partnership with Willis Hall produced the brilliant play and film *Billy Liar*. You can bet that somewhere in the world tonight one amateur theatrical body or another will be playing this time-honoured production. The partnership of two writers with a South Leeds affiliation was not only fruitful but at times unique. On one occasion they worked in their London office and despatched a junior member of staff to travel by train to Leeds (first class of course) and bring back a couple of pork pies from Newton's in Kirkstall Road.

Keith is pictured in City Square outside the Queens Hotel where a Leeds tapestry featuring Waterhouse and Hall was unveiled.

***

Waterhouse, I must tell, you was part of a talented Leeds quartet, all of whom – my research shows – have said they hated covering chip-pan and chimney fires. Quite frankly I find this hard to understand because in their time in Leeds, in the early 1950s, newsprint was in short supply, newspapers were restricted in the number of pages, and there were sub-editors, armed with carefully sharpened carving knives, out to ensure that space was not made available to the more insignificant of fires.

For my part I didn't get many if any. Maybe I was lucky. But don't misread this. I'm not suggesting that in any way I was more gifted, or more talented, than any in an incredible and legendary group. I am referring of course to Waterhouse, Barbara Taylor Bradford, Peter O'Toole, and Willis Hall, sometimes described as the ratpack!

But that I feel is unfair because, despite the undoubted and admitted roistering of three of the group, the youthful Barbara Taylor Bradford will, I'm sure, be remembered certainly in Leeds as that beautiful but always perfectly behaved Armley-born lass. Heads turned as Barbara joined the *Yorkshire Evening Post* typing pool and this was repeated as she was drafted into the editorial department, little realising that one day she would become a multi-millionaire writer of best selling novels, despite that brief letter she had published as a child in a girlie (i.e, girls) magazine.

Waterhouse and Malcolm Barker, later to be editor of the YEP, encouraged her to write and within a short time she was contributing to the women's pages and knew that she had found her niche in life.

In London, at the age of twenty-one, she helped to edit a women's magazine and eventually married her American television and film producer husband. They now live in the USA, where Barbara Taylor Bradford continues to write, although she nevertheless occasionally returns to her Yorkshire roots so often reflected in a prolific run of books.

On one such occasion there was a civic reception after which there was a visit to the *Evening Post*. Bets were laid. Which former colleague would the renowned author recognise first? The answer was slimline Frank Metcalfe, by now district news editor. The greeting was warm and affectionate, so much so that someone was prompted to say: "Small wonder she didn't spot you, your waistline's extended over much."

I didn't say much. I'd put five pounds on Frank.

Willis Hall and Peter O'Toole worked for the *Yorkshire Evening News*, one hundred yards away from its rival, the *Yorkshire Evening Post*, both newspapers then in the very much alive, near dead centre, of Leeds.

Frank Carlill, picture editor of the News, would often complain to me that his trainee photographer, O'Toole, kept disappearing to rehearse amateur theatre lines in a set of gents toilets tucked away in a convenient far corner of the building.

"The only useful thing about it is that at least I know where to find him, but it really is hard on the shoe-leather," Carlill would routinely add.

As O'Toole became more and more famous in later acting days, those same toilets became a much respected, almost hallowed place, where reporters would sit and draft out in shorthand their stories ahead of publication. In so doing, they would wonder whether they were occupying a seat the great O'Toole had once used in those formative and so important early days.

Some reports have said that O'Toole was a reporter, but that was never so, although some say he might have made an outstanding one bearing in mind that he has produced two volumes of autobiography of considerable merit.

Of one, Sheridan Morley wrote: "Far and away the best book to have been written by an actor since Dirk Bogarde first took to the typewriter."

Old pal Waterhouse agreed. "Sickeningly good. By and by, it will turn out that the bugger can paint too!" he said.

***

Willis Hall was famous for his lunches. He started work at 6.0am each day and worked until noon when it was time for a good meal and several glasses of wine. He rarely worked again until the next morning. It proved a great recipe for solo success, as well as jointly with the wonderful Waterhouse, someone I recently heard described as a prolific writing machine and a genius. Each loved good lunches and fine

Those of us fortunate to work in the editorial room at the *Yorkshire Evening Post* when Barbara Taylor was on the staff fell in love with the lady destined to become a world-renowned author. She was probably the most beautiful girl ever to enter local journalism. But it is doubtful if she realised that male eyes turned in her direction whenever she walked round the room. We worshipped from afar the Leeds lass who joined the typing pool at the age of fifteen and admits that her typing was not exactly error-free and her shorthand, at times, was unreadable.

Editor Barry Horniblow encouraged Barbara to write features and another of her mentors was Keith Waterhouse. Success as a novelist – home and abroad – came her way and she is now Barbara Taylor Bradford – author of *A Woman of Substance* based on her life in Leeds. One newspaper recently put her earnings in the £6 million class and others believe she is worth millions more than that figure.

Barbara was born in Armley. She is sentimental about her birthright and loves to visit the scene of her childhood and her teenage years. Barbara says: "I feel a little cheated by how much the city has changed. But it is wonderful and the rebirth is stylish and exciting. I still love both the *Yorkshire Post* – the best in the North of England – and of course the *Yorkshire Evening Post*. That is where I was given my first education in the art of writing stories."

wines, and whiling away time playing board games. But it never appeared to affect the memorable quality of their work or output with Willis, it seemed to me, routinely matching his pal's performance.

Willis Hall was born in Leeds, just off Dewsbury Road, and educated at Cockburn High School where he said his first claim to everlasting fame was sitting next to the future Mrs Frankie Vaughan. Much regarded as Cockburn was, Willis left aged fourteen, to fulfil a boyhood dream of becoming a ship's cabin boy. But his enthusiasm for the sea didn't last long. After only three months he was on his way and eventually found a job writing about racing on *The Sporting Pink*.

For five years Willis was in the Royal Corps of Signals mixing army duties in the Far East with spells of broadcasting, one radio station taking him on as a writer of plays, scripts and short stories. He was also introduced to some of the mysteries of stagecraft.

Willis Hall returned to Leeds journalism. He wrote a weekly column for the Yorkshire Evening Post largely based on his early life in South Leeds. The journalistic wheel had turned full cycle you might say.

His contribution to books, plays and television productions continued until his death in 2004. At a church in Covent Garden there was a memorial service where they sang 'On Ilkley Moor Baht at' and, bearing in mind that Willis was a Hunslet supporter, the famous Rugby League anthem 'We've Swept the Seas before Boys'.

That was a song Willis once sang with Peter O'Toole in an aeroplane at 40,000 feet on the way to the USA. The reason for the rendition was to attempt to get their performance in a Rugby League record book. They failed.

When Peter O'Toole was galloping across the desert as *Lawrence of Arabia* I wonder if his thoughts ever drifted to his job in the photographic dark room at the *Yorkshire Evening News*, Leeds? No doubt he had other things on his mind but it was at the YEN where the editor advised him to find a job outside the newspaper industry. He gently indicated that he did not believe young Peter was of journalistic material.

Peter attended St Anne's RC School, Leeds, where Jimmy Saville was also a pupil, and it was there he probably had his first theatrical part in the Christmas Nativity play.

Peter dabbled in amateur dramatics as a teenager and he was seventeen when he appeared in a play at the Civic Theatre in Cookridge Street, Leeds.

When Peter completed his National Service he won a scholarship to the Royal Academy of Dramatic Art. This was followed by three years at the Bristol Old Vic where he played every role imaginable from Shakespeare to falling-about-farce including pantomime. It was invaluable experience and in 1959 he was awarded the title 'Best Actor of the Year' for his part as Private Bamforth in Hunslet-born Willis Hall's epic play The Long and Short and the Tall.

Peter eventually turned to films with immediate success and his role in *Lawrence of Arabia* resulted in mass adulation of the handsome star. He was feted as a discovery of international standing and immense ability and charisma. However, audiences and theatre critics can be fickle and cruel. Peter was hammered as actor and director of *Macbeth* at the Old Vic. The play was a sell-out but the reviews were vicious and vindictive. The experience would have shaken the confidence of lesser men but Peter recovered from the mauling and it was not long before he regained his West End eminence.

Peter and his mates Willis Hall and Keith Waterhouse were members of a hell-raising coterie of seasoned drinkers and I recall one session at a pub in Pool In Wharfedale where landlady Dora Scott and her husband Wilf always entertained Peter when he was appearing in the Leeds area. One could not count the empties.

Drinking stopped abruptly for both Peter and Willis. But memories of theatrical triumphs as well as unbridled celebrations will never fade.

When I first wrote a story about Willis Hall he requested: "Don't say I was born in Leeds because I first saw the light of day in Hunslet." Willis was proud of his birthright and never surrendered loyalty to his native Hunslet. He watched the local Rugby League team in action as a boy and rarely missed a match at historic Parkside. After travelling the world, and settling for a protracted spell in London, he eventually returned home to resume his support of the club called Hunslet Hawks.

Willis was renowned for lengthy lunches and he is pictured at one of his favourite Leeds haunts – La Grillade.

Many of us gathered at St Paul's Church, Covent Garden, for a service to celebrate Willis's life and work. It was November but the carol 'While Shepherds Watched their Flocks' did not appear to be out of season and also fitting was a rousing rendition of 'The Battle Hymn of the Republic'. Never was 'Glory, Glory Hallelujah' sung with more gusto. And the final 'hymn' was five verses of 'Bless' Em All – The Long and the Short and the Tall'. It was a most enjoyable occasion with the Hunslet anthem 'We've Swept the Seas Before Boys" also in evidence.

Now for a few other most notable names, again with no messages to be drawn from the order in which I present them.

Allan Shaw's journalistic enthusiasm is legendary. In his early days he'd emerge from any one of a number of telephone kiosks at the end of the *Yorkshire Evening Post* reporters' room, shouting to his nearest colleague: "We've done it again." Then (less modestly): "I'm on to another absolute cracker kid." In terms of exclusivity this was almost invariably the case. That enthusiasm has continued ever since.

Allan served the YEP in Albion Street as a reporter and industrial correspondent and then became the first news editor of BBC Radio Leeds. After leading the setting up of another BBC local station at Middlesbrough he was appointed manager of Radio Manchester. When the challenge came to establish satellite stations he suggested that redundant mill chimneys should be used to provide aerial facilities. He then asked Fred Dibnah to act as opener, which also worked a treat.

After retirement from the BBC he worked in public relations for the Countryside Commission in the North-West. Cuttings of the articles he produced on their behalf measure in yards, not column inches, when stacked high. In a Radio 4 broadcast he was lauded as one of the true pioneers of local radio in the North of England in particular. Now he does much voluntary work aimed at improving race relations, not the least through publication of a newspaper dedicated to the cause.

\*\*\*

A few days before John Helm disappeared from the *Yorkshire Evening Post* newsroom, I invited him to become the newspaper's aviation correspondent. That would mean an improvement in his salary as a general reporter and at the same time offer new challenges and new prospects. But John left for Radio Leeds and I was mystified and upset that we should lose someone of such apparent potential.

Many years on, via a contribution to a video recording marking my retirement, John – by now a renowned television and radio broadcaster – said he thought that when I'd offered him that job I'd said 'aviary' correspondent. He had felt he was destined to a lifetime covering pigeon racing, about which he knew 'nowt', especially the way to chase up maybe complicated results.

Anyway, whatever the truth, John Helm, like others in this list, sought pastures new, which in his case included in addition to Radio Leeds, time at the BBC in Manchester and of course Yorkshire Television. He has covered the Olympic Games, golf, Association Football and many other sports as a broadcaster now known nationally but quite frequently returning to the printed word. As an after dinner speaker he's known as one able to recite –always correctly – the names of the England football clubs in alphabetical order. His record is a matter of seconds not minutes

***

Paul Truswell is included because he's the first of the hundreds of reporters I've worked alongside who has ended up at Westminster. We've had our differences, one outcome being that, at a fairly recent reunion of *Yorkshire Evening Post* former editorial staff, he said: "I well know that my election to Leeds City Council went down like a lead balloon in the eyes of some at the evening papers, particularly yours."

And it was true: the regular absence of a valued reporter on council business can cause problems in even the best-run newsroom.

Imagine my surprise when an election pamphlet dropped through my letterbox revealing that Paul had been adopted as a prospective candidate for my own constituency of Pudsey. I wondered what I'd say if I met him canvassing on my doorstep. Time heals, however and, Paul is rapidly developing a considerable career at Westminster. Nearer home, he is well known as an MP immersed in local matters large and small.

He must have learnt something from his time at the YEP. His photograph appears everywhere. He's become the big picture-fixer.  He also writes a fortnightly column for the local free sheet, one of the best I've seen, with sentences accurate and rhythmical, something about which he says he is fastidious.

***

**In addition, might I mention:**
- The freelance who said he had not filed a story about a Bengal tiger being kept in a council house because: "It was a right rubber-stamp job, and in any case, what with calls, conferences, court, council meetings and committees, I've enough to do without        worrying about tigers."
- The sub-editors who produced headlines such as: 'Dead Man was not Ill', 'Slate Thief left on Tiles' and 'Giant Jump in Leeds Abortions', or even 'Leeds Firm gives Kidney Sufferers new Heart' and 'New Head for John the Baptist'.
- The crime reporter who said: 'In the days before Ryan was hanged the vicar pulled many strings to make life easier for him.'
- The air correspondent who wrote: 'Leeds Bradford airport is operating normally except there are no aeroplanes.'
- The municipal correspondent who claimed: 'Eighty five per cent of Leeds housewives are satisfied with the services of their milkmen!'

# 5: This Sporting Life

## Leeds United

'Marching on Together' is Leeds United's anthem and fans continue to thunder the song of loyalty whenever the occasion demands. Another ballad is one sung years ago by the late Ronnie Hilton and is often given an airing at functions staged by branches of Leeds United Supporters' Club. The sounds conjure an immediate picture of the Elland Road scene during Don Revie's thirteen-year reign when he transformed a struggling club into one of the most powerful forces in British and European football. The song goes:

*Manchester can boast about their Summerbee and Best,*
*Then there's Liverpool and Arsenal and Spurs and all the rest.*
*But let us sing the praises of the team we love the best*
*As Leeds go marching on.*

*Chorus:*
*Glory, Glory, Leeds United;*
*Glory, Glory, Leeds United;*
*Glory; Glory, Leeds United;*
*They're the greatest football team in all the land.*

*Little Billy Bremner is the captain of the crew,*
*For the sake of Leeds United he'll break himself in two.*
*His hair is red and fuzzy and his body's black and blue,*
*But Leeds go marching on.*
*Chorus, etc.*

*Once we won the Fairs Cup and before so very long*
*The Inter-Cities champions were really going strong.*
*And when we get to Wembley you'll hear us sing this song*
*As Leeds go marching on.*
*Chorus, etc.*

*From the paddock to the Scratching Shed you'll hear our voices sing,*
*We'll get behind United and make the rafters ring.*
*We've a team we can be proud of, and Don Revie is the king,*
*As Leeds go marching on.*
*Chorus, etc.*

The Leeds United Supporters' Club has former player Eddie Gray as president. He succeeded the late Elsie Revie and the chairman is long-serving Ray Fell. The Supporters' Club came into existence in 1919 and, although secretary Eric Carlile denies that he was at the inauguration, he has served the club with diligence and for more years than he cares to count.

The Club has branches from Leeds to Australia. The Dublin Branch is 500-strong and other fan clubs are based in Sweden, the Far East and Norway. Members of the Norwegian Club are regular visitors to Elland Road and usually make a beeline for Peter Lorimer's pub in Holbeck.

Leeds United was formed in October 1919 after the disbanding of Leeds City – a club that struggled for existence and was finally ejected from league membership in 1913. It was accused of mismanagement, illegal practices and rule-breaking payments to players. When Leeds City folded a famous auction took place at the Hotel Metropole, Leeds, on October 17th, when each City player was sold to the highest bidder. It was the last act in a drama without parallel in football history. It was a local reporter who tagged it 'the flesh and blood sale'.

United played their first season in the Midland League and were elected to the Second Division of the Football League on May 31st, 1920. The public's financial support of the new company was poor and benefactor J. Hilton Crowther loaned the club £35,000 with the agreement that he would be repaid when United achieved promotion to the First Division. This came in 1924 and the debt to Mr Crowther was liquidated by an issue of debentures, of which £15,000 remained unpaid.

The first captain of United was Jim Baker, who played in 167 consecutive league and cup games. In 1927 he became licensee of the Smyths Arms in Gelderd Road, Leeds. United's first colours were blue and white stripes. The change to blue and old gold was made in 1934 in a match with Liverpool.

United were relegated at the end of the 1926-1927 season. But they were promoted with Manchester City in 1928. In May 1931 they again made the drop with Manchester United and returned to the First Division the following year with Wolverhampton.

United retained First Division status until 1946-1947 when they were relegated with Brentford. The club finished at the bottom of the table with a record of played 42 matches; won 6; lost 30; drawn 6; goals for 45; goals against 90; total points 18. Top scorer was George Ainsley with eleven and Aubrey Powell was runner-up with nine.

Mr Hilton Crowther was still waiting for his money. It is believed the debt was never settled.

Jack Charlton was a one-club player and joined Leeds United as a fifteen-year old schoolboy. He made more appearances for Leeds than any other player and grew to love his adopted city. Jack was capped for England with the undisputed highlight his contribution to England's epic World Cup victory over Germany.

When Jack retired from playing for Leeds he became a manager and he was headhunted by the Irish Football Association to take over their international side.

"It was St Patrick himself who chose Big Jack," was the comment of eminent Irish statesman Albert Reynolds who travelled to Leeds from Dublin to praise Jack's contribution to international soccer. Albert has obviously 'kissed the Blarney stone', but he was sincere in his praise of the player fans nicknamed 'The Giraffe'.

Albert said: "Jack had ten happy years managing the Irish team. My country loved him. He was an Englishman who came from Leeds to work a miracle. He formed a team into a family and gave them the confidence and class to challenge the world. Jack is well known for his shooting and fishing and I think I'll ask the Irish president Mary Robinson to create a job for him – he could be Ireland's first 'Chief Fishing Officer'."

My favourite story about Jack is his thrift and his cadging of cigarettes. We spoke together at a dinner and Jack asked me what I thought of his new suit, which he had collected that day.

"It is very smart," I replied.

"It is but I have left my cigs in the old one" said Jack reaching out for my packet of twenty and helping himself through the rest of the night.

Don Revie frowned on players smoking but he never caught Jack puffing fags. When Don came into view Jack – with great dexterity – always ensured that Billy Bremner was holding the cigarette.

The late Billy said: "I don't know how Jack transferred the fag to my fingers. He once did it when we were in soapsuds in the bath. The door opened and Don gave me a real telling off. Trying to explain to Don that it was Jack's cigarette was a waste of time."

# 'King John'

There was a no more majestic sight in soccer than to see John Charles heading for goal with the ball almost tied to his bootlaces. Little wonder he was tagged 'King John' when he reigned supreme at Elland Road, with 309 appearances and 153 goals before leaving for Juventus where he inherited the tag 'Il Gigante Buno' – 'The Gentle Giant'. His record with Leeds is all the more impressive when you consider that he played half the games at centre-half – a position he confided was his 'favourite'.

John was a modest character. He was never truly aware of his sky-high eminence in sport. He was unaware of the magnitude of his achievements and equally at home with fans in the tap room at Peter Lorimer's Holbeck pub as he was sipping wine with British and Italian aristocracy.

John was not a paragon. He was not a saint. Neither was he one for kicking over the traces. He never indulged in the behaviour of many present-day football stars whose seedy exploits make lurid media headlines.

John was not ambitious. He told me that his happiest days in football were spent at Merthyr Tydfil when he was player, coach and manager in the twilight of his illustrious career. He even manned the turnstiles on occasions and shared the most mundane duties with the chairman known to all as Mostyn.

When John signed for Juventus the city of Leeds went into mourning. But part of the agreement was a match at Elland Road between the Italian side and a team of veteran stars recruited by John. Spectators had their first glimpse of the South American Omar Sivori, who ignored the protection of shin pads and turned in a bewitching performance with socks down to his boot tops.

In goal for John's side should have been the former Charlton Athletic keeper Sam Bartram who was managing York City at the time. Sam came out of retirement to take his place between the posts for the usual warm-up with members of his side taking pot shots at goal. Sam was famous for his trick of knocking the shots out with his elbows but he did not allow for John's power. Sam was stretchered off before the match started. He nursed a suspected broken arm and was taken to Leeds Infirmary where a badly bruised arm was diagnosed.

John's shooting was fierce and accurate but former player Frank Soo – who was on the training staff at Leeds – gasped with disbelief when the centre-forward let fly with one mighty kick which missed the net and happily avoided the keeper. The ball hit the wall at the side of the upright and rebounded almost to the half-way line.

Frank turned to me and said: "If that had hit the goalie he would be dead."

The ball at that time was not the modern lightweight type. It was made of thick leather panels stitched together and when rain poured and the mud was flying it resembled a heavy suet pudding.

John was also a magnificent header and the callous on his brow was the result of his gift for powering the ball with unerring accuracy.

During John's brilliant career with Juventus the players were taken to a hideaway on the hills surrounding Rome where they drank wine by the gallon much to the anger of the coach. He growled: "You must stop this and listen to me. I want you to profit from new tactics."

Sivori interrupted the well-intentioned member of the backroom staff to say: "The only tactics that matter are simple. John kicks off by passing the ball to the inside left. He passes the ball to me. I run down to the corner flag. I cross the ball to John's head. He goes 'pow'. We are one up. Now let's get back to the wine."

I was John's ghost-writer before he went to Italy. We did a weekly column. Sometimes he never saw it in advance or even helped by giving me a subject to develop. However he was always in advance with his invoices. He was supposed to put in a bill monthly but this became weekly and often he was weeks in advance with his demands for the modest fee. He always seemed to have trouble with finance.

John lived at Middleton opposite the Park gates. He was one of the few players with a car and my favourite story about this humble man concerns the day he stopped his vehicle outside the Middleton Arms pub. Two young lads sporting blue and old gold colours were standing near the tram stop and John wound down his window and shouted: "If you are going to the match get in."

The boys sat in the back seats and, when the car arrived at Elland Road, John stopped and said: "There you are boys. Out you get."

One of them murmured: "We're going to Headingley to watch Leeds rugby, mister."

'Mister' simply laughed and drove the lads to Headingley before returning to the home of Leeds United. In those days both clubs played in similar colours.

'King' John Charles captured in typical action as he soars to head another brilliant goal.

Heading was one of the great features of his play at centre-half or centre-forward. When he played at Juventus his colleague Sivori outlined the team's method of playing. Sivori said: "We kept things simple. We did not have any frills. John kicked off by passing the ball to me. I ran down the field and crossed the ball. John climbed like a bird and headed the ball into the net. It was as easy as that. We did not complicate things."

The theory worked well. John was leading scorer for three years in Italy. Sivori was also a great player and John was one of his fans. But if you asked the late Leeds United favourite to name the best he ever played with or against he had no hesitation in nominating Di Stefano.

Can you imagine many of the millionaire players of today even stopping their car to pick up fans? John was a kind man but one lacking essential business sense, although he knew how to make a bob or two.

When he returned from Juventus for a second spell with United we teamed up again to pen stories about his career in Italy. They were colourful and tantalising. For instance one of his colleagues was 'Player of the Year' and his prize was 'a famous actress for a month'. We were unable to give her name. She would have taken John, me and my newspaper to court for millions. She is still alive today.

Unfortunately John thought the articles belonged to him. He sold them to a Welsh newspaper and my editor decided that we would end the series. But we remained firm friends. We were on the after-dinner speaking circuit together. The name Morgan stood me in good stead with the affable Welshman and we enjoyed a long and happy relationship.

My reward for our friendship came at a small dinner party in Leeds where John, his wife Glenda and close friends and relatives believed they were present to celebrate a birthday. It was my privilege to reveal that John had been awarded the CBE for services to football.

Fans will never forget the adopted son of Leeds and the most pleasing aspect in recent times was the unveiling of a magnificent bust of John at Leeds Civic Hall and the fact that his name is associated with the splendid South Leeds Stadium.

The Supporters' Club paid £30,000 for the bronze bust and it stands in the Civic Hall as a tribute to arguably the greatest player to wear a United shirt. Ray Fell said: "We originally hoped to find a permanent place for the bust at Elland Road. But we had to change our plans after the wife of club chairman Ken Bates unexpectedly commissioned her own sculpture of the great player. Leeds City Council came to our aid. We are grateful to the City Fathers for giving us the opportunity to display the bronze in a spot which certainly would have met with John's approval. He was held in high esteem by football lovers world-wide. We were lucky to have him at Elland Road."

Perhaps an honour will be forthcoming for Glenda, who nursed John through his grave illness in Italy and on his return to Leeds. He did not survive in spite of the best possible medical attention and he was laid to rest. Leeds and his native Wales shared the grief and Nat Lofthouse – the Lion of Vienna – paid a huge tribute to John when he said: "Charles was the greatest centre-forward and the greatest centre-half ever to pull on a pair of football boots."

Jack Charlton echoed that view. So did many more great players. Who are we to argue?

It was 'many happy returns' at Elland Road on August 22nd, 1962, when John Charles signed for a second stint as a Leeds United player. Manager Don Revie was the most delighted man in soccer when he persuaded John to return to the scene of so many triumphs. Don echoed the view expressed by thousands of fans: "The King is with us again. Long may he reign."

**Don Revie, manager of Leeds United in its golden age from 1961 to 1974.**

# Don Revie

Don Revie's reign as Leeds United manager remains a magnificent chapter in the history of a club once beloved by millions. During his twelve glorious years he could never have visualised that the Elland Road outfit would one day flirt with bankruptcy, sample relegation and almost be threatened with closure. Happily the fight back has started. although it will take years for the club to recover even a semblance of the Revie golden area.

Don cut an imposing figure. Many journalists – including me – were often awe-stricken in his presence. He defended his players against the mildest criticism. He was a father figure to his charges and they responded with superb soccer performances as one of the most feared teams in Europe.

The last time I spoke to him was an occasion I did my best to avoid. He was seated in a wheelchair – a frail figure and a shadow of his former athletic build. Motor-neurone disease had taken a devastating toll. Pain and sadness were in evidence as the late club physio Eric Brailsford propelled Don's conveyance down the empty tunnel leading to the Elland Road pitch.

The stands were packed with thousands of fans, who 'knighted' 'Sir Don' and they waited to deliver a thunderous salute to their hero.

My brief that night was to make announcements from the side of the pitch before the kick-off to a match sponsored by my newspaper the *Yorkshire Evening Post*. During the build-up commentator John Helm and I had a bit of a spat with Manchester United boss Alex Ferguson. But that was of little consequence as I skirted by him to walk up the almost empty tunnel.

I didn't want to meet the lonely figure in the invalid carriage. I wanted to remember Don as a fully fit player and a healthy manager, who plucked Leeds United from veritable obscurity and transformed them into a team of international notoriety. The microphone stint finished early simply because of a fault in transmission and the only way out from the pitch near the dugouts was up the tunnel. It was impossible to avoid Don who waited for the reappearance of Eric to wheel him onto the pitch.

Don held out a limp hand in greeting. We embraced. We didn't speak. There were tears in his eyes and a couple of half-stifled sobs from me as I bent down to attempt to whisper a few comforting words. They did not come and Don patted my head before we separated. Eric returned to fulfill his duty and I walked out to gaze at the starry sky with tears cascading. That poignant and distressing experience will remain until hopefully we stand together on some celestial terrace watching a couple of immortal teams locked in a game of seraphic soccer.

Don Revie signed for Leeds as a player in November 1958. He has six full English caps. In March 1961 he was appointed United manager. He led his team to victory in the 1963-64 Second Division championship. In 1964-1965 the team finished runner-up in both the First Division and the FA Cup. In 1966 United won the league Cup and the Fairs Cup. In 1970-71 they won the Fairs Cup, and the following season the FA Cup. In 1972-1973 they won the FA Cup. In 1974 they won the First Division Championship. In July 1974 Don Revie became England manager.

# Peter Lorimer

Peter Lorimer enjoys a love relationship with Leeds having spent infinitely more years in his adopted city than he did in his native Dundee. He was 15 years and 289 days old when he became the youngest player to appear in Leeds United's first team. It was a debut against Southampton in September 1962, and spectators saw for the first time the potential and awesome shooting power of the talented goal scorer.

This explosive brand of finishing was destined to strike fear in the hearts of opposing defenders especially goalkeepers. It was spectacular and inspired United fans to thunder the incessant chant: "Ninety miles and hour." Peter was given the nickname 'Lash' and he was described as 'The Cannonball Kid' because of his ability to blast the ball. But he is the first to concede that the 'ninety mph' claim was a myth.

He said: "I was timed in the mid-seventies by scientific methods. My kicks reached 76.5 miles an hour definitely not ninety. But it was confirmed that I was the hardest kicker in football at that time."

The eloquent Scotsman was thirteen years old when he realised that he could shoot straighter and stronger than his schoolboy mates. His football fame spread beyond the confines of his native land and vigilant scouts learned that the youngster actually scored 176 goals in one season.

Peter said: "I have to say that many of the goals were against diminutive goalies. Some of them were so small they could only reach half way to the crossbar. But 176 goals was not a bad tally for any lad."

The flood of goals – plus the local newspaper coverage – saw agents and managers racing for his signature and it was Leeds United's boss Don Revie who secured the signing.

Peter said: "My mother was impressed by Don's honesty and the promise that he would look after me. He adhered to his word. He sent my family regular bulletins and assured my parents that I was being well cared for. Don was like a second dad."

When Peter eventually made his debut for Scotland his mother hired a coach to take family and friends to the match. She told them not to worry about tickets because Peter would provide them. He recalls that he was £300 out of pocket. But the expenditure was 'worth every bawbee'.

Years after Peter retired from the game his Elland Road colleague Norman Hunter talked of the Lorimer contribution to the glory days under the late Revie.

Norman said: "We had a truly great side, brimming with internationals. Other teams gave us nothing. They packed defences but it was amazing how many times a goal from Peter broke the deadlock. When he was buzzing it was a case of 'stand by for blasting'. You could hear the ball whistle and few goalies had much of a chance with his pile drivers. I almost felt sorry for players who formed a wall to face a Lorimer free kick. He could have ruined a lad's marital future and many wisely turned their backs to the ball. I was glad to be on the same side as Peter, although I did face him in internationals."

Peter said: "I often wonder why I can't hit a golf ball 300 yards and the reason is I don't have the essential timing. Hitting a dead or even moving football is much easier for me. When I kick a ball I don't have to think about rhythm or power. It is a natural ability, an automatic action and a gift for which I was always grateful."

He is still playing charity matches with Leeds United's Ex-Players' Association but the chants from the fans dropped to 'thirty miles an hour' before rising to 'sixty'. Peter thinks the 'nineties' are over but he enjoys the banter and the enduring friendship of his Elland Road mates and the United fans.

When his career finished he had the chance to move from Leeds and return to Dundee but he did not give it a second thought. He said: "Leeds is now my permanent home. I played here for twenty-three years and the area has been good to me. It is the ideal place with a magnificent city centre and close to the Commercial Hotel, Holbeck, which is my business. We have the superb Yorkshire Dales more or less on our doorstep and within an hour I can enjoy the most picturesque countryside.

"Dundee will always be special. I lived in a small fishing village and go back as often as possible to see my folks. But you can say that Leeds is my first home and Dundee now my second. I have family here. I am a director at Leeds United. And I still see my old friends, Eddie Gray, Norman Hunter, Mick Jones, Jack Charlton and the rest. We often get together and being in Leeds makes it possible for me to keep in touch with so many friends."

Peter added, with a hint of mischief: "Leeds United could do with a few Scotsmen. They haven't had much of a side since the team was about 75 per cent Scottish. However we can look to the future with confidence."

Peter has vivid memories of the Revie reign. He said: "We had many triumphs and we also had little frustrations and this is summed up in Billy Bremner's book You Get Nowt For Being Second. There was the disallowed goal against Chelsea which cost United a place in the FA Cup Final. We were robbed in the European Cup Final in Paris. And I will never forget the horrendous match with AC Milan in Greece after which the referee was banned for life because the game was rigged in favour of the Italians. However we did have happy results like the League Championship and 1972 Centenary Cup Final. And I did play twenty-three internationals with Scotland."

The Commercial Hotel, which Peter runs with his partner Sue, is a target for football fans from round the world. There is a steady influx of bed and breakfast clientele from Norway and increasing bookings from the 500-strong Dublin-based Leeds United Supporters' Club.

Peter is often asked to display medals, trophies, shirts and caps that he gained in his distinguished career. He has plenty to show for his sporting endeavours. Even in the dark period when business failures, plus regular support of slow racehorses, contributed to financial problems Peter was never tempted to part with cherished symbols of his soccer status.

Peter said: "It seems an eternity since that first game for United. I thought I would never leave the club. But manager Jimmy Adamson transferred me to the North American soccer scene in the 1978-1979 season. I had four seasons with Toronto and Vancouver and returned to Leeds United when Eddie Gray was manager. I was thirty-seven and took my appearances to 690 and my goal tally to 238. This enabled me to beat the record established by the late and great John Charles. John was one of the first to congratulate me. John was a regular at my pub and my big regret is that I never saw him play. He must have been one of the greatest."

Billy Bremner took over Leeds United and in 1985 told Peter that he was surplus to requirements. Peter said:" I had the chance to play and coach in Israel but decided to hang up my boots. I enjoyed every minute with Leeds United. I will always follow the club with loyalty and great affection."

**Peter Lorimer was one of the Elland Road stars in the Revie era and his dynamic shooting power did not exactly endear him to opposing goalkeepers. Peter's career finished with him at the top of the Elland Road goal-scorers and he is now a successful landlord at the Commercial Pub, Holbeck, and also a director on the United Board.**

# Brian Clough

The guest list was like a page from a sporting Debrett with Len Hutton, Fred Trueman, Lewis Jones, Brian Close, Billy Wright and many others mingling with Prime Minister Harold Wilson and the outspoken Derby County manager Brian Clough. It was January 28th, 1973, and the 500-strong audience – with one notable exception – gathered to salute Peter Lorimer, winner of the Yorkshire Sportsman of the Year Trophy.

Peter was given special permission by Don Revie to travel to Leeds from Wolverhampton where United's players were booked in a hotel on the eve of a vital championship game. The Scottish international accepted the award and immediately embarked on the return journey to the Leeds United camp, missing a subsequent eruption of insults, indignation and total embarrassment.

It was the most bizarre dinner in my long experience. I must have covered over one thousand and more. I have spoken at many. But the Leeds function was venomous, acrimonious, sad and bordered on grotesque. Brian Clough's brief was an invitation to reply on behalf of the guests and he was introduced to the expectant audience by Peter Stone, chairman of Leeds Variety Club. But the former England striker did not begin his speech. He declared an unscheduled break in the proceedings.

Clough told us: "I have been sitting here for two and a half hours and before I respond to anyone I am going for a pee. You can do the same and, when you return, you can sit down and bloody listen to me. You will bloody pay me attention."

He kept the audience waiting for eleven minutes before returning to the microphone to launch a verbal attack on Lorimer. It was a disjointed outburst interrupted by jeers and catcalls.

Clough shouted: "Despite Lorimer falling when he hasn't been kicked or tackled and despite the fact that he protests when he has nothing to protest about....."

The remainder of his remarks were lost in shouts from the guests of "Get off. Sit down. You are disgraceful."

Clough appeared to be annoyed at the fact that his name on the toast list was given as 'Brian Clough manager of Derby County'. He claimed that it should have read 'Manager of Derby County – First Division Champions'.

He rounded on his hecklers and hollered: "I am not particularly happy with the idea of speaking to you lot. I have to stand up here but you are sitting in the crowd and hiding. If you have anything to say please say it. You are mumblers. We are becoming a nation of mumblers. Stand on your feet if you have anything to say. Come up here if think you can do better. Get off my bloody back. Give me a bloody chance. Sod off."

One man pointed at Clough and claimed the speaker had made a mockery of Yorkshire sport. Clough interspersed his reply with more strong language and added: "If I have made a mockery of Yorkshire sport I apologise. I was told before I came that no matter what I made of the speech the dignity of the occasion would prevail."

Clough continued to harangue Leeds United fans and many of the guests were furious and staged a walkout. He eventually sat down to a furore of boos. Harold Wilson listened to his performance without smiling or comment.

Peter Stone said: "I contemplated interfering and interrupting Brian's speech but thought it unwise to get involved in a slanging match."

Clough was certainly abrasive and abusive. But he signed autographs in the hotel foyer and made no excuse for his contribution which lacked a theme. He simply lost the thread of his material and did not return to the subject.

The full report of the incident appeared in the *Yorkshire Evening Post* and it was attacked by Danny Blanchflower in his *Sunday Express* column. Danny accused a local hack (me) of trying to make a name for himself to which the reporter (me) replied in a front-page open letter to the former Tottenham and Irish international footballer. It stated: "O Danny Boy your pipes and gripes are galling me..."

Years later Danny and I became firm friends. We both contributed to Yorkshire Television's sports output.

Later I spoke at a dinner with Brian Clough and Geoff Boycott. Brian said: "Please don't remind of that night in Leeds. He then started a row with the audience at the Darrington Hotel, on the A1 and took over the running of the dinner.

I was of the opinion that Brian Clough committed 'soccer suicide' as far as Leeds United were concerned on that fateful night at the Queen's Hotel. Little wonder he only lasted a matter of six weeks when he was appointed manager at Elland Road. But there was no doubting his coaching genius. He was possibly the greatest manager not to govern the England side.

It was said of the late Brian Clough that he could cause trouble in an empty room. This rang true on his first day as manager of Leeds United when he embarked on clearing out anything to do with his predecessor Don Revie. The story is told how he set about moving Revie's goods from the office and in between he made several calls to the apprentices' room asking for 'tea and biscuits to be sent up immediately'. Half an hour passed and the tea and biscuits had not surfaced.

He again rang the apprentices and one answered with Brian shouting: "Do you know who this is?"

The voice at the other end of the line replied: "Yes you are Mr Brian Clough our new manager!" The apprentice continued: "Do you know who this is?"

Brian answered: "No."

The youngster murmured: "Well get your own ruddy tea and biscuits."

It was a story that went the rounds. The culprit was never identified and Brian probably     saw     the funny side of the incident.

However there wasn't much fun at the Variety Club Sporting Dinner when Brian trod on a few toes and neither was it a laughing matter at another function where Brian and his hero Geoff Boycott were on the speaking list. Once again Brian upset the audience. But Morgan, the man in the middle, was able to smile. Here (left to right) are Brian Clough, John Morgan and Geoff Boycott.

Brian Clough played twice for England but his career as a player came to a premature end at the age of twenty-nine when he was seriously injured. His goal scoring was phenomenal – he scored 251 goals in 274 games. He was a brilliant manager and the pity is that he never got the chance to guide Leeds United to European success. He was sacked after 44 days. Brian guided Nottingham Forest to League and European Cup victories.

# 'Leeds Rhinos'

An epic meeting at the George Hotel, Huddersfield, in August 1895 resulted in Leeds becoming one of the founder members of the Northern Rugby Football League. The split from the England Rugby Union was caused by the fact that many clubs were paying compensation to players who missed work because of sporting injuries and lost wages.

Leading Yorkshire and Lancashire clubs – twenty-two in all – resigned from the Union and changed the playing numbers on each side from fifteen to thirteen. Both codes were miles apart for decades but it is true to say that Rugby League and Rugby Union are now closer than they have ever been since that momentous decision over a century ago.

Leeds has never lacked fervent support and the club boasts a record of achievements the envy of lesser teams. The sport is described by many fans as 'The Man's Game' and it is certainly a pastime not for the faint-hearted. Leeds has produced countless players and sterling performances over the years to delight those who regard Headingley's famous ground as their second home.

Honours include memorable Championship victories and Challenge Cup triumphs. Successful performances in the Premiership, Yorkshire Cup, Yorkshire League, Regal Trophy and BBC Floodlit Trophy finals have brought coveted silverware to the home of a club with a golden history. Few will ever forget the feat at Old Trafford on October 16th, 2004, when Leeds Rhinos powered to a memorable Championship victory to break a gap of thirty-two years. At that time Leeds had only lost four times in thirty-two matches. It was a team threatening to justify a tag of 'invincible' and fans were entitled to view the future with justifiable anticipation.

However luck has not exactly shone on Leeds in recent seasons and loyal fans will be hoping for improvements and perhaps 'new faces' in the players' ranks. But the fact remains that competition at the top echelon of Super League is formidable and none can take success for granted.

Leeds Rugby League history is a story of outstanding players and my memories invariably hinge on Arthur Clues and Lewis Jones. Arthur was a friend from the day he arrived from Australia and one of my escapades with 'Big A' occurred when I lived in Poole in Wharfedale. It was four o'clock in the morning and Arthur, golfer Hedley Muscroft and me – sporting dinner jackets and bow ties – were enjoying 'one for the road' when our local milkman approached the front window.

He looked in, rubbed his eyes and, having placed two pints of milk on the front step, he took another glance in the window by which time we had retired to a room at the back of the cottage.

At lunchtime the same day I met the milkman who told me he had 'suffered an experience' on his rounds. He continued: "I could swear that I saw you, Arthur Clues and another big fellow in your front room drinking and dressed as though you were going to a dinner."

"What did you do?" I asked.

"I went to see a doctor. He told me to go home and rest. It could have been an hallucination brought on by overwork," he said.

I didn't have the heart to enlighten him but it was noticeable that he always took a curious second look at my window whenever he passed.

Arthur arrived in this country with New Zealander Bert Cook. They were good mates and shared digs at first, although Bert did not subscribe to Arthur's leisure-time antics. The pair were popular with fans and Bert justified his signing for the club with 1,169 points in 210 games. He took size four in boots and could kick goals from any angle.

Arthur was one of the greatest forwards of all time and also a fine cricketer. He represented Leeds at the summer game and would have walked into the Yorkshire side had the stringent county 'birthright' ruling not been in operation at that time. Arthur came for a couple of seasons and intended returning to his native Australia but he stayed and the church at Roundhay was packed to overflowing for his funeral. It was a privilege to attend.

Lewis Jones was tagged 'The Golden Boy' during his career with Leeds. His signing upset the Welsh Rugby Union selectors and I remember the great Welsh player Cliff Morgan telling me an almost unbelievable story. Cliff came to Leeds to pay tribute to Lewis in a Yorkshire Television production and we shared a pint and a story or two in the bar. He told me that he was 'warned off' attending Lewis's wedding by the Welsh rugby authorities. He was threatened: "If you go to the wedding you will never play for Wales again."

When Australian Arthur Clues and New Zealander Bert Cook arrived in Leeds they were welcomed with a flurry of snowflakes. It was a new experience for the men destined to play major roles in the history of Leeds Rugby League Club. Arthur was under the impression that snow could be eaten but one mouthful was enough for the big fellow who signed for two years with the Headingley club and spent the rest of his life in the city he grew to love. Arthur became a great favourite with the Leeds fans. He was one of the best forward's ever to wear the famous Leeds colours and he was equally gifted at cricket.

Bert Cook wore size four boots. They were small but were possibly filled with dynamite such was the length and accuracy of his goal kicks.

Both players were so impressive Leeds directors moved swiftly to ensure that the talented duo would stay with Leeds for some considerable time. Bert became a successful businessman and he was Master of his local Lodge and Captain of his golf club. Arthur was also in business with his own sports shop and he became a Minister's Representative with the Sports Council. He raised thousands of pounds for the Sports Aid Foundation.

Our picture shows Arthur Clues being welcomed by Leeds Rugby League Club secretary George Hirst. On the left is Leeds manager RW Watson and in the centre is Bert Cook.

Lewis Jones shocked the Rugby Union world in November 1952 when he turned professional and joined Leeds Rugby League club for a then record fee of £6,000. Union fans in the Principality turned their ire and backs on the player once known as 'The Golden Boy'. He gained the tag when he was capped ten times for Wales and twice by the British Lions. Anger and venom replaced the cheers Welsh fans once had for the man born Benjamin Lewis Jones in Gorsienon in South Wales.It was there he learned his rugby skill and also showed great talent for cricket.

Lewis did not have a happy start to his career with Leeds. He fractured his arm within two months of switching codes. But he quickly made an impact and established records that stand today. In 1956-1957 he recorded 496 points with 194 goals and 36 tries. His total points of 274 on the tour to Australia in 1954 was also a record. He played fifteen games for Great Britain and left Leeds for Australia in 1964 to become player coach at Wentworthville, Sydney.

Lewis was skilful. He was equally at home as a centre, stand-off, full-back or winger. He had an amazing change of pace and could jink and dummy with the best. When he returned to Leeds he became a teacher.

Wales eventually forgave Lewis for turning to Rugby League. He was no longer ostracised and was able to return to clubs that once banned his presence.

Cliff ignored the message. He was Lewis's best man and he did represent his country again. Wales needed his wizardry.

When Cliff received his cheque for taking part in the televised tribute to Lewis he handed it to me and said: "Put that in the *Yorkshire Evening Post* Half and Half Appeal for the hospices."

I was asked recently to try and persuade Lewis to take part in a series of recordings featuring Rugby League's legends. He is very shy and we had to respect his gentle refusal. Lewis said: "Rugby was an important part of my life but now it is over. Rugby is in the past. But thank you for the invitation. I would rather not participate."

When you think that Lewis kicked 1,244 goals and scored 2,920 points in his career with Leeds you must agree that he is a legend. Add to that the fact he scored thirteen goals in one game and scored thirty-one points in one match with Bradford and you have a fair estimation of his kicking talent. He kicked 166 in 1956-1957 and scored a total of 431 points in that season. Thankfully this star of yesterday is now as welcome as daffodils in his native land and in the world of Rugby Union.

I must mention John Atkinson, Sid Hynes, Alan Smith, Les Dyl, Phil Cookson, Kevin Dick, Garry Schofield, David Ward, Roy Dickinson and countless others. They were all members of John Morgan's All-Stars – a charity cricket team of great renown.

When I was on the *Yorkshire Evening Post* staff I was asked by a young reader if Roy Dickinson would send him a souvenir. Roy sent him a sweaty sock he had worn in a match. Roy's mother was most upset. The young fan was delighted.

# Hunslet Rugby League

When the curtain descended on historic Parkside a million ghosts trod the turf that for many years was the hub of Hunslet's social life. There was a discernible air of decay hanging over the hallowed arena where crowds once turned up in thousands before the decision was made to sell the sporting acreage for industrial development. It was the start of a trek from threatened oblivion for Hunslet Rugby League Club to its permanent home at South Leeds Stadium – now bearing the additional name of John Charles.

Parkside was the pride of South Leeds for decades with memorable victories recorded by gallant men who proudly sported the famous myrtle, white and flame strip. Elderly fans still look back with never fading affection for the ground where the shutters were erected in April 1973. Old timers still recall Hunslet at its rugby zenith. They remember with satisfaction watching Hunslet beat Leeds in the 1933 Rugby League Championship Final by eight points to two. It was decided before a record crowd of 54,112 and it was staged at Elland Road.

Reporters were constantly reminded of that epic encounter by the late Bill Duffy, who played in the Leeds team. Bill was a publican who fronted a sporting quiz called 'Off the Cuff with Duff' and rarely a session ended without a mention of that outstanding Hunslet triumph. Bill often fractured the English language. He became a bit part actor on television but never forgot the highlight of his life – the clash with Hunslet at the home of Leeds United.

Elland Road again beckoned when Hunslet Rugby League Club was threatened with extinction and Geoff Gunney remembers that era with total recall of the controversial circumstances. Geoff was a leading player. He received the MBE for his services to the game. He made a record number of appearances with the club he supported as a schoolboy. He even collected jam jars to raise vital revenue for the team he followed with an obsessive passion.

Geoff said: "The directors told the players that they had bad news in store but refused to go into detail. You can imagine the shock when I read in the evening newspaper that the ground had been sold. I was rooted to the spot. I can still feel the chill that hit me. It was like the death of a loved one. My world had come to an end."

But Geoff and his colleagues refused to be beaten. He rang John Kennedy, who was general manager of the Leeds Greyhound Stadium, and asked if he could accommodate a Rugby League team. With the help of financial backers the deal was done. Geoff and his mates removed fixtures, seats, goal posts and training gear from Parkside. New Hunslet was born at the Elland Road dog track. New Hunslet should have been Hunslet Phoenix – having risen from the ashes – but the local press jumped the gun and labelled the club with its 'New' title.

Over four thousand watched the opening game with Huyton and I remember a request made to the *Yorkshire Evening Post* for a reporter to participate in the grand opening. That is how I was dressed as a jockey and rode a donkey round the track tossing lollypops to children who hurled them back at the overweight rider.

However, it was not long before Hunslet – having dropped 'New' – was again on the move with the decision by Ladbrokes to sell the greyhound track. Batley's Mount Pleasant took in the Hunslet lodgers for a couple of seasons before Elland Road again entered the picture. The late Leeds United chairman Manny Cussins invited Hunslet Rugby League Club to share United's facilities. Manny's gesture was not simply out of friendship. He wanted cash for the deal because Leeds United were feeling the financial pinch. Hunslet contributed handsomely to the United coffers and Manny and his fellow board members were grateful for the monetary lift.

Almost £250,000 poured into United's coffers before Leeds City Council leader John Trickett made a momentous announcement designed to secure the future of Hunslet Hawks RL Club. He said: "Hunslet will play one season at Bramley's McLaren Field ground before moving to the new South Leeds Stadium. There will be a capacity for five thousand with many other benefits."

Excitement was given free rein. South Leeds Stadium was no more than a couple of drop kicks from the ground that once housed Parkside. Hunslet Rugby League was coming home.

Mr Trickett – now a Member of Parliament – was correct in his description of facilities at the state of the art structure. But the Hawks supporters are still waiting for the five thousand and preferably a ten thousand seater. Will that upgrade ever take place? Geoff Gunney and his friends are prepared to wait and see. And pray!

South Leeds Stadium is luxurious compared to one or two stadiums housing Super League clubs. Hunslet Hawks are the envy of many when it comes to facilities. The pitch is now returning to the standard lovingly cultivated by the late groundsman Brian Cartwright.

Ten years have elapsed since Hunslet Hawks relinquished their Elland Road lease and established residency at South Leeds. The decade resulted in fluctuating fortunes with the highlights a place in the Silk Cup Plate Final at Wembley and victory in the Premiership Grand Final against Dewsbury at Headingley.

It was heartbreaking for all connected with the club when entrance to the ranks of Super League was denied. The scandalous decision was made by the infamous Independent Franchise Panel, which gained the derision of people with only a remote interest in rugby but sticklers for fair play.

The sporting world at large criticised the sickening sequel. Hunslet Hawks's victory and the shattering decision resulted in the immediate loss of over a thousand fans.

Club president Grahame Liles said: "We invested thousands of pounds in the drive for promotion. The decision was not only sad. It almost finished our club. We are still reeling and feeling the effects of the panel's findings. The problems are on-going, but hope springs eternal and the future depends on home-grown talent of youngsters from the immediate locality"

Hunslet remains a hot bed for rugby with many aspiring teenagers eager to wear the distinctive Hunslet colours. Grahame's contribution to the club has been phenomenal. He has devoted twenty-six years and colossal amounts of money to the cause. Without his continued backing Hunslet would not have a Rugby League team at the South Leeds Stadium.

Grahame said: "Hopefully the missing fans will return. We have to engender the spirit and the message behind the club's famous anthem: 'We've Swept the Seas Before Boys, And So We Shall Again'."

He added: "We are proud of our association with South Leeds Stadium and anticipate many more years with the management and City Fathers. But we make no apology for reminding them of the promise to increase the seating capacity. Only then will we qualify to bring Super League status to the land which nestles south of the river."

# Leeds Tykes

The first reports of Rugby Union taking place in Leeds can be traced to 1864 with a club formed at Headingley in 1877. The game spread throughout Yorkshire with strong teams in the Leeds area and in 1899 Headingley temporarily disbanded and eventually reformed to play at Clarence Fields, Kirkstall.

Roundhay Rugby Union Football Club was formed in 1924 with headquarters at Chandos Park and, in May 1991, Leeds RUFC was created with the amalgamation of Headingley and Roundhay. The first game took place on September 1st, 1992 against Hull Ionians with Leeds RUFC initially based at Clarence Fields and Chandos Park.

The appointment of former Wales international Phil Davies as Director of Rugby preceded the move by Leeds RUFC to Headingley where they became tenants and played their first game on August 17th, 1996, against Swansea. Two years later Leeds were promoted to Premiership Two with their sights firmly fixed on a place in the top division.

July 1988 saw another important stage in the rise of the Leeds Rugby Limited with Headingley chairman Paul Caddick establishing the world's first dual code partnership with one company controlling both professional Rugby League and Rugby Union clubs. Leeds RUFC was renamed Leeds Tykes with the future guaranteed.

There were many highlights in the offing. The first Leeds Tykes international was Stuart Reid who was given his Scottish cap against France on April 10th, 1999. Scotland triumphed by 36 points to 22.

In May 2001 Leeds Tykes were promoted to the Zurich Premiership and this brought top flight Rugby Union to Headingley and heralded the international recognition of Tom Palmer. He became the first Tyke to play for England when he came on as a replacement against the USA.

September 2nd, 2001, saw Leeds defeat Bath in their opening game in the Premiership and on December 7th, 2003, Leeds played their first ever game in the Heineken Cup. They beat Neath-Swansea Ospreys at Headingley by 29 points to 20. March 13th, 2004, resulted in Leeds appearing in their first ever Cup semi-final but they lost to Sale Sharks away from home. They went down by 33 points to 20.

There were better things in store. On April 16th, 2005, Leeds defeated Bath at Twickenham to win the Powergen Cup with tries from Chris Bell and Andre Snyman. There was a man of the match performance by Gordon Ross. However, the 2006 season was unkind to the Tykes. Relegation spelt thee loss of a few big name players but the target remains a push to return to the top echelon. Leeds Tykes are not short of ambition and there will be a concerted effort to achieve the target. All in Yorkshire Rugby Union will wish the Leeds team well in their quest.

# Len Hutton

The majority of journalists are renowned partakers of strong drink and invariably check out the most convenient pub or bar when detailed for a long spell of duty. We did not have to look far at Headingley – the home of Yorkshire County Cricket Club – where a county game or five-day Test match resulted in persistent patronage of the watering hole governed by a   motherly character called Madge.

She looked after gentlemen of the Press and even those news hounds unworthy of the title. When the premises overflowed with thirsty customers we were usually able to jump the queue. This was the case one particularly hot day when Madge's Bar was crowded and she took my order ahead of other customers. There was a tap on my shoulder and a voice observed: "You seem to have some influence here young man. Will you order me three large gins, with ice and tonic please?"

It was my idol Len Hutton accompanied by another cricket great Denis Compton and the retired England wicket-keeper Godfrey Evans. In those days fans believed that Len and Denis did not exactly see eye-to-eye. But they were definitely friendly on that occasion. Len was present to watch the game. Denis was commentating and Godfrey was a representative for bookmakers Ladbroke and advising on the fluctuating betting odds as the match proceeded.

Madge answered my call. She served the drinks and I handed them one-by-one to Len before paying the lady thirty shillings. I then turned to collect the cash from Len but the trio had disappeared in the belief that I was in an ultra-benevolent mood.

Malcolm Barker, who was editor of the *Yorkshire Evening Post*, was quite happy with my thirty bob expenses, which were attributed to gaining exclusive interviews with three cricketing giants. He waited patiently for the stories to be filed and eventually forgot them as the weeks rolled by.

My next meeting with Len was on the Headingley pitch during the Test match where supporters of the 'Free George Davis Campaign' had desecrated the Test match arena with oil and tar before digging huge holes in the cherished turf. Len surveyed the damage with tears threatening to roll down his cheeks. He turned to me and said: "This is dreadful. This is where Don Bradman batted. Have the perpetrators no soul?"

You will note that Len did not mention that he made centuries on that hallowed pitch. His thoughts were with Bradman who he rated above all others.

That night I was due to attend a meeting at Pudsey St Lawrence Cricket Club with Yorkshire Television producer David Lowen. Len offered to drive us there and he dropped us outside the club where he learned his cricket. He said: "I won't come in. Folk there tend to make a fuss."

The night Len acted as our 'chauffeur' was more than sufficient compensation for the price of three gin and tonics. He was my hero

Len was usually generous in his praise of other players. He said: "Herbert Sutcliffe was the best opener I played with and Wally Hammond was the best England batsman during my career. But the best in the world was Don Bradman. He was as light and quick on his feet as Fred Astaire. He lacked nothing in style and confidence."

Of his own batting Len was in no doubt about his personal best performance. Mere mortals like you and me would expect Len to plump for the marathon innings of 364 at The Oval against Australia in 1938. We members of the 364 club meet with our president Keith Moss at Headingley in July to remember and celebrate that brilliant display of courage, stamina and a full array of beautiful batting strokes.

However, Len believes that his double century against the might of Australia's Ray Lindwall and Keith Miller was a much better innings than the record-breaking test of endurance. Len said: "When the 364 is mentioned I actually feel fatigued. But the battle against two of the world's greatest bowlers will always give me a tinge of excitement and satisfaction."

Len was lost to cricket for the duration of the Second World War. Hitler robbed us of the Pudsey man's sporting prowess and almost cost him his career. Len – later Sir Leonard – dislocated his left arm so badly in a gymnasium fall it required three operations and numerous plaster casts.. The accident and treatment reduced his arm by two inches and reduced movement by fifty per cent.

He said: "I felt at the time that my cricket career was over. I never thought I would bat for Yorkshire and England again. But happily I made a comeback and owed much to a Leeds surgeon Reg Broomhead. It was a case of adapting my left arm to the demands and thankfully I was able to resume my career."

Len did that to some tune. He became the first professional captain of England. He led his country in twenty-three Tests and in 1953 he skippered his country to victory over the Australians and retained the Ashes in 1954-1955. In the 1950-1951 tour of Australia he scored 533 runs and averaged 88.83. In 1953-1954 he scored 677 runs in Tests against the West Indies for an average 96.71.

Len indeed was a run machine. He played in seventy-nine Test matches. He scored nineteen centuries. In his First Class seasons with Yorkshire he scored 40,140 runs including 129 centuries. Can you imagine what figures he would have achieved but for the lost six years?

Perhaps Yorkshire will one day unearth another young cricketer with the gifts to follow in the hallowed Hutton footsteps. I would cheerfully stand such a chap a double gin and tonic.

# Hedley Verity

Hedley Verity was born at Headingley, Leeds, on May 18, 1905, and was destined to become one of cricket's greatest left-arm spin bowlers. He died of war wounds on July 3rd, 1943, and he is buried at Caserta, Italy, where white roses and Yorkshire CCC ties often appear on the grave of this hero.

Jim Kilburn produced countless enthralling features in the Yorkshire Post and none was greater than his recollection of Hedley and, in particular, September 1st, 1939. Yorkshire had won the county championship for the fifth time by defeating Sussex and the team boarded a coach for the return journey to Leeds.

Jim wrote: "Herbert Sutcliffe had recorded his 50,000th run. Len Hutton was blossoming. Brian Sellars had developed into a strong captain and, as the charabanc proceeded through silent towns, it was evident that a blackout was in force. The threat of war was not only imminent but certain. The war would see Hedley Verity killed in action; Bill Bowes incarcerated in a German POW camp; and others serving their King and country with cricket a distant memory."

Hedley was a captain in the Green Howards. He was killed leading his men into action on a July night in Sicily. Bill Bowes languished for four years in the prison camp and returned at the end of the war to play again for Yorkshire. He eventually retired and wrote about the game he loved in the Yorkshire Evening News and later the Yorkshire Evening Post.

Jim Kilburn recalled that epic coach trip from Hove, Sussex, and said: "When the vehicle approached Leeds men were dropped off at different locations. When it reached City Square it was empty and one of the finest county teams of all time was no more. The men united in the bond of cricket each nursed their own fears for the future of themselves and their families."

Hedley Verity paid the ultimate penalty for his bravery. But he will never be forgotten.

Cricket crowds loved the quiet man who waited until he was twenty-five to make his Yorkshire debut. He followed in the footsteps of Wilfred Rhodes, another famous spinner of the ball.

Hedley's record was amazing. He took 200 wickets in each season from 1935 to 1937. In 1932 he collected ten wickets for ten runs against Nottingham including a hat-trick. In 1934 for England against Australia he took seven for 61 and eight for 43. Fifteen wickets in one day remains a record. He played in 40 tests and hit a total of 669 runs. He also took 144 wickets. His First Class record reads 5,605 runs with a highest score of 101. He took 1,956 wickets at an average of 14.90.

# Fred Trueman

When Fred Trueman was a patient in the Yorkshire Clinic a few years ago he accepted a telephone call from me. The fact that I was included in a select coterie of journalists enjoying Fred's trust and friendship was good for the ego.

But our affinity did not stretch to Fred giving me a free copy of his latest book or even quoting a knock-down price. Fred was the archetypal Yorkshireman – loyal to a point of affection – but careful with his money.

It was the late Harold Wilson who described Fred as the world's greatest living Yorkshireman and the recipient of the accolade would be the last to argue with the eminent politician.

Cricket fans of my era blessed the day Fred was born in Scotch Springs, Stainton, near the pit village of Maltby, Rotherham. So too do a flock of after-dinner speakers who regale audiences with Trueman tales. One or two would not have a speech were it not for the exploits of Fiery Fred. But he always expressed a chuckling denial about the authenticity of his so-called swash-buckling, hard-living, drink-swilling days with Yorkshire and England.

Half the oft-quoted experiences and incidents never happened. Many of the yarns were apocryphal and Fred was a much gentler person that his rough, tough public image – and the invented stories – would suggest. There was a soft side to the man who hurtled into furious action against the 'enemy' and struck trembling fear into the most intrepid and talented batsmen.

Legend has it that when Fred Trueman retired from cricket and settled in a picturesque village near Gargrave, he offered his services to the local club. He wasn't surprised when one committee man rejected the idea of creating a place in the first team for the newcomer.

"Nay Fred lad. We are well off for bowlers. It's batsmen we want," said the cricket club spokesman.

Fred loved life in the country. It was his refuge and home with his wife Veronica and at one point Willy, an Old English sheepdog, who loved to nestle at his owner's feet. When Fred retired from bowling his heart out for Yorkshire and England he settled for the quiet life. But newspaper columns, radio and television work, kept him busy and the telephone was never quiet with journalists – like me – forever asking Fred for his views on anything to do with cricket.

Life in the Dales was relaxing. He even found time to write about the beauty of this part of what Yorkshire men proudly claim is 'God's own country'. Fred would never disagree with that assumption and he was never happier than striding along the country lanes with Willy for company. It was a far cry from the hurly-burly of releasing cricket balls at ninety miles an hour or fronting the hectic television show 'Indoor League'.

Fred was versatile. His cricket books made compulsive reading and his after-dinner speeches were worthy of television coverage. We will miss Fred. The Dales will not be the same without the fiery sportsman who liked nothing more than the quiet life.

Fred Trueman made his peace with Geoffrey Boycott after a protracted spell of animosity which often reached fever pitch. But advancing years saw Fred sympathising with Geoffrey's cancer problems. Boycott described his one-time cricketing colleague as: "A great man, a funny man, who should have been elected to the role of Yorkshire President."

Geoffrey added: "Fred had the most classical action. He was one of the all-time great fast bowlers."

This unique picture of four England and Yorkshire legends – together for the first time in thirty years – shows (left) Brian Close, who was born in Rawdon, Leeds, on February 24th, 1931. He became the youngest England player when he turned out against New Zealand aged 18 years and 149 days. Brian was a great all-rounder – batting and bowling (left handed and right). He was a brilliant fielder and an ace tactician. He skippered England in seven Tests, winning six and drawing the other. He led Yorkshire to four championships. There was a rumour that when he was eighteen he gave England colleague Denis Compton a black eye. Denis said the damage was done when he bumped his eye on a tap. I must ask Brian for the facts next time we meet.

Raymond Illingworth, with hand on Brian's shoulder, was born in Pudsey on June 8th, 1932. He captained Yorkshire, Leicestershire and England, leading his country to victory in twelve matches including four Tests at Headingley. He is rated Yorkshire's greatest off-spin bowler in post war years. He was also a great batsman. Ray first made the headlines when he played truant from school and climbed a wall to gain entrance to a Headingley match. His escapade was captured by a cameraman and the photograph appeared in the Yorkshire Evening News. Unfortunately for Ray his schoolteacher also saw the offending picture.

Geoff Boycott was born in Fitzwilliam and he achieved greatness as a batsman with the peak of his career the scoring of his 100th Test century at Headingley in 1977. The fact that it was made against Australia made the achievement all the more memorable.

He had his problems. Slow scoring did not endear him to everyone. But he is back on the Yorkshire scene after a successful battle with a life-threatening illness. Hopefully his presence at Headingley will rejuvenate a team which has struggled to return to its former all-conquering eminence. (painting by John Blakey)

One example of his concern for fellow men helped Geoff Cope when the Yorkshire spinner's career collapsed with allegations of a suspect action. The heart-broken young bowler was hounded by the media and the situation was uncomfortable for the likeable Leeds-born lad. But reporters searched for Geoff in vain. It was Fred who sized up the situation. He collected the distraught sportsman and sheltered him at his lovely cottage near Gargrave until the hue and cry died down. Fred then helped Geoff to re-build his career with advice and encouragement.

My first meeting with Fred took place in Albion Street, Leeds, outside the Yorkshire Post building. Retired England and Yorkshire fast bowler Bill Bowes was on the *Yorkshire Evening Post* sports staff and the young Trueman called in the office for advice from Bowes who figured in the infamous 'bodyline' tour of Australia. The pair startled a few shoppers and office workers walking down Albion Place as Bill attempted to improve Fred's already graceful and streamlined action.

Fred had half a dozen Yorkshire appearances to his credit by the time he was eighteen. He made his Test debut at his beloved Headingley when he was twenty-one having returned from National Service in the RAF. We were both stationed at Hemswell RAF Base in Lincolnshire. Fred played cricket so well there was no way the Station Team officer-in-charge would sanction a trip overseas for the ace sportsman. I couldn't play cricket so I was sent to Egypt.

Fred's England debut was sensational. He took seven wickets against India including four for twenty-seven in the second innings. Yorkshire Evening Post photographer Harry Fletcher produced a set of pictures recording Fred's achievement. I did the captions and the three of us remained mates from that day.

Fred's career with Yorkshire resulted in a record 2,304 wickets at only 18.29 runs each. However, mere statistics do not tell the full story of Fred – a funny man with a joke and wisecrack for all occasions.

He made his debut as a 'comedian' at the Ace of Clubs, Woodhouse, Leeds, with a spectacular entrance. There was a paper-covered hoop on the stage and Fred, in cricket gear with ball in his hand, burst through the flimsy screen with a scream of 'Howzat'! It was just as well he kept a tight grip on the ball. Those in the seats adjacent to the stage ducked with genuine apprehension.

Fred was a 'no frills' straight-talking individual. He loved cricket. He had little time for those who took liberties with the game. He was a leg-puller with an impish sense of humour and he told anyone prepared to listen that "Ian Botham could not bowl a wheel down a hill." He also claimed: "A Test match without Ian Botham is like a horror film without Boris Karloff."

When an Australian boasted about the Aussies' superiority over whinging poms, Fred readily agreed and added: "Of course you were sent to Australia by the best English judges."

When Fred's career ended he excelled with a column in the *Sunday People* and he was always the star turn at the staff's annual Christmas party. Fred's sports editor Neville Holtman described it as: "The high point of the evening. Fred's speech was always a model of un-PC and ribaldry which had even the most cynical hacks collapsing with laughter."

Fred was also the man who dropped to his knees with prayer and humble supplication at his village church each Sunday. It was where Fred's funeral took place and where cricketing colleagues gathered to say farewell to a man of cricket excellence, a man blessed with a thousand quips and millions of fans.

Years ago Fred and I were in Radio Leeds and he told me that he had contacted John Nash, the Yorkshire County Cricket Club secretary, and told him he was prepared to come out of retirement to help the team out of its current difficulties. The story made the headline 'Trueman Bombshell' in the Sunday Mirror, which scooped Fred's own paper the Sunday People.

I never told Fred that I wrote the tale. I was working for the local *Mirror* correspondent at the time and did not realise that Fred had not done the story. He got a rollicking. I got £25.

Sorry Fred! No doubt he would have forgiven me had he known.

Three Yorkshire cricketing 'greats' walk out at Headingley for a Test mach. Two of them played junior cricket together and the third is a man who skippered his country to victory and won 'The Ashes'. 'Young' Dickie Bird is easily recognisable with capped Geoffrey Boycott. They played for Barnsley as teenagers. The third man in this retouched picture is Raymond Illingworth who would have made a brilliant groundsman. The lawn at his Farsley home is better than any Test wicket.

It was a case of 'Hats off the Queen' when the world's most famous umpire Dickie Bird was called to Buckingham Palace to receive an MBE. But Dickie felt he had to call in at Lord's Cricket Ground before his appointment with royalty. Dickie used to register a little annoyance when folk addressed him with the famous nickname. He was christened Harold. But he is 'Dickie' and always will be to the supporters of cricket at home and abroad.

# Dickie Bird

Dickie Bird is often given to flights of fancy with thoughts winging to nostalgic moments in his colourful sporting life. It was a career packed with incidents and he is still hailed throughout the cricket-playing universe as the greatest umpire of all time. Dickie also has medical gifts denied lesser mortals and it is no secret that he saved my life.

My health problems started on Waterloo Station, London, where I was struck with a dizzy attack and was taken to Guys Hospital. A course of steroids was recommended and I embarked on a daily intake of the tablets.

It was weeks later when I met Dickie at York races. He had broken the pledge of a lifetime and taken notice of a cricket-loving racehorse trainer Sir Michael Stoute and plonked £20 on one of the eminent horseman's tips. Up to then Dickie had preached the gospel: "Put your money in the building society." But Sir Michael was so persuasive he convinced Dickie the horse was a certainty and the retired umpire won well over a hundred pounds.

Dickie was flushed with success. I had never seen him so animated – not even on that wonderful evening we spent at the Queens Hotel, Leeds, where we both spoke at a sportsmen's dinner. I remember Dickie telling the assembled audience that wild horses would never drag from him the amount of money he had rejected when Aussie Kerry Packer had asked him to join a breakaway cricket circus. Dickie, blissfully unaware of what he had just vowed, continued; "Packer offered me seventeen thousand pounds and I knocked him back."

But he was happy to count the cash he received from the bookies and he suddenly changed the subject and asked me  – as elderly gentlemen often do: "What pills are you on these days?"

I told him "steroids" and added that they did not appear to be doing me much good.

Dickie thundered: "I'm not surprised. I say I'm not surprised. I was on 'em and they had me rolling round the room and hardly able to stand up. Kick 'em into touch. Tell your doctor you are coming off them. Throw 'em in the dustbin. They are killing you."

The following day I informed my doctor, Andy Mawson, of Dickie's diagnosis and the medical man murmured: "You know John – he could be right."

I was weaned off steroids. I was a new man. I've never felt so well.

Dickie feels he is now justified in informing anyone prepared to listen that he saved my life. And who can argue with this assertion? I certainly won't.

Neither will I dispute the story he told me about his trip to Barbados where he decided to have a swim and he happily floated on his back unaware that he was about to collide with an object of immense bulk.

Dickie said: "I thought I had hit a liner. The breath was knocked out of me and I swallowed a pint or two of salty water. When I recovered I realised I had bumped into Pavarotti, who was on holiday. We talked a lot and I quickly realised he didn't know the first thing about cricket.

"But he did tell me he was once a goal keeper and had a great passion for soccer. So I told him the history of Barnsley football club. I was surprised that he hadn't heard of the late Tommy Taylor, Danny Blanchflower or Skinner Normanton. Mind you they had probably never heard of Pavarotti.

"He was pleasant to me. We had a good laugh and he swam off like a big whale. Things like that encounter are always happening to me."

Cricket dominates his waking days. He fails to comprehend how anyone can lack his addiction to the 'beautiful game'. He wasn't a bad player himself. He represented Yorkshire and was a more than useful batsman. Dickie also opened batting for his beloved Barnsley at Headingley in the days when young Fred Trueman was about to burst on the county scene.

Michael Parkinson recalls: "I was at one end and Dickie was at the other when Trueman came on to ball. Fred's opening delivery was a corker. It fairly fizzed and struck Dickie on the chest and felled him. I helped Dickie to his feet and Fred shouted: 'Is he all right?'

"I replied: 'I think so.'

"Fred gripped the ball and turned to start his run-up with the far from comforting words: 'Now think on lad – you're next!'"

Dickie spoke from the heart at Fred's funeral. It was a tribute befitting the occasion. It was Dickie expressing our love and admiration for one of the greatest bowlers the game has known. It was a speech many of us would have been proud to make.

# Jack Berry

When an august panel of horse-racing experts voted Jack Berry 'Trainer of the Year' he could have been excused had he bought a larger size in titfers. But fame and a dramatic rise from rags to riches will never change the industrious horseman who was born in modest circumstances and was destined to soar to the summit of his chosen profession.

Jack was born on October 7th, 1937 at 57 Glensdale Grove, East End Park, Leeds. He was one of eight children and they were disciplined by a strict father, Harry, and loved and cosseted by their doting mum Nancy. Jack – always one for the hoary jokes – said: "We did not have much. It was a case of first up best dressed, although I jibbed at wearing frocks!

"I was the 'runt' of the family. I was small, thin, and hyperactive. I was running about within months of my birth and in doing so I damaged my knees so badly I had to wear leg irons. My limbs were so bad I was sent for specialist treatment to the orthopaedic wing at Harrogate General Hospital and that early contact with the medical world prepared me for the bumps and bruises – and heartbreak – I experienced in years to come."

Jack was plagued with glandular fever and tonsilitis as a child. He still conjures up the sickening aura of ether when he thinks of the hours he spent in Leeds General Infirmary. And he still winces when he recalls that he rode forty-seven winners as a courageous National Hunt jockey and suffered forty-six painful fractures – including a broken back.

Jack started riding when he was four years old. His father and grandfather were dealers and often had as many as thirty horses in boxes in York Road and in fields at Seacroft. The majority were earmarked for the family's horseflesh shop – a part of the business Jack was never happy about – but he was able to jog on the sound ones.

Jack and his brother Harrry had to be up before the 'crack of sparrows' to muck out before heading for school with the smell of sweat and stables a deterrent to those who had to sit next to the Berry boys.

It was Jack's introduction to the animal kingdom. When he was ten he rented a cage at Leeds Market and he bought and sold pups, chicks, rabbits, bantams, guinea pigs and even the mice which often accompanied him to school and, no doubt, had his teachers lifting up their skirts in terror.

Jack said: "My market job was a nice little earner and the money went to my mum who always had a struggle to feed ever-open mouths and make ends meet."

Jack's judgement of animls was fostered in his formative years. It stands him in good stead when he appears at the yearling sale rings at Doncaster, Newmarket, Ascot and Ballsbridge, Ireland. He spends well and wisely with an inherent Yorkshireman's gifts for securing a bargain. When Jack buys he does so with unerring skill and this attribute has taken him to the zenith of the training art. It has also led to mammoth offers – always refused – from multi-millionare owners who want him as their private trainer.

He produced 127 winners in one season – more than any other trainer in the British Isles – and he won £5,000 in side-bets that he would top the century mark. He saddled over seventy hand-picked two-year-olds and he has trained at least one winner on every Flat-racing course in the country.

Jack served his apprenticeship with Charlie Hall at Towton, Tadcaster. They were happy days – the occasional drink in the Rockingham Arms, a trip to Wetherby for the 'flicks' and weekly dances – and above all the chance to ride thoroughbreds in training work and the thrill of flying with steeplechasers over formidable fences.

Jack had a repulation for riding 'owt with three legs and a swinger'. When others shunned no-hopers and jumpers who couldn't rise six inches from the unyeilding terrain, the cry "Send for Jack Berry" used to ring out. And he often partnered horses capable of burying their fearless pilot.

Jack quit the saddle after one too many crashes. He took out a licence to train at a yard near Doncaster and one of his early winners was Don-Aire, owned by Leeds United footballers Peter Lorimer, Mick Bates, Mick Jones and Eddie Gray.

Life was lived on the breadline but he married his sweetheart Jo and, in 1972, they moved to a derelict farm at Cockerham near Lancaster.

Jack had nothing but a huge overdraft and bailiffs banging on his door. But lads from York Road, Leeds, are a tough and tenacious breed. He battled for survival and – with his lucky red shirt as an omen – his racing fortunes took a turn for the better.

Jack retired from training after a career which saw him at the top of his profession. He now lives in the Yorkshire Dales where he and Jo reflect on the triumphs and heartbreak often connected with the Sports of Kings and Commoners. Their son Sam was in a coma for five weeks after his mount fell in a race at Sedgefield. Brain damage robbed Sam of the use of his right side and he is in a wheelchair.

Jack wrote a book *It's Tougher at the Bottom* – an appropriate title for the man who sampled the lows and highs of life and the racing game. He was awarded the MBE for his work on behalf of the Injured Jockeys' Fund.

When Leeds-born Jack Berry rode his first winner his jockey silks were red and this became his lucky colour. Jack always wears a red shirt. Even when he went to the palace to accept his MBE he had a shirt to match his crimson look of delight. Pontefract racecourse stages an annual 'Red Shirt Night' organised by Jack to raise money for racing charities, especially the Injured Jockeys' Fund. Hundreds of punters turn up in red shirts to support the retired trainer.

# Pot Black

Leeds was once a hot-bed for snooker with every working men's club, political club, youth club and sports club equipped with at least a couple of the cosseted tables. The green baize was brushed and ironed with loving care and prized match balls – some made of ivory – were always under lock and key and only available for tournaments not practice.

Anyone who showed prowess at billiards or snooker was accused of 1eading 'a misspent youth'. Today lads who are highly proficient at building huge breaks in front of television audiences can earn fortunes for the skill they gained in clubs.

Leeds had a popular snooker saloon in Burton's Arcade, off Briggate. It was called 'Charlie Mahon's' and in supreme charge were the late owner's daughters. Although the saloon – with a dozen tables – was a male domain, swearing or bad behaviour was not acceptable or tolerated. One frown from either of the ladies was sufficient warning. Any repetition of the offence resulted in lasting expulsion. Charlie Mahon's premises were open from 10 am to 10 pm with a regular clientele, who potted balls with unerring accuracy, spending hour after hour in the dimly lit premises.

Jim Windsor's Commercial Club, in Vicar Lane, was another popular billiards and snooker venue, as were St Patrick's, The Brunswick, Judean Club, Ascot Bridge and Social Club, St. Anne's, Burley Liberals, Middleton Conservatives and other too numerous to mention. Rivalry was intense with weekly league and cup games. Newspapers filled columns with results and match reports and the area produced many outstanding players.

One of the greatest billiard exponents in the locality was Leslie Driffield. He owned a foundry in Leeds and was able to give himself time from work to practice. He won the World Amateur Championship when the finals were played in India. He spent hours on the tables at Smith and Nelson's Saloon, in the Lower Headrow, and his seemingly endless practice sessions certainly paid dividends.

Bradford-born Joe Johnson built up his bid for the World Snooker Championship with regular practice at Morley Snooker Centre. Joe was the underdog when he beat Steve Davies for the coveted title at The Crucible, Sheffield, and his days working as a gas fitter in Leeds were over the moment he potted the final black. Joe's success fired many youngsters to take up the game, which spawned the likes of Stephen Hendry, John Pulman, Ray Reardon, Dennis Taylor, Jimmy White and Alex Higgins.

Leeds now has another potential world-beater in Paul Hunter, who is facing a battle off the snooker table. Paul has a rare type of cancer, which has brought his career to a temporary halt, but hopefully he will be back in action before the next World Championship tournament. Paul is one of the most popular professionals with fellow players and also ladies who form a major part of his huge fan club. Apart from enormous skill, which has taken him to three Masters' titles. Paul is famed for his film star looks and various hairstyles

**Paul Hunter, who once slightly embarrassed his then wife-to-be by revealing that they once went to bed between match sessions to help Paul relax. The plan worked: Paul returned to action after the interval to win the match!**

# Beryl Burton

Northern folk tend to be possessive of their celebrities. Lancashire had 'Our Gracie', a lady with a magnificent singing talent. We in Yorkshire had 'Our Beryl' – a lady, housewife, mother, grandmother and an athlete of rare brilliance.

Beryl Burton lived for her sport. She was a dedicated cyclist who dominated the cycling scene at the peak of her international career. She was on the world stage for more than a quarter of a century and she was in the saddle of her beloved bike when her life tragically came to a premature end.

Beryl was the bane of journalists. She would never have been given the role of Beattie in the BT adverts because she didn't have a telephone. If we had a query or simply wanted a quick quote we had to ring Beryl's neighbour and ask her to bring Beryl to the phone.

There is a sexist club in Yeadon where chauvinists have a notice on the wall. It says "No telephone, no television set, no women." In Beryl's house the telephone and television were also banded. She told me that she had better things to do than waste valuable time gazing at a 'tele'. She would rather perch on the saddle of her bike than lounge in an armchair following the gripping adventures of Neighbours, Coronation Street or even Yorkshire's production of Emmerdale.

Beryl was a busy housewife. She loved baking her own bread and making delicious pies – particularly those of the rhubarb variety. She could clean and hoover with the best. She could also change tyres and tighten gears with the speed and attention to detail of any male mechanic. Had she lived on the continent she would have been feted and richly financed from her pedals to the top of her curly hair. But the Leeds-born lass, who worked in the rhubarb fields, preferred her native Yorkshire where she indulged her appetite for thrift and hard work.

The last time we met socially was at the Hull Road Club's Annual Dinner.
I rang the Paragon Hotel, pleaded a tale of poverty and secured a room for my wife and me at £30 including breakfast. Beryl howled when she saw the bill made out to two Wallace Arnold coach drivers. The night would have been free for Beryl but she refused to stay over. Beryl and her husband Charlie rode their bikes to Hull and rode them back home to Harrogate.

Another memory for me was spotting Beryl in Scarcroft, on the Leeds-Wetherby Road, where I was waiting for a bus to Leeds city centre. It was a cold but light night and in the distance was a familiar figure, bent over handlebars, with legs pumping like pistons.

'Our Beryl' stopped for a brief chat but our conversation ended in mid-steam with the arrival of the bus. We pulled off in front of Beryl but, when the bus arrived in Leeds, she was waiting at the terminus to finish the tale she had started. Beryl had been waiting at least ten minutes, which says much for her speed or shows what kind of tortoise-like bus service we have in Leeds.

Don't believe it. Beryl 's pace was the deciding factor that night, as it was in her days as a time-trialist, world track pursuit champion and road racer.
Beryl was five times World 3000 Metre Champion and twice World Road Racing Champion. She could compete with men on equal terms. She beat the British men's record for a 12-hour time trial in 1967.

The sport made relentless demands on her physique and Beryl was equal to any challenge. Had women's cycling been an Olympic sport in her heyday she would certainly have plundered Gold medals galore. Beryl won more than a hundred titles, national, regional and local championships. At her peak she was simply unbeatable. She was Women's Best All-Rounder twenty-five times and experts claim that this is a record which will stand forever.

Statistics make cold reading. But none will be able to comprehend or really appreciate her single-minded dedication or the relentless pressure the sport put on her slender physique.

Beryl was born in Leeds and, as a child, survived chronic ill-health, rheumatic fever and partial paralysis. She was Beryl Charnock in those days and already showing signs of her unquenchable spirit. She won the battle against sickness, left school and went for a 'Burton' in more ways than one.
She started work at Montague Burton's tailoring factory and met Charlie Burton – her devoted husband to be.

Charlie introduced Beryl to cycling. He became her tutor, trainer and inspiration. He sacrificed his own burgeoning career to groom Beryl to reach the zenith of the sport and climb the dizzy heights to world stardom. Beryl was seventeen when she married Charlie. Two years later she finished second in the National 100-mile Championship. A further two years later she won the first of her five gold medals.

Charlie was content to remain in the background. He shared in the reflected glory of his wife's triumphs and was comfortable in the knowledge that he had played a part of paramount importance in her golden career. He rejoiced in her victories and he celebrated when Beryl told him that she was pregnant. Beryl stopped cycling three months before the arrival of Denise because her bump prevented her squeezing behind the handlebars.

But it was not long before Denise, who was a happy little baby, perched on a seat above her mother's rear wheel. The Burton family were soon a regular sight with mum, dad and daughter touring Yorkshire's beautiful countryside simply for pleasure and that priceless feeling of togetherness. Denise also became a top competitive cyclist in her own right as well as producing two lovely grandchildren, who hopefully will maintain the Burton family's sporting tradition.

No story would be complete without mention of an incident in 1967 during the Otley 12-hour race. Mike McNamara must have tired of hearing the saga – often exaggerated – of Beryl handing him a liquorice all-sort as she caught up and passed him. Beryl said: "It was the only thing I could think of at the time."

Beryl Burton, the 'unbeatable' cyclist, preferred to lead her life away from the glare of publicity. She had no phone and loved making rhubarb pies.

The year 1967 was one of Beryl's greatest. She won the National Sportswriters' Award and the Daily Express Sports Woman of the Year Award. She was Vaux Brewery Northern Sports Woman of the Year and she was runner-up in the BBC Sports Personality of the Year poll.

Beryl Burton won the 100-mile title eighteen times in her long and distinguished career. She was awarded the MBE, granted an OBE and lived a life for us to recall with joy and sincere admiration. She will never be forgotten. She will always be 'Our Beryl'.

Beryl Burton collapsed on her bike when racing against the clock. She died in a competitive event known to participants as 'the race of truth'. Beryl was a true Leeds girl and proud of her birthright.

# Jane Tomlinson

**Jane Tomlinson has often stowed away her running shoes and dismounted her bike forever! But she has always bounced back after a short rest to attempt another gruelling challenge in the name of charity. Never has there been a braver person than this slip of a lady who packs so much effort and courage in her tiny frame. The Leeds lass is endowed with the determination denied lesser people and few gave her any chance of completing her recent American sortie. But Jane has never quit even when her condition has caused her unbearable pain. She is indomitable. She will never give in and I can imagine her back for another testing exercise when she recovers from the American ordeal.**

# Last Words

Leeds is nothing if not historic with over eight hundred years of memories. Every street and building tells a story and the current trend is one of success, expansion and a future ensured with a top ten niche in Europe. The City Fathers are entrusted with the task of maintaining the stature, eminence and progress launched by those pioneers eight centuries ago.

The well-being and development of Leeds in the coming years will depend on the magnificent youth of our fair city. One fine example is the worldwide success of a band 'Kaiser Chiefs' who have resisted to the magnetic lure of London and insist that they belong to Leeds.

The on-going affluence and investment in the City has made Leeds the financial capital of the North. We rely on the next generation to maintain the security and glowing reputation of a city, which is the envy of many. The Kaiser Chiefs will spread the gospel and the message – behave, be brave and ambitious. Long live Leeds!

Our picture of the Kaiser Chiefs shows (left to right) Andrew White, Ricky Wilson, Nick Hodgson, Nick 'Peanuts' Baines and Simon Rix.

## Further Reading

Briggs, Asa, 'Leeds: a study in civic pride' (*Victorian Cities*, pp 139-83, Odhams, 1963).
Cooper, Lettice, *Yorkshire West Riding* (Robert Hale, 1950).
Hartley, Marie & Ingilby, Joan, *Life and Tradition in West Yorkshire* (Dent, 1976).
Hey, David, *Yorkshire from AD 1000* (Longman, 1986).
Hickling, Michael, *Reporting Yorkshire: 250 years of the Yorkshire Post* (Great Northern, 2004)
Joy, David, *A Regional History of the Railways of Great Britain: Vol 8 South and West Yorkshire* (David & Charles, 1984).
Lennon, Patricia & Joy, David, *Grand Memories: The Life and Times of the Grand Theatre and Opera House, Leeds* (Great Northern, 2006)
Pevsner, Nikolaus, *The Buildings of England: Yorkshire The West Riding* (Penguin Books, 1959)
Singleton, Fred, *Industrial Revolution in Yorkshire* (Dalesman, 1970).
Thompson, James, *Leeds Born and Bred* (Dalesman, 1982).
Townsley, Don, *The Hunslet Engine Works* (Plateway Press, 1998).
Twidale, Graham H E, *Leeds in the age of the tram* (Silver Link, 2003).

# Subscribers

Ian Duthie Adams
John Adams
Christopher Ainslie
Richard Allison
Janet Lesley Alton
Leslie Ambler
John Armitage
A Ashworth
M J Atkinson
Mr Ralph Austin

Margaret Baker
Brian Bamford
Barbara Barlow-Wilkinson
R H & M M Barraclough
Mr W A Baugh
Madge Beaumont
John Pickard Beesley
Muriel & Bernard Berman
Mr Timothy Berry
David Bewell
Mr C Blackwell
Charles Edward Blakeborough
Florence Patricia Bonallie
Mr Henry Boot
Agnes Booth
Anthony P B Booth
Keith Clasper Borthwick
Peter & Pat Boyes
Mr John Richard Bradley
Peter H Breckin
The Broughtons
Mr Peter G Buckland
Thomas Buckton
Alex Butler

David Chance

Ron Chapman
Sue Child
Geoff N Clark
Olive Clark
Moreen Clayton
Trevor Coates
L Crosland
George Crow

Christopher Dale
R W & M Davis
Matthew Jacob Dawson
Peter Dealtry
J Dibnah
George Disley
Maureen Dobson
Frank Dodsworth
Philip Duffy
Barbara Durrant
Gail Dyson
Hazel Dyson

Betty Edwards

Phillip J Farnsworth
Yvonne Margaret Fearn
Mr Ralph Firth
Pat Fitzgerald
Frank "Frisky" Fletcher
Ian Foster
Jack & Betty Foster
Barrie Fowler
Michael Freeman

Olive Gager
John Gallagher
Mavis Garratt

Geoff & Sheila Gaunt
Neil & Wendy Gaunt
Phillip & Judith Gaunt
Winifred Gaunt
Harvey Goldman
Reg & Doreen Goulden
Joan V Green
R Green
Rose Green
Nigel Greenwood

Jean Hagan
Geoff Hallas
James Hammond
Martin Handley
Mr John Hart
Henry Heyworth
David Hodgson
Horace & Margaret Hodgson
B Holmes
Brian C Holmes
Trevor Holmes
Jack Hood
Steve Horne
Mrs Nancy Houlgate
Major Ian Ryder Hunter

E Ingham
Roy Ingle

Gary D Jackson
Don James
Mrs J Jellings
Brian Jenner
Frank Johnson

William Kaye

Maureen Kershaw
W J & B E King

Keith P Lambert
Bernard Langstaff
Mr & Mrs Robert Lawrence
Donald Laxton
Jim Leason
Mrs B M Lee M.B.E.
Mary Leeson
Mr Arthur Liley
Des Little
Miss M Lound
Graham Lunn

Bernard Mackie
Alan Makinson
James Malone
Chris Marks
Michael Matthews
Alec & Edith McLean
Mary McMahon (nee Morton)
John Lawrence Midgley
Colin Mitchell
David Mitchell
Florence Moody
Christopher Charles Moore
June Moore
John Michael Moran
Anthony Morrisroe
John Mounsey

Jack Naylor
James Naylor
David Ian North (Leeds)

S Osborne

June Padgett
Dennis Parkin
T Parkinson
Ada Pearson

Jack Peat
Colin Pegden
Brian Pickup
Rona Powell

E W Rayner
Gerry Redshaw
B & P Remington
Sylvia Render
John Lyndon Richards
Julie Riley
Peter Ripley
Mrs C D Roberts
Mr Harold Robinson
Stan Robinson
George Peter Ruane

Honorary Alderman
Stephen Sadler
Christine Schofield
Mrs C D Seipp
Donald Senior
Eileen Senior
O Sessions
Alan Shaw
Mary & Brian Shaw
Tracie & Dan Sillers
Eric P Simpson
Arthur Slade
Linda Anne Smalley
Andy Smith
Audrey Smith
Derek Smith
Dr & Mrs M V Smith
Yvonne & Terence Smith
Peter & Gwen Smithson
John A Snowden
Norah Spencer
Irene Stainburn
Eric & June Stephenson
F R A Stirk
David Stockton

Mo Stokes
Richard T Strudwick
John Sutherland

Gerald Tatham
Barbara Maureen Theakston
Fred Thistlewood
Howard H Thompson
Leslie Thompson
Linda Thompson
Ivon & Brenda Tirson
Denis Brook & Linda Townend
Doreen Tring
Maureen Turner

Granville Roy Wagstaff
John & Val Walker
Keith Walker
William Walker
Neil A Wallace
Ian J Ward (Thorner)
Jean Wardman
Robert Watling
Dr A N Watson
Margaret R Watson
Lyndon Richard Webster
Gary Wheelhouse
David Whitaker
Elaine Whitaker
Frank & Sheila Whitelow
Barrie Williamson
Mark Willingham
Leslie & Barbara Wilson
Andrew Keith Wood
Nancy Wooler
Helen & Andy Wright
Richard Wright
Florence Wrightson

G Wendy Youngman

C000018665

VOLUME 3

# MEASURING UP
## The Business Case for GIS

**Edited by
Cory Fleming, Christopher Thomas,
and Shannon Valdizon**

Esri Press
REDLANDS | CALIFORNIA

Esri Press, 380 New York Street, Redlands, California 92373-8100
Copyright © 2022 Esri
All rights reserved. First edition 2012
26 25 24 23 22      1 2 3 4 5 6 7 8 9 10

Printed in the United States of America

The information contained in this document is the exclusive property of Esri or its licensors. This work is protected under United States copyright law and other international copyright treaties and conventions. No part of this work may be reproduced or transmitted in any form or by any means, electronic or mechanical, including photocopying and recording, or by any information storage or retrieval system, except as expressly permitted in writing by Esri. All requests should be sent to Attention: Director, Contracts and Legal Department, Esri, 380 New York Street, Redlands, California 92373-8100, USA.

The information contained in this document is subject to change without notice.

US Government Restricted/Limited Rights: Any software, documentation, and/or data delivered hereunder is subject to the terms of the License Agreement. The commercial license rights in the License Agreement strictly govern Licensee's use, reproduction, or disclosure of the software, data, and documentation. In no event shall the US Government acquire greater than RESTRICTED/LIMITED RIGHTS. At a minimum, use, duplication, or disclosure by the US Government is subject to restrictions as set forth in FAR §52.227-14 Alternates I, II, and III (DEC 2007); FAR §52.227-19(b) (DEC 2007) and/or FAR §12.211/12.212 (Commercial Technical Data/Computer Software); and DFARS §252.227-7015 (DEC 2011) (Technical Data – Commercial Items) and/or DFARS §227.7202 (Commercial Computer Software and Commercial Computer Software Documentation), as applicable. Contractor/Manufacturer is Esri, 380 New York Street, Redlands, California 92373-8100, USA.

Esri products or services referenced in this publication are trademarks, service marks, or registered marks of Esri in the United States, the European Community, or certain other jurisdictions. To learn more about Esri marks, go to: links.esri.com/EsriProductNamingGuide. Other companies and products or services mentioned herein may be trademarks, service marks, or registered marks of their respective mark owners.

For purchasing and distribution options (both domestic and international), please visit esripress.esri.com.

*Library of Congress Cataloging-in-Publication Data*
Thomas, Christopher, 1963 Aug. 6–
Measuring up : the business case for GIS / Christopher Thomas and Milton Ospina.
    p. cm.
  Includes bibliographical references.
  ISBN 1-58948-088-0 (pbk. : alk. paper)
  1. Decision support systems. 2. Geographic information systems. 3. Industrial management. I. Ospina, Milton. II. Title.
HD30.213.T47 2004
658.4'038—dc22                                        2004013898

This book is dedicated to Cory Fleming of the International City/County Management Association (ICMA), who worked tirelessly to advocate for data-driven decision-making in city and county government. She began working with Esri® nearly a decade ago and became an advocate and ambassador for the use of geographic information systems (GIS) as a mission-critical management tool.

Cory's work as a GIS ambassador took the form of multiple book projects, citizen hackathons at ICMA annual events, writing executive briefings, leading panel discussions on performance-driven government, and formulating focus groups on GIS and economic development.

As director of the #LocalGov Technology Alliance, an initiative started with Esri, Cory helped local governments explore the world of big data, open data, apps, and dashboards, and what it all means for local engagement. She served as editor of *The GIS Guide for Local Government Officials,* a joint publication produced by Esri and ICMA released in 2005. A subsequent joint publication, *The GIS Guide for Elected Officials,* was released by Esri Press in January 2014.

This will be Cory's final project with the GIS community as she enters retirement. The GIS community will always be extremely grateful to people like Cory who bridge the technology and management communities.

# Contents

# Foreword

Marc Ott, executive director, International City/County Management Association (ICMA)

With heightened expectations from the public, a growing list of challenges, and limited resources, today's governmental leaders must prove the value of their technology investments. Recommending new approaches or promising enhanced operational efficiency is no longer enough. Any proposals for new technology must have a public-facing element. There is an even greater responsibility to support discipline-specific goals. Governmental leaders at all levels must take the lead in building a modern, data-driven organization. As facilitators of cross-departmental collaboration and providers of insight through performance dashboards, government leaders can open a new gateway and start a two-way dialogue on how to best meet the public's needs.

How do leaders and innovators drive change and improvements to the bottom line? In ICMA's experience, GIS capabilities allow leaders to accelerate the fitness of an organization. For the past 50 years, GIS has evolved from a conceptual approach used within various niches to a widely used solution. This not only provides guidance for better government decision-making but also helps break down barriers between government and its constituents, allowing residents to engage and gain information on everything from reporting crime to traffic congestion and available parking spaces—all with the click of a mouse or the swipe of a finger.

Nearly all programs and services provided by governments start from a neighborhood or from a geographic context, making the insight that GIS provides the key to better decision-making by community leaders. The past few years have seen the development of a proliferation of new apps, analysis tools, collaboration platforms, and operations dashboards. By integrating GIS solutions into daily workflows, leaders can achieve a deeper understanding of how to use location-based data more effectively. The key is knowing the right questions to ask to provide improvements to workflows and present opportunities to intervene in public policy.

It is truly astonishing to reflect on the evolution of GIS technology and its applications. GIS offers tremendous possibilities for communities and governmental operations. ICMA is proud to partner with Esri to publish volume 3 of *Measuring Up: The Business Case for GIS*. Together, ICMA and Esri hope to help support government executives as they explore how GIS has evolved and expanded its use in government workflows, understand opportunities for GIS to be applied, and recognize the business values that any community can develop with this technology.

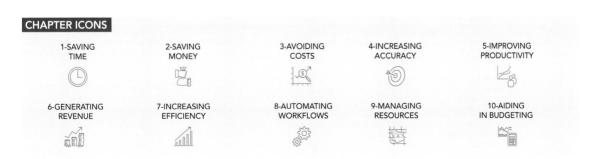

**CHAPTER ICONS**

| 1-SAVING TIME | 2-SAVING MONEY | 3-AVOIDING COSTS | 4-INCREASING ACCURACY | 5-IMPROVING PRODUCTIVITY |
| 6-GENERATING REVENUE | 7-INCREASING EFFICIENCY | 8-AUTOMATING WORKFLOWS | 9-MANAGING RESOURCES | 10-AIDING IN BUDGETING |

# Introduction: Embracing a geographic approach

Every few decades, something happens that makes organizations and their executives reevaluate how they do business. Economic downturns, advancements in technology, the worldwide spread of disease, and the need to address diversity and racial equity can alter our everyday work. And with that, professionals may find themselves in a position to justify their processes, expenditures, and operations. Today, there is perhaps no other technology as significant and ingrained in government as GIS. Organizations have used GIS across disciplines and industries to better understand problems and opportunities and drive real business value.

The intention of this book, *Measuring Up: The Business Case for GIS,* volume 3, is to offer you and your organization a resource to take you through your next challenge or simply show you how you can improve your everyday operations. The book can be used to demonstrate the benefits of GIS to your leadership, show best practices of GIS use that help justify your expenditure on the technology, and provide examples to help you calculate and document return on investment (ROI) from GIS. It features a wide variety of case studies and new applications designed to improve government operations and engage community residents more fully. For instance, in this volume, the city of Johns Creek, Georgia, explores the use of artificial intelligence for answering nonemergency questions, leaving staff time for more critical duties. To meet residents' demand for high-speed internet service, leaders in Potter County, Pennsylvania, used GIS to plan and develop a budget that minimized the digital divide. The volume includes 30 such case studies that can help policy makers and other decision-makers understand how GIS technology can be used in almost every discipline that government supports. The chapters

are aligned with the tangible and inspiring benefits organizations have realized from GIS, including:

- Saving time
- Saving money
- Avoiding costs
- Increasing accuracy
- Improving productivity
- Generating revenue
- Increasing efficiency
- Automating workflows
- Managing resources
- Aiding in budgeting

This is the third time Esri and the International City/County Management Association (ICMA) have come together to prepare such an educational book. As we worked together to produce this current volume, we concluded that there is an endless supply of such stories; it is now a matter of sharing them. The more we all share our needs and our stories with colleagues, the more they will spark innovation and creativity within our organizations.

Moving to the digital age requires merging communications with innovation. Change will continue to occur, and new technologies will continue to overtake the familiar. With education and training, however, government organizations can adapt and move forward.

My sincere thanks go to Christopher Thomas, Shannon Valdizon, and Leslie Barlow at Esri for their subject matter expertise, creativity, and other important contributions. Working on this project has been a tremendous privilege. We hope all of you will find this to be an important tool in your professional library.

**Cory Fleming**
ICMA senior technical specialist
Research and Policy/Publications/Bookstore

# ROI Benefits Matrix

| | Saving Time | Saving Money | Avoiding Costs | Increasing Accuracy | Improving Productivity | Generating Revenue | Increasing Efficiency | Automating Workflows | Managing Resources | Aiding in Budgeting |
|---|---|---|---|---|---|---|---|---|---|---|
| **Chapter 1 - Saving Time** | | | | | | | | | | |
| Arizona Department of Environmental Quality | X | • | • | • | • | | • | • | • | |
| Houston Police Department, TX | X | | | • | | | • | • | • | |
| Utah Department of Natural Resources | X | • | • | • | • | | | • | • | |
| **Chapter 2 - Saving Money** | | | | | | | | | | |
| Clay County Utility Authority, FL | • | X | • | • | • | | • | • | | |
| Rural Lorain County Water Authority (RLCWA), OH | • | X | • | • | • | • | | • | | • |
| New England | • | X | • | • | • | | • | | • | • |
| **Chapter 3 - Avoiding Costs** | | | | | | | | | | |
| City of Glendale, CA | | | X | • | • | | • | • | • | |
| City of Cayce, SC | • | • | X | | | | • | • | • | • |
| City of Escondido, CA | | • | X | | | | • | • | • | |
| **Chapter 4 - Increasing Accuracy** | | | | | | | | | | |
| City of Sarasota, FL | | | • | X | • | | • | | | |
| City of Columbia, SC | • | | | X | • | | | • | • | |
| Santa Clara County, CA | • | | • | X | • | | | • | | |
| **Chapter 5 - Improving Productivity** | | | | | | | | | | |
| US Census Bureau | | | | • | X | | • | • | • | |
| Denton Municpal Electric | • | | | | X | | • | • | • | |
| City of Thomasville, GA | | | • | • | X | | | • | • | • |
| **Chapter 6 - Generating Revenue** | | | | | | | | | | |
| Tippecanoe County, IN | | | | • | | X | • | • | | • |
| England | | | | | | X | • | • | | |
| Stafford County, VA | | • | • | • | • | X | • | • | | |
| **Chapter 7 - Increasing Efficiency** | | | | | | | | | | |
| Maricopa County, AZ | | | | • | • | | X | • | • | |
| City of Johns Creek, GA | | • | | | • | | X | • | | |
| City of Santa Barbara, CA | | | | • | • | | X | • | • | |
| **Chapter 8 - Automating Workflows** | | | | | | | | | | |
| Crawford County, PA | • | • | • | • | • | | • | X | | |
| Delaware Department of Agriculture | • | • | • | • | • | • | • | X | | |
| Massachusetts DCR | • | | | • | • | | • | X | | |
| **Chapter 9 - Managing Resources** | | | | | | | | | | |
| City of Glendale, CA | | | | • | • | | • | • | X | |
| Maricopa County, AZ | | • | | | • | | • | • | X | • |
| City of Palo Alto, CA | • | • | • | | • | | | | X | |
| **Chapter 10 - Aiding in Budgeting** | | | | | | | | | | |
| City of Brownsville, TX | | | | • | | • | • | • | | X |
| Potter County, PA | | • | | • | | | • | | • | X |
| State of Texas, Parks and Recreation | | | | | | | • | | • | X |

X Main Benefit    • Additional Benefit

# Chapter 1
# SAVING TIME

Time is a precious resource. There never seems to be enough of it, and once it's gone, it's gone. Organizations can overcome time deficiencies by adding staff, extending due dates, or streamlining workflows. But these solutions can be costly, not to mention that in many instances, time is critical—for instance, responding to an emergency call, improving wait times for citizens, or getting through a long list of projects.

Time savings are typically the first and most reported benefits of the application of GIS. The ripple effect of time savings can be felt in cost savings, improvements in productivity and efficiency, and real-time decision support. Most organizations witness tremendous time savings in GIS through automated mapping, mobile data collection, and keeping the public informed via mapcentric information hubs. Other organizations have experienced time savings in improving analysis and project reviews by leveraging GIS's superior spatial analytics. Organizations are also integrating new technologies such as the Internet of Things (IoT), drone imagery, and machine learning to find more ways to improve operational effectiveness. Decisions on allocating resources are being made in real time. Mobile field data collection is offset by automated data feeds. Artificial intelligence is redefining workflows, as opposed to simply automating them. GIS is connecting these processes and peer technologies through location and spatial thinking.

# Arizona Department of Environmental Quality saves inspectors time in the field

## Community profile
- Arizona Department of Environmental Quality (ADEQ)
- Population of Arizona (US census 2019): 7,278,717
- ADEQ fiscal year 2020 budget: $163,794,000
- Year GIS program was implemented: 2019
- Nature of the project: Create a radically simple, leading-edge inspection tool

**Community fact:** Around 27 percent of Arizona's landscape is made up of forests.

In July 2019, ADEQ embarked on a pilot project to streamline its solid waste compliance field inspection process and reporting system. ADEQ solid waste compliance inspector Justyn Beach began researching how the team could optimize its workflow, increase efficiencies, and reduce processing times for field inspections, cases, and reports throughout the inspections process and when providing compliance assistance.

With the support of his supervisor, Michelle Ogburn, Beach researched a variety of methods and tools to speed data collection and identified contacts with whom to consult. As a result, ADEQ's pilot project team reached out to the Washington Department of Ecology to discuss their experience and success using the survey tool, one of the tools under ADEQ's consideration.

ADEQ's solid waste team (SWT) regulates about 1,500 facilities statewide. Each year, the SWT's four inspectors are expected to complete about 500 inspections (including 150 complaint investigations)—and in doing so, contend with extreme temperatures during certain times of year. Critical to the team's ongoing success is finding ways to increase efficiency and customer service without sacrificing quality and while also supporting inspector field safety.

Beach recruited fellow solid waste compliance inspector Katherine Phillips to partner with him on the pilot project. Beach and Phillips saw an opportunity to take advantage of new technologies to improve their workflows. As compliance inspectors, both Beach and Phillips routinely collected field data, and they used these results to refine the architecture of the user experience for both the customer and inspector.

ADEQ's mission is to protect and enhance public health and the environment in Arizona, and its vision is to be the number one state in the nation in balanced, leading-edge environmental protection, through technical and operational excellence and radical simplicity for customers and staff.

As part of its mission work, ADEQ strives to reduce costs, improve service for customers, boost the economy, improve the environment, and provide transparency of operations. To this end, ADEQ has established aggressive goals and clear-cut metrics to measure and report progress. One of these goals is to issue 80 percent of in-compliance inspection reports while in the field. Notifying customers earlier of issues helps them address problems more quickly, which in turn protects the environment and allows the customer to return to compliance much faster. ADEQ's SWT was lagging behind the agency goal and issuing only 34 percent of its inspection reports in the field. The team also was completing on average only 250 of the expected 500 inspections a year. The pilot project aimed to issue 60 percent of inspection reports in the field, increase the total number of inspections, positively impact facility return to compliance, and provide radical simplicity

for customers, while maintaining or reducing time in the field.

ADEQ's solid waste compliance inspectors travel statewide to conduct routine facility field inspections and complaint investigations and to provide facilities with compliance assistance. This work involves collecting data, recording observations, taking photos, and securing signatures. Inspectors use this data to make compliance determinations for numerous and varied facility and media types, including landfills; transfer stations; waste tire and used-tire collection sites; biohazardous waste treatment facilities and transporters; used oil burners, marketers, processors, and transporters; composting facilities; mining operations; septage haulers; battery

ADEQ's solid waste compliance inspectors use GIS field tools to accurately conduct field inspections.

collection sites; special waste generators; and special waste receiving, shipping, and transporting facilities.

To increase efficiency and field-issued inspection reports, ADEQ needed a tool that could automate collection of a large volume of complex and varied data in the field. Also, this tool needed to stand up to challenges such as hardware crashing because of overheating in Arizona's sometimes extreme climate, as well as intermittent cell service in remote locations of regulated facilities. Selecting and using an inspection tool that could apply to all media and include location-based information was essential to maintaining quality data governance in the inspection process.

ADEQ's pilot project selected and evaluated the effectiveness of the survey tool as a tool to address these challenges. To ensure the final product would be a catch-all solution, the tool design had to encompass a wide variety of needs of both regulated facilities and ADEQ inspectors. ADEQ identified and documented the current state of factors affecting inspection efficiency to serve as pilot project metrics: battery life, connectivity, and existing tools and equipment (for example, laptops and tablets).

Because inspectors use compliance checklists to help document observations made at facilities with the goal of providing a completed checklist as quickly as possible, redesigning these checklists was of paramount importance. The SWT worked closely with ADEQ GIS technicians to craft groundbreaking user forms that allowed for powerful analysis of captured data and ease of use while in the field—all while maintaining the high quality that customers expect. Concurrently, Ogburn, Beach, and Phillips ensured that the inspection tool accurately reflected the environmental requirements outlined in solid waste rules, regulations, and statutes while also streamlining the actual inspection process through innovative user-experience design.

The SWT used ADEQ and Esri experts to achieve design success. The ADEQ GIS team developed processes through Integromat software to create an automatic reporting process to format and report inspection data with just the click of a button. This turning point significantly reduced the number of steps needed to field-issue inspection reports. Next, the SWT enlisted assistance from the ADEQ information technology team to develop a communication protocol between the survey tool and AZURITE, Arizona's database of environmental compliance and facility documentation. Through this communication protocol, information captured during an inspection automatically uploads to the database from the field instead of requiring inspectors to manually upload data after they return to the office. This feature also increased data governance, reduced costs to ADEQ, and reduced postinspection processing time.

At the end of the pilot project and data design phase, the SWT had created a revolutionary new set of inspection documents and data capture tools—one that would be dynamic in meeting the needs of both inspection staff and regulated facilities. After Phillips and Beach achieved full deployment of the survey app for all field inspectors, they saw an immediate increase in field-issued inspection reports, received positive feedback from customers, and began yielding record-breaking results in the standard metrics used to gauge team performance.

The first month of full implementation showed a 49 percent increase in field-issued inspection reports, which quickly increased to a record-breaking 83 percent, exceeding the pilot project and agency goals of 60 and 80 percent, respectively. The team also achieved the highest number of inspections conducted in a single fiscal year—496, nearly twice the prior record.

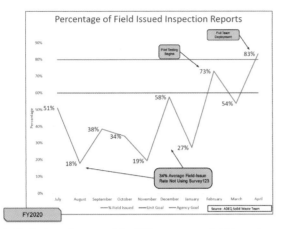

With the introduction of the GIS survey app, field-issued inspection reports increased by 49 percent in the first month.

To consider both inspector and facility user experience, ADEQ designed and implemented a user acceptance testing (UAT) protocol and forms.

Using the survey app, ADEQ also was able to collect, parse out, and track data to compare time spent (cost) for each inspection component for various me-

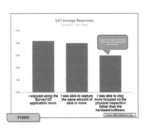

To continue to improve the usability of the app, ADEQ asked for feedback from inspectors and facility users.

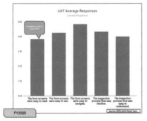

dia types: pre-research, phone, transportation, field, and postinspection.

The survey tool provided a more user-friendly back end, tailored for the inspectors' needs, while maintaining consistent reporting for regulated facilities and preserving customer experience.

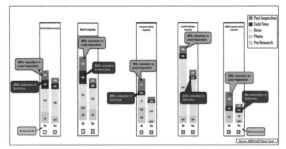

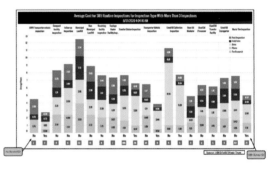

Using their survey results, ADEQ was able to report on the time spent per inspection and identify the data that was collected.

GIS technology made field data collection possible even during the hottest months in Arizona. Location-based data—such as coordinates, directionality, weather, and facility names—was watermarked onto the photos taken through the survey app. This functionality is critical to develop cases and help facilities return to compliance.

Data collected for the pilot project demonstrated a 35 to 70 percent reduction in field time and an average reduction in processing time ranging from

40 to 67 percent. After further testing with more than 100 additional test inspections, the average reduction in field time ranged from 35 to 65 percent, and the average reduction in processing time ranged from 45 to 75 percent.

Beach, Phillips, and Ogburn acknowledge that the survey app was easy to set up and use and provides access to a wealth of data that can be used for a variety of purposes to better serve the agency and its customers through reliable analysis that can respond to changing needs.

A solid understanding of the environment in which the GIS software operates was a crucial step. Although the tool can effectively support and refine existing processes, it requires a knowledgeable user and clear objectives. The biggest challenge and area of opportunity was in analyzing and revising existing inspection documents, tools, and facility needs.

The app provides an automated process that unlocks the potential of each inspector to collect quality data to better inform decision-making. The app sup-

The introduction of the GIS survey tool allows ADEQ inspectors to save time on data entry in the field.

ported the ADEQ project team in thinking outside the box on a larger scale and enabled the team to track progress from start to finish. Data-driven decisions using a metric-based approach are the foundation of best regulatory practice. As the ADEQ project demonstrates, decision-making can be significantly improved through comprehensive, frequent, and accurate data collection and analysis.

---

ADDITIONAL BENEFITS

# Purpose-driven apps save time, help Houston officers focus on solving crimes

**Community profile**
- Houston Police Department (HPD), Texas
- Population of Houston (US census 2018):
- 2.326 million
- Nature of the project: Crime data

**Community fact:** At 655 square miles, the city of Houston could contain the cities of New York, Washington, Boston, San Francisco, Seattle, Minneapolis, and Miami.

One of HPD's latest initiatives is to get data and analytics into the hands of officers as quickly and efficiently as possible. The HPD crime suppression teams (CST) are dedicated tactical units that consist of one sergeant and eight officers who work together to prevent crime by using analysis to identify crime trends and patterns and proactive policing methods to reduce criminal activity. But they needed a better way to get analytical products to officers. The HPD GIS unit was tasked with creating a mobile app that would help the officers get the most current information and promote situational awareness for all team members.

As with many other cities, Houston started 2020 enjoying a vibrant economy, but as the coronavirus disease 2019 (COVID-19) continued to spread and stay-at-home orders were issued, businesses shut down, and unemployment claims rose. As spring dragged into summer, many American cities, Houston included, began to experience increases in crime,

GIS technology has long been used by police to help identify crime patterns and make decisions about where and when to assign resources. But modern GIS technology can help police do much more by giving agencies the ability to create an enterprise environment that supports every police mission, including advanced analytics, dashboards to fit many needs, public engagement apps, and maps and apps that provide real-time situational awareness for officers in the field. HPD is one of these agencies, using enterprise GIS to save time, streamline operations, and better serve the Houston community.

including an alarming year-over-year increase in gun violence and homicides. HPD also began seeing rising incidents of street robberies and burglaries associated with two specific methods of identifying and targeting victims. These methods are known as jugging and sliding. Jugging is when an offender identifies a potential victim whom they suspect is carrying money, often perpetrated by watching locations such as ATMs or bank drive-throughs for potential targets. The offender then follows the victim to another location with the intent of robbing them or burglarizing their vehicle or residence. The common factor in jugging is not the crime incident type but how the victim is identified and followed before the commission of the

HPD officers can analyze patterns and hot spots of incidents in the field.

crime. Tracking jugging incidents can be difficult because the victim will not typically know that they were followed, and the incident will be reported as either a robbery or a burglary.

Sliding is another crime pattern that has increased in Houston, in which offenders target victims while they are stopped at gas stations and are preoccupied paying and filling their tanks at fuel pumps. The modus operandi of these kinds of thefts usually involves two or more perpetrators. The suspect vehicle, often with tinted windows to conceal the backseat passenger, pulls adjacent to the victim's vehicle, and the perpetrators then quickly enter, or slide, into the targeted car and steal whatever they can grab while the victim is distracted at the pump. The suspects then drive away before the victim even knows what has happened. As with jugging, sliding can be hard to identify, and incidents are often underreported or reported as other crime types.

The CST team was tasked with identifying and stopping jugging and sliding incidents, and they needed the help of the GIS team to build a mobile app to manage the problem. Working together, they created a dashboard that provides officers with an all-in-one self-service app that includes a map of current and historic crime incidents, the ability to filter them by incident type, and the ability to read reports within the app without having to go directly to their assigned crime analyst with specialized requests any time they need current information.

According to Lt. Freddy Croft, the GIS unit supervisor, "Staff wanted a way to do things out in the field, such as capturing data on-site and taking photos. The new app made data management much easier. Officers can use the app in their cars when on patrol. This saves time on data gathering, organizing, and presentation by the analysts. To get the information that is now automated through this application, analysts would spend two hours a day providing what this application offers instantaneously." Officers now have

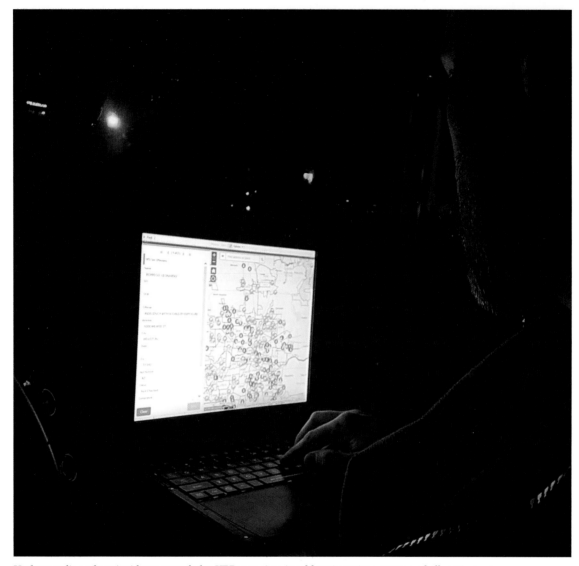

Understanding where incidents occur helps HPD save time in addressing crime surges and allocating resources.

the tools they need to answer when and where questions so they can focus on the who while conducting investigations.

This mission-focused app put the power of analytics in the hands of nontechnical users, but a one-size-fits-all approach doesn't work for all the agency's needs. Using the same technology, the GIS team has the flexibility it needs to build purpose-driven apps that fit the needs of the current agency missions they are supporting today, as well as the unforeseen missions of tomorrow. As new projects and requests come in, the GIS unit responds by identifying the appropriate tools to fit new missions and end-user needs. Other applications they have created include dashboards that show recent crime hot spots, current calls for service, and gang information, all of which is available at officers' fingertips on their in-car computers or mobile devices.

As the HPD unit has become more proficient at building these types of apps, they have also been able to assist other units and teams within HPD and help them identify the best GIS applications to fit specific business needs. Many of the ideas generated by the creation of the CST app are also making it possible to share information and best practices with other agencies and GIS users in the Houston community. The technology has the flexibility to fit any mission; the

key has been starting the conversation and identifying the need.

> *"The primary goal for our unit is to make our customer's life easier. The application made our patrol officers' jobs much easier and more efficient while they were out in the field. Being able to add new information is a huge improvement."*
>
> **—Lt. Freddy Croft**
> **GIS unit supervisor**

---

ADDITIONAL BENEFITS

# Developing tools to track ROI in Utah's Department of Natural Resources

## Community profile

- Utah Department of Natural Resources
- Population of Utah (US census 2019): 2,763,885
- Annual budget: $13.7 billion
- Nature of the project: Demonstrating the ROI of technology

**Community fact:** Utah is the second-driest state in the United States after Nevada. On average, Utah has about 300 sunny days a year.

Government leaders, policy makers, and the public at large want evidence of how technology is benefiting their organizations. A traditional cost-benefit analysis or consultant-prepared ROI study takes time, organizational commitment, and money to produce. The Utah Department of Natural Resources (DNR) wanted to break down these perceived barriers and develop its own GIS ROI report that would allow GIS staff to repeat a process to discover actual business results, clarifying their organizational impact and value.

To address this challenge, Utah DNR staff—including Wade Kloos, director of enterprise systems, and Eric Edgely and Buck Ehler, GIS managers—took on the challenge of building a standardized template for calculating GIS ROI. The department first promoted the ROI tool at a contest for DNR staff to gain acceptance of this new way of approaching GIS projects. Using the new mechanism, staff were able to record their GIS business results. The contest garnered 30 submissions over its first two years of operation and

> The DNR has created a new tool for deriving GIS ROI at the project level. In creating this tool, the DNR explored how it might establish repeatable processes for discovering ROI and communicating the business benefits delivered by GIS. The DNR encouraged documentation of various GIS-supported business improvements that resulted in roughly $450,000 in labor and cost avoidance after just two years of use.

provided documentation of approximately 19,000 hours of avoided labor.

Before beginning such an effort, an organization must ask key business operational questions. The most relevant one for Utah DNR was what business processes the DNR needs to invest in today to achieve the desired outcomes for the future. Documenting and communicating the impact of GIS requires knowing the cost of conducting business before and after a GIS enhancement. Having actual business data is necessary to tell a compelling, evidence-backed story to the organization's leadership. The resulting ROI tool is a simple one-page spreadsheet, but it asks relevant before and after questions to gauge actual impact and help in setting priorities.

The DNR's intent was to create a tool that any GIS professional could use. The tool helped collect the essential business data needed to show costs and benefits as well as ROI. The simple approach to ROI required an abbreviated methodology. Key to this approach is a focus at the project's scale, not historical data for the entirety of a GIS program. Chasing down organizational expenses from years ago or asking people to recall GIS-related business gains, from dim or faded memories, is impractical. At DNR, they realized that significant benefits were created as a result of their GIS projects, so why not limit the scope of ROI investigations to GIS projects?

This approach leaves a few important questions unanswered. First, what is the total organizational investment in GIS? The second question concerns the total benefit derived from GIS-related work in quantitative as well as qualitative terms. Determining the answer to the first question is relatively easy. The second question involves much more consideration and investigation.

Moving to a GIS project-based approach makes the question of total costs and benefits a nonissue. IT departments are viewed as essential for running a business or government, an accepted cost of doing business. Investment in GIS technology—particularly at the enterprise level—should likewise be considered an essential business support function. The more relevant questions for this approach are: What type of project is being considered? What impact is a project expected to make? Can staff see and prove the value of GIS projects within their departments and divisions?

The DNR wanted an ROI tool that fit on one page, and that was what they created—a one-page spreadsheet. Within the spreadsheet are the typical calculated cells to derive the math part of ROI, but there is also a fair amount of room for narrative associated with a complete picture of the business benefits the GIS created. "Not all GIS projects can be distilled into financial or ROI terms," Kloos said. The best part of the GIS ROI and Benefits Report is not the reveal of

### GIS Project ROI and Benefits Report

Project Name:
Department or Division:
Project Manager/Sponsor:
Project Completion Date:

**Executive Summary:** (Concisely state the problem and its impact on the organization then describe the solution and its impact on the organization)

**Describe current workflow or limitation:** (Be as detailed as needed)

**Describe proposed enhancement:** (Be as detailed as needed)

**Current Workflow Costs** (Enter values for hours, wage - see note below, and occurrence. Dollar values are calculated, no need to enter these values)

| | | | | |
|---|---|---|---|---|
| Hours to complete current workflow | 6.0 | | Current workflow cost | $150.00 |
| Hourly wage rate* | 25.00 | | Current annual cost | $11,250 |
| Annual occurrence of workflow | 75 | | | |
| **Enhanced Workflow Costs** | | | | |
| Hours to complete workflow after enhancement | 2.0 | | Enhanced workflow cost | $50.00 |
| Hourly wage rate* | 25.00 | | Enhanced annual cost | $3,750 |
| Annual occurrence of workflow | 75 | | | |
| **Enhancement Production Costs and Savings** | | | | |
| Hours to complete enhancement | 20.0 | | Enhancement cost | $500.00 |
| Hourly wage rate* | 25.00 | | Annual Savings | $7,500 |
| Annual maintenance costs of enhancement, if any | $0.00 | | 3 year savings | $22,500 |
| **Projected ROI** | | | | |
| ROI=Savings-cost of improvement/cost of improvement | | | 1 Year ROI | 1400% |
| | | | 2 year ROI | 2900% |
| | | | 3 year ROI | 4400% |

**Tangible Benefits to the Organization:** (i.e., quality or quantity improvements, effects to throughput, cost avoidance, better decisions, etc.)
Benefit 1:
Benefit 2:
Benefit 3:

**Tangible Benefits to Others Outside the Organization:** (i.e., other divisions, state agencies, stakeholders, public, etc.)
Benefit 1:
Benefit 2:
Benefit 3:

**Meaningful Measures of Success:** (Describe how can/will the project be measured - what is needed to implement regular measurement?)

**Measurement Observations:** (interval varies depending on project, typical may be 3-6 months, 1 yr., 2 yrs., and 3 yrs. after completion date. The purpose of these observations is to record measurements, validate ROI projections, and adjust workflows as necessary for continued improvement)
Date:
Date:
Date:

| | |
|---|---|
| Submitted by: | Date: |
| Project Sponsor/Manager Confirmation by: | Date: |

*Generalized wage rates are used for simplicity and consistency: Intern $15/hr., General Clerical $20/hr., GIS Analyst $25/hr., GIS Manager $30/hr., Division Professional $35/hr.

The team at Utah DNR developed the GIS Project ROI and Benefits Report to document ROI from their efforts.

the resultant ROI percentage but the report authors' explanation of the tangible benefits that could be realized by the proposed GIS project.

The Division of Wildlife Resources (DWR) within the DNR routinely provides reports on essential sensitive species impact and proximity. A considerable amount of data is created by logging requests, performing spatial analyses, creating maps, and producing a final report. More than 400 requests on sensitive species impact reports were received annually, which amounted to 500 hours of staff time. This time-consuming, time-sensitive, and repetitive workflow ultimately led to the implementation of automation enhancement through GIS.

Like many GIS projects, DWR's program had the authority to initiate an enhancement project without projecting an anticipated ROI. The resultant automation project eliminated the time of a GIS analyst from

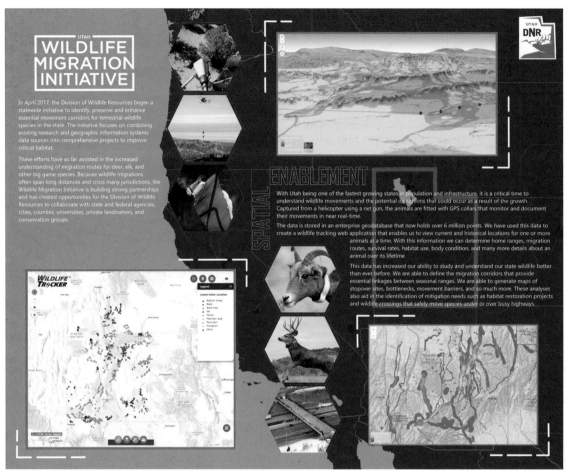

An example of a successful project that is shared internally and externally to showcase the success of GIS use.

the workflow. Although the project avoided 500 hours of required labor, it also took 350 hours of GIS time to create a solution. The resulting ROI was less than hoped for: 58 percent for the initial year.

This raises the question: Should projects that initially might lose money be undertaken? An ROI of 100 percent would be needed to earn back the initial investment. The answer is not necessarily no but dependent, rather, on the possibility of longer-term returns and other tangible benefits. After three years, the DWR's project ROI would be 326 percent. After its first year of deployment, the project produces 1,000

reports annually, operating 24 hours a day, 7 days a week, and 365 days a year—a service level that was never possible before. The value of increased customer service should also be considered when assessing a GIS project's impact.

DNR's initial contest was a great start to ramping up the use of the new GIS ROI and Benefits Report and helped motivate department staff to participate. Yet relying only on the staff's intrinsic motivation did not yield the level of results needed. However, many staff members embraced the discovery process and the education they received by asking the relevant business questions and learning how their organization values their work.

GIS managers are the primary decision-makers about which projects to pursue. This prompts two questions: (1) What kind of projects are they doing? And (2) How much business value are they creating? The pyramid on the left in the figure illustrates, at a high level, a list of general GIS activities (what GIS does). The inverted pyramid on the right identifies the likely outcomes resulting from the associated GIS activities. The purpose of the figure is to suggest the relationship between common GIS projects and the possible value recognized by an organization. Taking a more businesscentric approach, GIS activities would likely deliver higher potential value.

The takeaway is that without measurement and documentation of GIS results—for example, using an ROI tool such as those included in the one-page GIS ROI and Benefits Report—an organization cannot clearly see the GIS outcomes or have a basis to determine the value of GIS. What is left is just a wish list of things GIS could do and probably some anecdotes about how GIS was useful in the past.

In creating this ROI tool, DNR wanted to be able to provide a response to the executive request to show the evidence that GIS is creating value for the organization. What is GIS-created business value? Subsequently, DNR has realized that a stack of spreadsheets is not the best mechanism for communicating with one's organization. Therefore, the department is currently developing a 2.0 version of the GIS ROI and Benefits Report in the form of a web survey, central database, dashboard, and report generator.

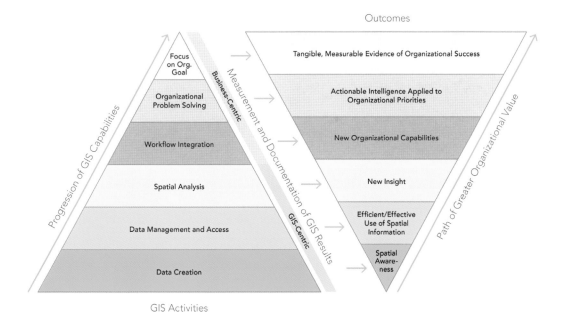

Internally, Utah DNR promotes the valuable outcomes from GIS.

ADDITIONAL BENEFITS

# Chapter 2
# SAVING MONEY

The concept of saving money in government and business often induces fear in the minds of employees. Typically, the phrase is associated with reductions in levels of service, layoffs, and an inability to perform one's job. Budget reductions in troubled economic times are often a Band-Aid approach to getting through a rough patch. However, organizations that practice sound financial management as a normal part of doing business are more resilient and sustainable.

GIS has paved the way in providing innovative ways of approaching operations and service-level improvements. Efficiency gains from staff provide the opportunity to maximize money savings. Organizations are typically in a use-or-lose situation when executing their budgets, and efforts to reallocate funds can spur them to find new ways to apply GIS technology to save money in one area and shift monies to neglected programs. The most common applications of GIS leading to budget surpluses involve streamlining processes that formerly required higher personnel cost. The automation of processes such as field data collection can ensure that data-entry efforts are not duplicated. Applications via mapcentric web interfaces provide staff and citizens with a self-service model for information, while incorporating location builds confidence that the information includes context and insight. Applying GIS can improve navigation and logistics, which increases fuel savings and reduces the number of vehicles required. Optimizing the location of services such as social services, fire stations, polling places, and licensing offices ensures that aid is in the right location and eliminates poorly performing or less-trafficked locations.

Money saved is an opportunity earned. Budgets can be shifted to programs and offerings that would otherwise be tabled, delayed, or eliminated. Using GIS to improve financial management allows organizations to ask where money can be saved and to find effective solutions.

# Clay County, Florida, saves lives and saves money

## Community profile

- Clay County Utility Authority, Florida
- Population of Clay County (US census 2019): 219,252
- Nature of the project: Asset management

**Community fact:** Clay County was once a popular destination for tourists visiting from the northern states. Steamboats would bring visitors to enjoy the therapeutic warm springs and mild climate. President Grover Cleveland was the most prominent of such tourists; he even had spring water from Clay County shipped to the White House.

For many years, the Clay County Utility Authority in Florida used a dated legacy system for conducting hydrant inspections, one of the key tools firefighters use to save lives and property when a fire breaks out. Properly maintaining hydrants assures that the system is in good operating condition when crews are sent out. During this annual inspection, emergency professionals record data, analyze it, and provide it to the fire department and county officials for review. It is equally important for staff to know the exact physical locations of hydrants. Under its existing legacy system, Clay County had no mapping component. The system was strictly a tabular paper-based system that required three staff members working throughout most of the year to prepare for the annual inspection. In addition to being time consuming, this system was not cost efficient.

Fire hydrants require flushing once a year. Clay County maintains over 3,500 hydrants, and completing maintenance work used to take anywhere from 9 to 11 months. With an average processing time of 30 minutes per ticket, leaders saw an opportunity to realize significant savings in costs and time. Using GIS technology, Clay County Utility Authority has improved its operations and reduced the time frame to four months.

Clay County began researching asset management solutions to determine what the right system was for the county. Before deciding which system to procure, the leadership identified their operations requirements. The first GIS project using this new platform began with the establishment of an open data portal. Employees were supported in their desire to learn how to use the technology, which allowed them to do their jobs more efficiently.

The main goal of the fire hydrant mapping project was to improve operations overall using GIS technology. The county had many legacy processes that the utility kept for various reasons. Over the years, staff had worked hard to think outside the box and bring their utility to the forefront of technology. Through the rollout of the new asset management system, staff were able to drastically improve team operations. Once the system was in place, staff members discovered new ideas and uses for the technology and built new apps.

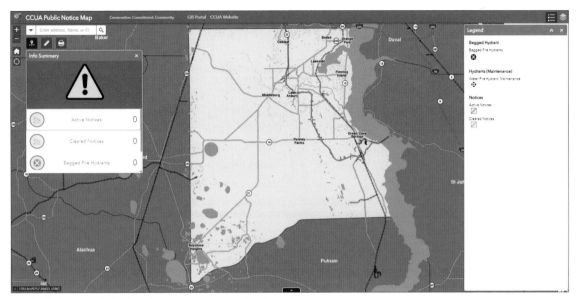

Public-facing maps help the utility communicate with the public.

The organization's GIS portal allows staff and stakeholders to access and share data, reducing duplication of effort.

New GIS technology has allowed the county to speed up the collection of data and data entry. In some cases, the new apps have allowed staff to collect data in real time. The apps also have paid substantial dividends in terms of the amount of time and effort it takes to retrieve data from the system; it also helps eliminate redundancy. The estimated cost savings is over $110,000 in labor reduction. Many departments now rely on the GIS team to provide them with new tools to do their jobs.

Mobile accessibility is a good example of how the departments of Clay County Utility have jumped on the GIS app bandwagon. Field crew members can send data from the GIS platform directly into the hands of all employees, whether they are in or out of the office. And they also have the capacity to quickly send a presentation to show different components and milestones.

In the broader utility industry, there is a concern about aging infrastructure, and users are asking how GIS can be used in new ways and what it will take to capture the data needed. The value of GIS data is high.

Yet Daniel Johns, formerly with the city and now GISP director of geospatial technology for England-Thims & Miller Inc., cautions GIS staff not to "try to do too much on your own." Early in the project, he says, "I was trying to get a lot done in a short amount of time and had created my own custom environment along the way. Over the years, I realized we had gone off the path a bit. We had created a headache in that the systems didn't work together. We went back to a utility industry model that we had customized earlier and consulted with subject matter experts."

The customer and user buy-in to the new apps has been fully embraced within the organization. Government professionals use it routinely in their work. Perhaps the best change was discontinuing the paper processes. Now, GIS technology can do what needs to be done, adding considerable value to the annual project. The future of GIS in Clay County has been geared toward asset management. It also can be used as a budgeting tool, helping leaders determine what to spend to keep their infrastructure strong.

---

ADDITIONAL BENEFITS

# Smart community practices in rural Lorain County, Ohio

## Community profile
- Rural Lorain County Water Authority (RLCWA), Ohio
- Population of Lorain County (US census 2019): 308,461
- Nature of project: Digital water meters

**Community fact:** Prior to the formation of RLCWA and construction of the water system, residents of southern Lorain County and surrounding areas were unable to depend on groundwater or other sources of potable water and thus relied on cisterns, individual wells, and tank deliveries for their water needs.

In the past, Lorain County secured the services of third-party vendors to do this work. "This approach represented additional costs and less oversight than when we can do the work in-house," said Joe Waldecker, assistant general manager of RLCWA. Although RLCWA hired some temporary workers to do some of the work during this project, the bulk of the immense task fell to existing staff, who changed the meters out. This involved opening the old meters, recording old data, installing a new meter, and recording that new number from a digital reading. Once the new workflow was completed, staff were able to send data back to the office in real time. At each meter, GPS identified the exact location for significantly greater accuracy.

The county realized considerable cost savings by completing the work in-house. In addition to the cost savings, other variables that contributed to the success of the project included greater accuracy and

Monitoring water resources being used by community residents and area businesses is critical to providing a steady source of revenue and ensuring standards for safe drinking water for the public. In rural Lorain County, Ohio, RLCWA had approximately 21,000 service connections and 1,200 miles of water lines covering a six-county area of 680 square miles. The utility serves 21 contiguous townships, four villages, and one city. The challenging task before RLCWA was how to switch out 19,000 existing water meters with new smart meters, enabling the water district to save the water utility $1.5 million.

*"GIS enabled RLCWA to make a successful shift to a new water meter system with little or no drama. Establishing a GIS hub, our top priority, enabled us to better manage our billing logistics. We have easy access to real-time and accurate data for billing purposes as well as tracking metrics."*

**—Joe Waldecker**
*Assistant general manager of RLCWA*

programming of the available GIS data. Moving forward, the county's key benefit is having more accurate data. "We can make corrections in-house rather than sending out a third-party contractor after the project was in place," Waldecker said.

As the new technology was implemented, staff collected data to construct interactive maps that could be recorded and accessed through an enterprise system as well as on the web. This allowed staff to provide live updates after the meters went into the ground. Without GIS technology, there would have been a great deal of paperwork—including using fieldworkers to record data in the field and bring it back to the office for analysis.

The new platform allowed RLCWA to execute the meter change-out program more efficiently. Meter change-outs increased from an average of 15–20 meters per day to an average of 70 meters per day. Traditionally, it would take a clerk two to three hours to enter the data into the billing system. Now, data on 1,000 meters can be loaded in 15 minutes. Implementing the new platform allowed RLCWA to perform all the work associated with the meter change-out program in-house, saving the utility $1.5 million in contractor costs.

Initially, RLCWA prepared only internal reports that were submitted to the board of directors monthly. However, the new platform provided the tools needed to collect, visualize, and share information via web

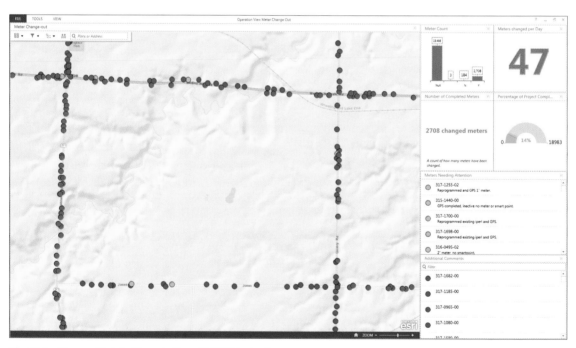

The Meter Change-Out dashboard allows RLCWA to track progress.

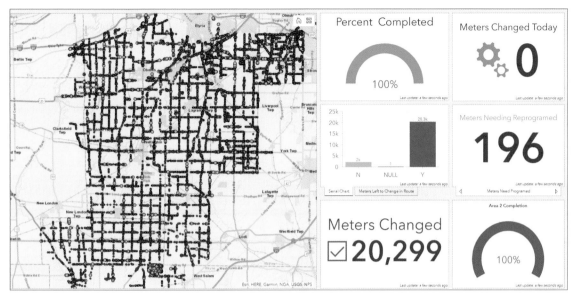

With insight into overall progress, RLCWA can monitor performance and adapt in real time.

maps and dashboards. The dashboard allowed the public to access the data to track and monitor water usage by location. Management was able to receive up-to-the-minute progress reports of the field crews and provide easy-to-understand updates to the board of directors.

RLCWA eliminated thousands of paper-based work orders and prevented hours of costly and time-consuming data entry by personnel in multiple departments. "The massive scale of our project necessitated a more efficient method of tracking the meter installations. Our operations dashboard and apps allowed us to be able to keep the project on schedule and avoid creating a backlog of work orders waiting to be processed," Waldecker said.

*"This project was beneficial for me [as a GIS technician] to have a better understanding of how this technology works—both as to how it is implemented in the field as well as to how I can use it in the office. I learned having clean data is incredibly important, and staff should not be afraid to go to a paperless system."*

**—Orin Babcock**
*GIS technician*

ADDITIONAL BENEFITS

# New England cities are future-ready with smart LED streetlights

**Community profile**

- New England cities: 70 midsize and rural communities in Maine and New Hampshire
- Nature of the project: LED street lighting

**Community fact:** Though New England is home to six states and about 14.8 million people, its total area of 71,992 square miles means it is only slightly larger than the state of Washington.

Cities and towns across the East Coast have implemented LED and smart lighting programs for several years. To date, smart streetlight work has touched more than 25,000 lights in innovative ways to audit, inventory, and manage projects. In addition, the state departments of public works helped facilitate education sessions in more than 70 midsize and rural communities in Maine and New Hampshire. These sessions have featured many of the positive economic and sustainability impacts of implementing GIS mapping technologies—opening new opportunities for GIS use beyond lighting.

The state departments of transportation, together with local governments in the region, worked to retrofit older, inefficient high-pressure sodium bulbs into streetlights with smart LED bulbs. The new bulbs have a more uniform, less harsh distribution of light for better driving safety at night. The switch has also significantly reduced carbon dioxide emissions and energy consumption, up to 75 percent in some cities. Optional smart-enabled nodes enable the lights to

The streetlight of the future is here, and it does much more than lighting city streets. GIS technology is being used to turn older, high-pressure sodium-lit streetlights into efficient, interconnected LED lighting networks in communities across New England. The streetlights are not only budget reducers and energy savers but can become precisely managed and monitored networks, with future-focused technology built in. The streetlight of the future is the foundation of a smart community.

Providing staff with mobile GIS tools allows for quicker data collection and increased coordination.

Web maps allow for insight into the progress of LED retrofitting efforts.

provide additional public safety, environmental reporting, and communication abilities.

GIS technology was an integral component of the project from the start. A standardized geodatabase stores lighting data as well as field data. The entire process was managed in real time, allowing field auditors to conduct their fieldwork and assess progress via dashboards. Once the field auditing process of verifying community lights was complete, lighting staff analyzed the results and developed a proposed LED retrofit lighting plan that detailed the wattage and fixture styles to be installed. The information was presented to participating communities for review through a web app, which supported an interactive design review process that simplified municipal staff review and comments.

Following lighting design approval, electrical contractors helped complete the installation process. An LED installation map helped electrical contractors pinpoint the location of each light, the recommended new fixture and its proposed wattage, and additional field audit comments.

After streetlight conversion to LED, the electrical contractors updated the status of the streetlight. The dashboard was used to engage stakeholders by translating technical information into a friendly, easy-to-use communication tool that tracked LED conversion locations and status in real time. The community could track the progress of LED conversion on specific streetlights in real time via live status maps.

A cloud-based mapping platform was also built. The technology allowed teams to create and share maps with electrical installers; upload data; track staff using tracking layers to visualize installation crew routes; collect points, lines, and polygons data; and efficiently upload information in the field via wireless sync.

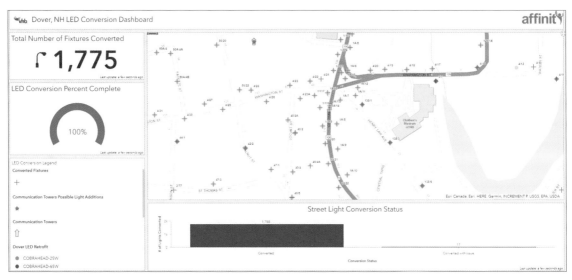

The Conversion Dashboard enables communication to stakeholders on overall progress.

"Communities do not have to be large or wealthy to reap the benefits of smart technology," said Steve Anderson, GISP, director of applied technology for VHB, a project partner. "The communities we are working with in New England are smaller, rural communities with as little as 50 to 100 streetlights that need upgrading to LED. They are seeing the benefit immediately."

The city of Dover, New Hampshire, has approximately 1,800 streetlights that serve a population of more than 30,500 residents. Dover is saving over $140,000 annually by replacing the older bulbs with new LED bulbs and reducing its annual carbon footprint by 482 tons. Electric consumption was reduced by approximately 65 percent. The initial cost to convert is recouped in future savings, with most municipalities expecting a return on investment like Dover's within two to three years.

Some municipalities can apply for rebates to implement the switch to energy-efficient bulbs, further contributing to cost savings. The City of Keene, New Hampshire, received $100,000 via rebate through its utility provider and expects a savings of more than $1.5 million over 20 years due to the conversions.

It is the smart-ready aspects of LED streetlights that may have the most enduring impact. Many cities decide to enable the sensor-ready technology inherent in LED streetlights to make the jump to a smart city.

Municipalities across the US are planning and implementing smart city initiatives—programs that leverage technology and community input to improve the places residents live, work, and play, with a focus on sustainability, resiliency, and social equity. Streetlights are an important tool in smart community development, in part because they are widespread and strategically located sensors. The myriad uses for data that could be gathered by the smart streetlights involve virtually every municipal department, from transportation, energy, and wastewater to public safety and recreation.

By implementing smart-ready node plug-ins in the LEDs, communities gain valuable capabilities, data, and insight that reach far beyond lighting. The streetlights' smart nodes are sensors that can be connected and used to build wireless networks. A wireless network can be used as the foundation of many smart community applications, including supporting 5G and connected vehicles; detecting loud noises, such as gunshots; pinpointing individual lights to brighten and dim when needed; monitoring the environment for air quality; and conducting video surveillance.

For communities large and small, the first step of retrofitting inefficient streetlights with GIS technology results in a smarter, sustainable, and more resilient future.

*"GIS technology was critical to the success of these projects in every stage, from data collection and analysis to reporting and stakeholder engagement. The smart streetlight projects are an innovative use of GIS technologies in municipalities and generate more interest in GIS for applications in other departments like stormwater or traffic."*

**—Steve Anderson**
*GISP, director of applied technology for VHB*

---

ADDITIONAL BENEFITS

# Chapter 3
# AVOIDING COSTS

Though some may say they are one and the same, there is a clear distinction between cost savings and cost avoidance. GIS is always touted for saving money by streamlining processes, enhancing field data collection, improving navigation, and optimizing services. But it can also help organizations avoid costs altogether. Cost avoidance comes when an organization can eliminate a costly workflow from the budget or rethink how a service or operation is delivered.

Think decades back when organizations were able to eliminate paper and printing costs as they moved files and documents from filing cabinets to computers and digital filing methods. This eliminated a cost forever. GIS, too, can initiate a process change or modernize a workflow that removes a cost permanently. For example, governments have been able to bring GIS operations in-house and eliminate third-party data management and processing needs. GIS allows organizations to host on-demand access to data and information that helps avoid customer service costs, especially as the public demands more transparency and accountability. Also, GIS can improve the management and life cycle of public assets such as roads and utility networks, which can lead to better maintenance routines and prevent costly breaks or repairs. Mobile GIS technologies enable work crews to feed data back to the office, directly from the field, and avoid travel time and data postprocessing. Adding GIS to routing and logistics operations can ensure optimal routing and rerouting of fleets that avoids fuel and mileage costs.

Cost avoidance is sometimes referred to as soft savings, but the impact is real. Expenditures are avoided because processes and workflows can handle new demands without additional staff or tools. With the introduction of GIS, organizations can eliminate outdated or costly workflows and modernize operations. In many cases, cost avoidance occurs as a by-product of well-constructed workflows assisted by GIS.

# Glendale, California, looks to eradicate brush before fire season begins

## Community profile

- Glendale Fire Department, California
- Population of Glendale (US census 2019): 252,381
- Nature of the project: Preventing wildfires

**Community fact:** Grand Central Airport, in Glendale, California, also known as Grand Central Air Terminal (GCAT), was an important facility for the growing Los Angeles suburb of Glendale in the 1920s. It was also a key element in the development of US aviation. The terminal was built in 1928 and still exists, owned since 1997 by The Walt Disney Company. It was the departure point for the first commercial west-to-east transcontinental flight flown by Charles Lindbergh; Laura Ingalls landed at the airport on the first solo female flight across the country; and Amelia Earhart bought her first plane there.

Glendale sits along the San Gabriel mountain range and presents a moderate wildfire risk to residents. In the past few years, the city has experienced several destructive fires that have caused tremendous damage to area homes. The city covers 30 square miles of homes that are mixed in with brush areas. Traditionally, the city has maintained a rigorous brush abatement program as part of its wildfire management programs. Using flat and line-drawn maps, inspections took an intensive amount of manual labor to complete.

In 2019, fire department officials in the city of Glendale, California, completed over 9,000 inspections to identify locations that needed work or might be susceptible to dangerous conditions that could result in wildfires. The development of new GIS tools has enabled community leaders to better understand exactly how many parcels the city has and how many homes are in the high fire danger areas.

To better prepare for the fire season in 2020, the city partnered with a consultant to help identify areas that needed work. This partnership helped city staff understand exactly how many land parcels the city has within its boundaries and how many homes are in the high fire danger area. Further, GIS technology has provided staff with better insight into the actual threat of fires by examining the potential fuels, such as brush and dead trees, that could interact within the community. The technology has also helped the city demonstrate the importance of the program to its residents.

The city has defined three main goals for its brush abatement programs. First, staff want to achieve 100 percent completion of all initial inspections, which amounts to more than 9,000 inspections a year. In this phase, an initial inspection is made, and the site either passes or doesn't pass. After the first inspection, the

Providing inspectors with parcel maps allows the city to track and monitor the efforts of field crews.

Example of a photo taken by inspectors of a parcel with brush that could lead to fire danger

parcel owner is informed of what needs to be done to pass inspection. However, Silvio Lanzas, fire chief for the City of Glendale, did not anticipate that the city would make its 100 percent goal in the first year of a new system.

After the repairs or adjustments have been made by the property owner, a second inspection takes place. The goal of the project is to improve communication and cooperation with area residents so they know what to expect. Inspectors take a picture of the violation, share it with residents, and explain how important it is for them to act. The real key to a successful program is education.

Finally, the city works hard to continually improve and maintain the quality of public service and safety. Brush fires are of concern throughout California. Such fires can ravage cities, neighborhoods, homes, crops, and wildlife in a heartbeat. Taking preventive steps can greatly control damage should a wildfire get started.

Initially, Glendale worked to identify areas that clearly needed inspections. City staff collected data on how many parcels needed to be inspected, what time commitment would be required for the project, and how to ensure the appropriate staff members were assigned to complete the project. Additionally, the city afforded staff an opportunity to review aerial views of the homes and hillsides via drones and GIS technology by identifying partial layers within the neighborhoods. GIS technology offered an important ability to make better use of time and be more efficient. In the fire service and safety field, this capability can be a transformative technology.

Before adopting the new initiative, the Glendale team was required to make a presentation to the city council. The presentation outlined the initiative's

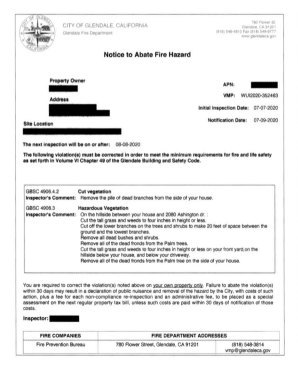

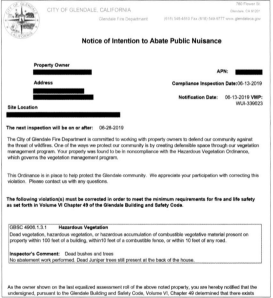

The fire department generates notices to residents to abate fire hazards.

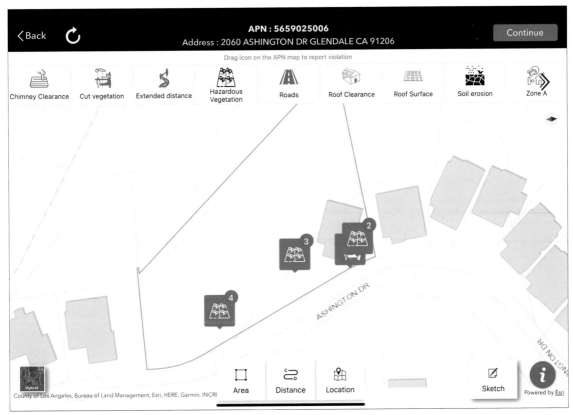

Field inspectors are empowered with GIS tools to collect data easily on types of fire hazards on each parcel.

goals, required staff hours, and estimated time to completion. Team members also took on the challenge of calculating ROI. With this new digital data available, the team was able to demonstrate the benefits for workforce and staffing and the associated cost benefit. For example, project labor can be reduced by two-thirds, saving time for work on other more critical projects.

The brush abatement project began in January 2018. The team had three main milestones to address as they started the implementation. The first milestone involved obtaining approval to use GIS technology for the project. Training helped encourage more buy-in from the staff involved. Finally, implementing

and conducting inspections provided a vetting process to ensure that the system worked as planned.

Inspections based on the new technology began in April and ran through December 2019. Internally, staff shared reports to help department executives understand the nature of the work. Once a month of inspections has been completed, reports are submitted to department executives. And annually, the staff is required by law to report on certain inspections in the fire prevention section to Glendale's city council.

The city has implemented all phases of using GIS technology to give the scope of a project, time requirements, and mapping results over time. GIS binds different datasets to create a view of what is happening on the ground. Having multiple layers and systems in a GIS provides a huge benefit, enabling staff and the public to see how the local landscape changes year over year.

Typically, different staff and the tenure of those staff members pose challenges with technology. Teaching all the team members how to use the new software is critical. Project leaders need to locate people within the organization who have the interest and desire to change the way they work. The ability to deliver and get staff onboard with the new procedures is important; good communication is key. Staff need to understand how all the project pieces fit together and what their role is in ensuring success.

Encouraging the community and the organization to embrace change can be a challenge, but by realigning resources, the City of Glendale made great

The fire department will often conduct controlled burns to abate brush.

gains in working with its residents to prepare for a possible future disaster. Inspections were historically done by engine company personnel ( first responders), who don't specialize in that type of work. Reassigning responsibilities for brush abatement to the department's fire-prevention section created ownership of the projects that aligned with personnel skills and interests. "Finding the best way to deliver our service is what we should focus on as leaders. What's best for our employees and the people we serve. That should be at the forefront of how we make our decisions," Lanzas said.

> *"GIS has been a great example of how we can make a difference in our communities."*

—**Silvio Lanzas**
*Glendale fire chief*

---

ADDITIONAL BENEFITS

# Building a cohesive GIS structure in Cayce, South Carolina

**Community profile**

- Cayce Utilities Department, Cayce, South Carolina
- Population of Cayce (US census 2019): 14,009
- Nature of the project: Constructing GIS inventories and implementing GIS technology

**Community fact:** In the early 1900s, "Uncle Billy" Cayce opened a general store, and locals referred to the area as Cayce Crossing. When the town filed for incorporation in 1914, the name was selected to honor the Cayce family.

The city of Cayce is a major suburb of Columbia, the capital of South Carolina, and has a rapidly expanding economic base. One of the most significant challenges the city faces is the collection and management of spatial data. A cohesive GIS structure has enabled the city to organize the collection of an inventory of utility assets that can be used for multiple purposes. Before that, little had been done to build out a structure for GIS in the city. City documents were not digitized for easy access. Referencing legacy maps—paper maps—took up a significant amount of the utilities staff's time, more than 50 percent.

The department hired its first GIS analyst, Robert Hawks, in 2017. Hawks took the lead in setting up a cohesive GIS infrastructure for the city, including training for staff on how to use GIS products as well as educating leadership and employees alike on what can be accomplished with GIS. The main goal of these

> The Utilities Department for the City of Cayce, South Carolina, has developed an extensive GIS data collection structure designed to avoid costs, generate value, and reduce duplication of effort. Robert Hawks, utilities GIS analyst, points out that the city's GIS structure enables the collection and consumption of data by city staff. This allows the city to avoid expenses by sharing data between departments. In 2019, the total amount of cost avoidance ran a little over $60,000. By 2020, the amount had increased to approximately $120,000.

efforts over the last four years has been constructing the city's GIS inventory.

In the past, utilities staff would spend about half their time referencing materials (such as record drawings, as-builts, CAD files, online maps, and others) to locate assets. That level of effort has been significantly decreased through the availability of online GIS apps and web maps. Having quick access to the data has also allowed the city to secure buy-in for needed funding to tackle the scope of new GIS projects.

The city updates its regular GIS datasets every three months. The city also maintains a mapping gallery. Several other milestones have been implemented over time, and these benefits to the city are quantified by tracking cost avoidance generated each year from these operations. One example is performing

## MUNICIPALITIES CLOSE TO CAYCE MAP
ALSO SHOWING COLUMBIA METROPOLITAN AIRPORT (CAE)

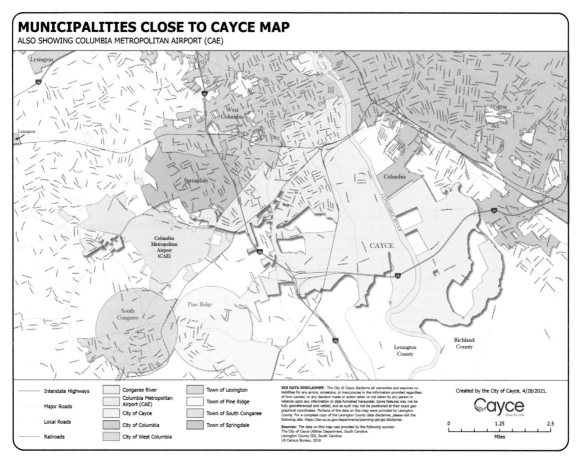

| | | |
|---|---|---|
| Interstate Highways | Congaree River | Town of Lexington |
| Major Roads | Columbia Metropolitan Airport (CAE) | Town of Pine Ridge |
| Local Roads | City of Cayce | Town of South Congaree |
| Railroads | City of Columbia | Town of Springdale |
| | City of West Columbia | |

GIS DATA DISCLAIMER : The City of Cayce disclaims all warranties and assumes no liabilities for any errors, omissions, or inaccuracies in the information provided regardless of how caused, or any decision made or action taken or not taken by any person in reliance upon any information or data furnished hereunder. Some features may not be fully georeferenced and vetted, and as such may not be positioned at their exact geographical coordinates. Portions of the data on this map were provided by Lexington County. For a complete copy of the Lexington County data disclaimer, please visit the following site: https://lex-co.sc.gov/departments/planning-gis/gis-disclaimer.

Sources: The data on this map was provided by the following sources: The City of Cayce Utilities Department, South Carolina. Lexington County GIS, South Carolina. US Census Bureau, 2019.

Created by the City of Cayce, 4/28/2021.

0    1.25    2.5
Miles

The city has built one authoritative geospatial database that allows multiple departments and agencies to operate from one source.

GIS-related projects in-house rather than contracting out to external firms.

The city has undertaken many projects over the years, all of which have taken advantage of the power of GIS. One of the first major successes was the rollout of a master utilities web map. The city provided electronic devices to field crews for the immediate consumption and collection of these GIS products. Once implementation was in place, all field utility crews had access to this data at their fingertips. Before that, everything was on paper or CAD, and referencing was problematic and time-consuming.

*"Every year or so, I review our GIS capability and reassess what the city and its departments need. Our first milestone was the rollout of an ArcGIS® Online master web map for the utilities department. This project was incredibly well received and grew from there. One good outcome that was not anticipated was how receptive city staff were about adopting the new technology."*

—**Robert Hawks**
*Utilities GIS analyst*

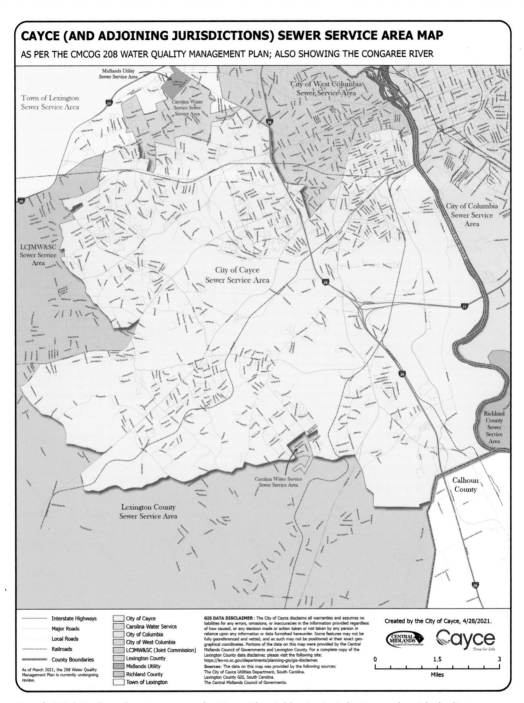

**CAYCE (AND ADJOINING JURISDICTIONS) SEWER SERVICE AREA MAP**

AS PER THE CMCOG 208 WATER QUALITY MANAGEMENT PLAN; ALSO SHOWING THE CONGAREE RIVER

Cayce's GIS data allows for stronger coordination with neighboring jurisdictions and avoids duplicate data creation.

The second project focused on emergency management operations. Beginning in 2019, Hawks began producing a series of utility structure emergency management reports. This project was well received and has taken the place of reports that were previously produced by a paid outside vendor.

One of the most critical recent projects completed was the creation of a cohesive fire hydrant feature. This represented the first time that Cayce assets have been referenced to a high geographic accuracy using GIS-based methods. The fire department has also begun using this data. Hawks has trained the fire crews in the use of web maps so that they no longer need to find hydrants using physical books and are able to access this data on smartphones, tablets, and other devices.

*"We do an ROI analysis at the end of every year that is used for strategic GIS planning purposes. This enables us to look for other opportunities where we can avoid costs and generate value."*

**—Robert Hawks**
*Utilities GIS analyst*

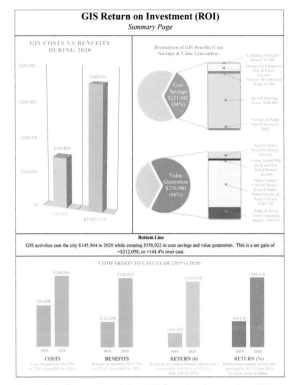

Cayce has documented the ROI from implementing GIS.

ADDITIONAL BENEFITS

# The City of Escondido taps into volunteer power

**Community profile**

- City of Escondido, California
- Population of Escondido (US census 2019): 151,625
- Nature of the project: Volunteerism

**Community fact:** The City of Escondido was incorporated in 1888 and is one of the oldest cities in San Diego County, California.

Residents decide to volunteer in their communities for various reasons. For some, there is a particular issue or concern they want to support. For others, it might be a desire to contribute to the community in a meaningful way or a longing to find new social connections. In the end, however, local governments can't provide all the services residents want and need solely through the efforts of government professionals. Local governments rely on volunteers to do what needs to be done.

Enter Rob Van De Hey, information systems director for the City of Escondido, who took over ownership of the volunteer effort shortly after he joined the city. Van De Hey had learned about the hub tool at a conference for executive leaders and matched the technology with a practical application that he believed would be the best fit for addressing Escondido's needs. Van De Hey created a team to research the feasibility of establishing a new system, using updated technologies to make government processes work better for citizens and local businesses who were seeking opportunities to contribute philanthropically to the community. The new system was installed

> The City of Escondido has secured the talent and time of over 1,500 volunteers who donated 60,000 hours of community service in 2019. The result of this effort was a cost avoidance of $1.5 million, based on the average value of volunteer labor nationwide at $25 per hour and California's hourly average of $30 per hour. With the launch of the city's volunteer hub in November 2019, it received more than 80 volunteer and internship applications from people wanting to make their community a better place. The hub now has received nearly 7,500 online visits from individuals excited to be helping in their community or the city at large.

and implemented in record time. Within a two-week period, the city had the initial platform set up. Just a few months later, the system went live, and it has been operating successfully ever since.

As a result, city leaders have adopted a philosophy that centers around meeting people where they are. Van De Hey said the new system works significantly better than previous efforts at identifying residents for available volunteer opportunities. "There are plenty of people who want to be involved to make their community better," he said. "Oftentimes, residents have a limited number of hours to do that during the day, so the city created a technology platform that allows people who have a few minutes to jump on the hub to see what's going on in the area and determine

The City of Escondido uses GIS to encourage and amplify volunteer efforts.

The city's Volunteer Escondido hub makes it easier for residents to find volunteer opportunities near them.

*"The cost was very minimal and the return on that investment was community engagement or, some might say, priceless. What made the project successful was the creation of our vision and bringing the right people together."*

**—Rob Van De Hey**
*Information systems director for Escondido*

how he/she can get involved and become part of the community."

One of the primary goals of the volunteer hub is to streamline the volunteer onboarding and tracking process. "We want to increase community engagement, remove barriers for people to become involved, and interact with them in less formal ways," said Joanna Axelrod, director of communications and community services. But higher volunteer placement in Escondido is not the only use for the volunteer hub. City staff also use the hub for managing community advisory groups. "We needed to bring our process to a 21st-century standard," Axelrod said.

A volunteer program can achieve many things. The volunteer hub provides one means for fostering greater community engagement by providing communities and local businesses a platform to be heard. No government can afford to offer all the services desired by community residents. At the same time, government needs to provide residents with the opportunity

The hub tracks the success of volunteer projects, including the number of events hosted, volunteers who participated, and the hours contributed.

The hub allows the city to promote the value of volunteer opportunities.

to add input on the services they want. Working in collaboration with government, community volunteers can assist the city in improving its services.

Communication is another significant goal. "Part of my job is to make sure that presentations are professional and represent the city in the best way possible," Axelrod said. "Hub data and story map technology allow us to incorporate map data and visualize elements of products and descriptions of staff reports that show the city council exactly how city data can be used in real time." Good communication helps governments keep expenses and taxes down and supports creative and innovative ideas from sources not normally associated with government planning. For example, Escondido has worked with volunteers on hosting "cleanup days" in many of the city's parks. City staff approached the leaders of a neighborhood group to post an announcement on the hub site, suggesting a cleanup at a particular park. Using the hub's volunteer portal to recruit volunteers, the city and the neighborhood made the project happen. A similar process has been used for volunteer work on particular streets or in neighborhoods that need support. The goal is to hear the citizens' concerns and ideas, and the city hopes to build that kind of collaboration throughout the whole community.

People want to do more, so giving them a mapping layer in the volunteer hub helps paint a picture of what efforts are being undertaken throughout the community. Users can see what volunteers have accomplished and what is left to be done. People want to see what's going on and where things are happening; the mapping element allows volunteers to visualize how their participation contributes to the community's quality of life. The city has also used the hub's ability to visualize data to create an interactive, engaging presentation tool.

The idea behind the volunteer hub is to have a wide range of projects available and something to fit all interests. Volunteers do not need any experience or special skills to use the hub technology. Notices about new projects can be put up on a map along with an outline of the project. This helps residents select projects they are interested in, from assistance at the library to painting fire hydrants.

The Escondido team recommends procuring a platform that has a full life cycle. A system that is only public facing is half a solution. The technology must include a back end to be a complete solution that establishes processes, workflows, and data collection and facilitates communication behind the scenes. On the back end, the city has a way to track everything, to know what's going on, to see where, and to review what's been accomplished to date.

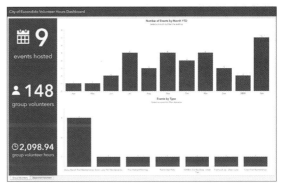

Dashboards for city officials allow them to manage volunteer waivers and events per month.

Other departments in the city have quickly embraced and adopted their own visions for what a hub could do for their teams. This transformation was not anticipated, but improvements continue in Escondido. The takeaway is that leaders should never underestimate the value of data-driven decisions. Having mechanisms in place to manage and improve decision-making is crucial. Any time an organization spends on creating a platform to collect data will lead to quicker improvements and greater innovation.

ADDITIONAL BENEFITS

# Chapter 4
# INCREASING ACCURACY

With people today having easy access to a reliable smart device in their pocket and organizations having access to more data than they know what to do with, it is understandable that citizens expect governments' decisions to be highly accurate. Citizens expect governments to know where to shut off the water main before it ends up on the nightly news or to fix the pothole on the most trafficked street first. But without accurate and reliable information, governments would be unable to make these informed decisions.

Today, organizations use GIS to standardize data models and establish an authoritative system of record to increase accuracy. The basemaps used to build the foundation of the GIS are generally derived from an original source such as surveying or engineering drawings. GIS allows organizations to clean their data through comprehensive checks that ensure they always have high-quality, accurate data. For instance, several departments might input address data as a key field. By cross-referencing these data sources and defining data standards, governments can create a more authoritative geospatial infrastructure. The integration of new precision support technologies—such as drones, high-resolution aerial imagery, remote sensing, GPS/GNSS, and laser measurement devices—increases the validity of GIS databases. Data derived from smartphones, the Internet of Things (IoT), citizen sensors, and location-aware apps that replace reliance on paper provide up-to-the-minute awareness and increased understanding of current conditions.

Accurate information contributes to an organization's effectiveness and benefits the entire community. For example, in hurricane recovery efforts, taking high-resolution aerial images of the devastation can empower insurance companies to make claims decisions the day the imagery is collected. And the pinpoint accuracy of the imagery gives them confidence that they know exactly which customers need to be taken care of.

Accuracy fuels better decisions and performance. GIS is recognized as a technology designed to apply spatial analysis to address the world's problems, but the results of these insights are highly dependent on accurate sources of spatial data. GIS ensures that accuracy: patterns are clearer, relationships become more obvious, and questions get answered.

# Sarasota, Florida, uses GIS to increase accuracy while traditional workloads decrease during the COVID-19 crisis

## Community profile

- City of Sarasota, Florida
- Population of Sarasota (US census 2019): 433,742
- Nature of the project: Field data collection to support asset inventory

**Community fact:** Sarasota has been ranked as the best small city in the US by Time magazine and is known as a tourist haven because of its beaches and warm temperatures.

Located on Florida's Gulf Coast, the city of Sarasota is a full-service city. IT director Herminio Rodriguez was hired to rebuild the city's IT department, including its GIS program, from scratch to better meet the city's needs. "We want to be able to make data-driven decisions, and GIS is a big component of that," Rodriguez said. "I wouldn't even list what you can do in a GIS. I would just say there's probably very few things you cannot do with GIS. A robust and accurately updated GIS database is the key in making these decisions."

The city had existing plans to rebuild the IT department from the bottom up using its GIS system as the platform. Rodriguez hired GIS coordinator William Rockwell to use the city's enterprise agreement (EA) with Esri and rebuild its GIS, starting with the data. In the past, Sarasota had outsourced its GIS data collection to outside firms, but the data collected was outdated and unreliable. Rodriguez and Rockwell determined they would need to either update or re-create all the city's assets. They estimated the

The COVID-19 crisis has had wide-ranging implications for governments, not all of which are fully known yet. One surprising change has been decreasing workloads for many government employees whose projects have been delayed. In the city of Sarasota, Florida, a parking-enforcement officer and city clerk took up the challenge to make use of unexpected downtime. Their idea is not only keeping employees busier and more productive, but the city's GIS initiative has significantly cut down on third-party data-collection costs to the tune of hundreds of thousands of dollars.

costs to be in the hundreds of thousands of dollars in outsourced labor over the course of at least five years.

That was before COVID-19 hit.

As COVID-19 struck Florida, Sarasota began locking down its municipal buildings. One by one, local businesses discontinued service. Development projects were put on hold as investors tracked the status of the economy. As workloads took a dive, government managers had to think creatively about how to keep staff fully engaged and productive. City manager Tom Barwin put out a notice to all departments to consider new and creative ways to productively occupy these city workers.

Rockwell, who had only been with the city for a short while, proposed that workers collect accurate location and attribute data on the city's much-needed assets. This would speed up the city's existing five-year plan to rebuild the GIS system, and it would cut down on six-figure quotes for outsourcing the same work. Rockwell and Rodriguez ran a funding exercise to determine the cost of such a project and found it to be reasonable.

The city also had a supply of extra iPhones on hand, left over from a service provider migration, which could be turned into offline data-collection devices. The only new costs would be for professional-grade GPS receivers to enhance the iPhones' accuracy.

One of the first tasks was to prioritize the asset data to be collected. Rockwell met with city subject matter experts and decided to focus on asset types that could be collected within the time extent of the

*"The financial commitment was small for the city, but the return was huge. We could start capturing this massive amount of data that we really needed. Once we put the whole picture together, the city management really liked it."*

**—Herminio Rodriguez**
*IT director for City of Sarasota*

project. Priority was given to streetlights because of the numerous requests for information from outside organizations, such as Florida Power and Light (FPL) and the Florida Department of Transportation (FDOT). "Everyone agreed it would be better to undertake mapping campaigns that could easily be completed," Rodriguez said. "We decided streetlights

City of Sarasota map of streetlights and signs.

would be the first assets we could tackle in order to better answer requests for information."

As road signs were easy to map concurrently, their inventory would also be done at the first stage of the campaign. Mapping the city trees would come in a subsequent phase.

Trees have historically been an important part of Sarasota's luscious green landscape. Local regulations even dictate rules for residents about cutting down or swapping placement of trees, including on private property. "Just about every city commission meeting includes some kind of tree initiative," Rodriguez said. "So having an accurate count of our trees is important."

The immediate task at hand was how to get staff prepared and trained to take on their new responsibilities. During the training, the employees took great care to stand six feet apart while Rockwell explained the basic concepts of data collection. During these sessions, the employees took turns collecting sample data so Rockwell could address any concerns. Under perfect satellite-visibility conditions, the accuracy

obtained was as good as seven inches, but averaged 2.5-foot (or 0.8-meter) accuracy. Rockwell handed out reflective vests, printed maps, and markers. The printed map series consisted of 28 full or partial grids of the city. This allowed the newly improvised data collection workers, most of them not familiar with GIS, to easily mark off where they had collected data each day.

"Some of the old-school employees prefer to keep track on paper of what they map each day," Rockwell said. "Once they're done, they text or call me, and I can give them a new quarter-section to take on." At the end of each day, after the workers synced their data, Rockwell could assess the team's progress. In the first few days, this allowed him to quickly spot errors, such as not collecting pictures with the assets, and then take immediate corrective actions before it was too late.

Planning technician Billy Cooney usually spends his time assisting senior planners in tasks such as measuring rights-of-way. Now he is committed to spending two days per week doing field data collec-

City workers offer their support and are trained on GIS data collection to stay busy during COVID-19 when city offices are closed.

Volunteer city staff use a city-issued phone to complete asset mapping in Sarasota.

*"We're collecting a lot of high-quality data. This same work would have otherwise cost us hundreds of thousands of dollars if we had outsourced it."*

**—William Rockwell**
*GIS coordinator for City of Sarasota*

A city employee uses the data collection app and high-accuracy global navigation satellite system (GNSS) receivers in the field.

tion. "I try to help out wherever I can," Cooney said. "It's nice that I have a project that gets me out and walking around, especially now that I'm working from home and socializing less."

In the first round, seven fieldworkers collected data on 1,463 of the city's 6,000 streetlights and 2,998 of the city's 16,000 road signs. After that, they planned to collect data on the city's 35,000 trees. The project was initially approved for 30 days but could be expanded based on encouraging initial results and COVID-19 developments.

Other departments have also requested their assets to be collected if time allows. For instance, one proposal is to map the city's parking meters, which were previously collected by manually dropping locations on a map. "This would be an opportunity to have an inventory of all the parking meters with submeter accuracy and bring them into the GIS world," Rockwell said.

The city of Sarasota has managed to turn the unprecedented COVID-19 pandemic into an oppor-

tunity. Not only is the city accelerating its planned GIS database improvements, but it's also keeping city staff from becoming idle. Overall, the response to the project has been overwhelmingly positive.

*"I'm thrilled the city is supporting this initiative. To be able to take employees doing very, very different jobs and put them in the field—this wouldn't have been possible in a normal environment. We are excited that everyone is chipping in."*

**—Herminio Rodriguez**
*IT director for City of Sarasota*

ADDITIONAL BENEFITS

# Columbia, South Carolina: Building a smart community

**Community profile**
- City of Columbia, South Carolina
- Population of Columbia (US census 2019): 156,714
- Nature of the project: Managing resources

**Community fact:** One of the first planned cities in America, Columbia was laid out in a two-mile square surrounding the site of the State House. The city's streets, designed in a grid, were named for heroes of the Revolutionary War and for the state's agricultural products, such as rice, wheat, blossoms, and indigo.

Because GIS solutions are locationally based, numerous datasets can be used and reused to create new apps, analyses, and other tools. The GIS team for the City of Columbia has found that integration of different enterprise programs has been useful for improving efficiencies.

For example, to improve data sharing for the 911 service the city shares with Richland County, which supports the police and fire departments, the city used GIS to deliver a simple, centralized information system to collect, deposit, and store routine data. The system can also analyze daily calls and review call trends for the various public safety agencies. With multiple stakeholders operating from the same information, agencies can now improve coordination and accurately dispatch first responders where they are needed.

In another example, the GIS team built a public-facing interactive web app to support the

> In the city of Columbia, South Carolina, GIS technology has provided a new way to manage resources and conduct analyses that helps reduce the amount of staff time needed for projects. Columbia opted to implement an enterprise GIS that would be integrated with other enterprise systems for use by various city departments. These GIS applications have allowed city departments to work together more efficiently and effectively and, above all, build a smarter community.

Columbia water utility's Advanced Metering Infrastructure (AMI) project to replace old analog water meters with an automatic meter-reading system. The app for the public allowed customers to view the work calendar of where and when the utility intended to install new meters. Utility customers were able to accurately determine when their service might be interrupted as crews replaced the meters.

The GIS team and its applications are also helping to improve the health and safety of residents in their community. The team worked with the Columbia Customer Care Center to improve outreach on boil water advisories by incorporating location intelligence into their efforts. Through the common language of location, the team was able to integrate the boil water advisory notification system with a GIS application. The system now allows the Customer Care Center to identify individual callers and determine whether they

The Calls for Service Response Dashboard allows public safety agencies to better understand 911 call patterns and allocate resources.

The AMI Schedule Information app allows utility customers to look up when their water meter is scheduled for upgrade and when service may be interrupted.

The GIS app built for boil water advisories helps the city communicate more accurately to residents in affected areas.

are in a boil water advisory area. This information, in turn, helps the Customer Care Center provide necessary information and instructions to the public with greater accuracy.

In the city of Columbia, the GIS team has taken impressive steps to expand GIS use across various functions. Their work—whether it is a web app that renders locations and counts of 911 calls for services, a tool that helps identify customers in a boil water advisory area, or a public-facing application that provides utility customers with new water meter installation information—allows the city to achieve improved accuracy and deliver greater levels of service to its residents.

ADDITIONAL BENEFITS

# No more slippery slopes: Santa Clara County, California, creates a parcel slope application

## Community profile

- Santa Clara County, California
- Population of Santa Clara County (US census 2019): 1.928 million
- Nature of project: Measurement of parcel slopes

**Community fact:** Home to Silicon Valley, Santa Clara County is an economic center for technology and has the third-highest GDP per capita in the world (after Zurich, Switzerland, and Oslo, Norway).

> *"Appraisers need to know the slope percentage in order to determine the value of land parcels for assessment purposes."*

—**Yoko Myers**
*GIS manager for Santa Clara County*

There are about 500,000 land parcels in Santa Clara County, with a large percentage of the land located in hilly areas. The high ROI that the tool introduced was discovered when the county hosted a GIS Managers Summit. During the summit, county staff shared their user stories to explain how they produced an ROI analysis. The story was a compelling example of how GIS can be used to calculate slope of parcels for their appraisers.

The landscape in Santa Clara County is varied, running the gamut from flat and highly desirable for development to so steep that the parcels are not suitable for any commercial or residential purposes. These differences in slopes greatly influence land values. After the county's GIS team developed a new slope calculation tool in its SCCMap app, they discovered that the technology saves at least 30 minutes of staff time for each use. They further determined that the county saves $350,000 of staff time annually. The cost to build the new app was roughly $37,000. The tool has been running for six years, resulting in more than $2.1 million in ROI.

While developing SCCMap, the GIS team began with listening to the users. What tasks were part of departmental staff's responsibilities? What did stakeholders need to complete those tasks? What would increase data accuracy? As the team's understanding of departmental needs deepened, the county GIS team realized how long it took to complete each task or step involved in their job. This led to creation of a new tool.

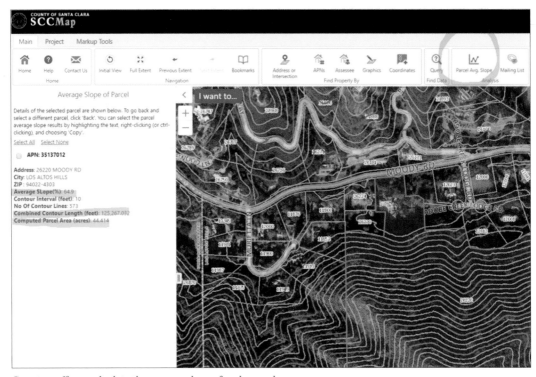

County staff can calculate the average slope of each parcel.

SCCMap is now being used in several departments and cities within the county. The app has roughly 300 users. One of the first departments to use the app widely was the assessor's office. The county has about 80 assessors who use the app when collecting data for appraisals. The key data element is average slope, which is required to conduct a GIS analysis of the slope percentage. To calculate the property value, they had to incorporate slope percentage in their calculations. Although the app involves lots of clicking and entering data for each parcel being appraised, that time cost has been greatly reduced. It takes about an hour to manually calculate the average slope versus 10 seconds with the app.

The GIS team ensures that they document and communicate ROI from GIS use across the organization.

*"We did not expect to have such a huge time savings. But if we listen to our users' comments diligently and always look into the return on investment, then we know we will have happy customers."*

—**Yoko Myers**
*GIS manager for Santa Clara County*

$$S = \frac{(0.0023)\,(I)\,(L)}{An}$$

Where:

I = contour interval in feet
L = total contour length of lot in feet (within net area)
An = net area of lot in acres
S = average lot slope in percent

Calculate S to the nearest 0.1 %

Using this formula, appraisers can calculate slope percentage—the steeper the slope, the lower the property value.

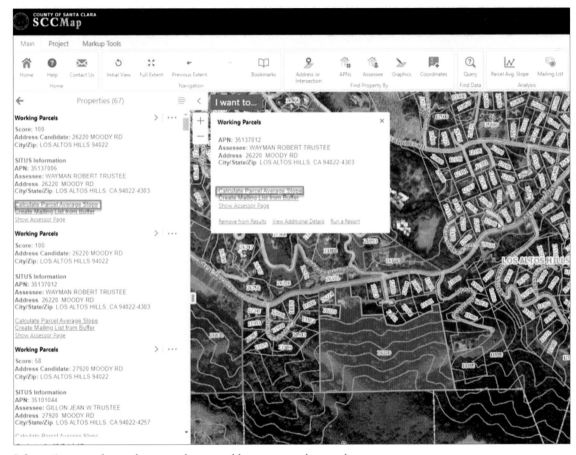

Information on each parcel can reveal owner, address, average slope, and more.

ADDITIONAL BENEFITS

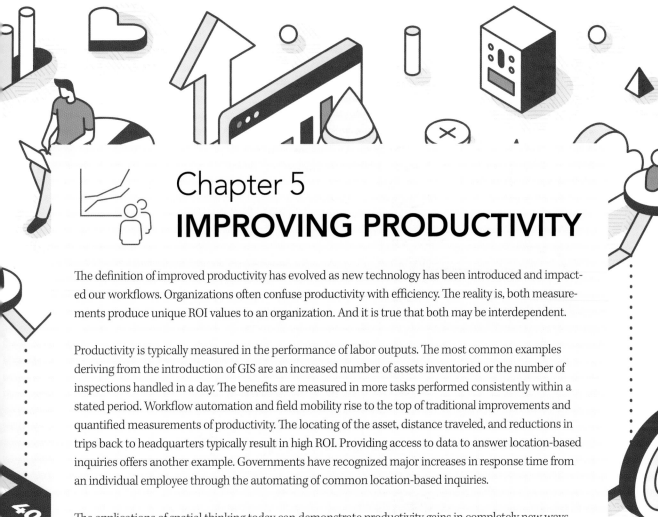

# Chapter 5
# IMPROVING PRODUCTIVITY

The definition of improved productivity has evolved as new technology has been introduced and impacted our workflows. Organizations often confuse productivity with efficiency. The reality is, both measurements produce unique ROI values to an organization. And it is true that both may be interdependent.

Productivity is typically measured in the performance of labor outputs. The most common examples deriving from the introduction of GIS are an increased number of assets inventoried or the number of inspections handled in a day. The benefits are measured in more tasks performed consistently within a stated period. Workflow automation and field mobility rise to the top of traditional improvements and quantified measurements of productivity. The locating of the asset, distance traveled, and reductions in trips back to headquarters typically result in high ROI. Providing access to data to answer location-based inquiries offers another example. Governments have recognized major increases in response time from an individual employee through the automating of common location-based inquiries.

The applications of spatial thinking today can demonstrate productivity gains in completely new ways. For example, applying the use of drones with GIS can improve overall productivity. Take, for example, the use of drones and captured imagery for asset management and inspections. A drone operated by a human can increase overall productivity, and the number of inspections completed can be increased by eliminating many steps in the inspection process, data collection process, and postprocessing analysis.

Longer term, productivity gains will be realized by maximizing staff productivity and outputs at the point of data collection, reducing decision-making time to mobilize staff and allocate resources, and acknowledging the opportunity to use complementary technologies to augment workflows, such as data derived from sensors, drones, and augmented and virtual reality.

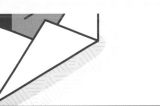

# The US Census Bureau advances productivity through GIS

## Community profile

- US Census Bureau
- Population of US communities (US census 2020): 329.5 million
- Nature of the project: Modernization of workflow

**Community fact:** In 1790, under the leadership of the secretary of state, US marshals conducted the nation's first census, which asked six questions.

Preparing for a national census is a mammoth undertaking. It requires planning and preparation carried out in a transparent and accurate manner. Preparation for the 2020 census began shortly after the 2010 census ended. With the rapid evolution of GIS technology, bureau executives understood that the Census Bureau's existing national geospatial database with addresses, roads, boundaries, and other data should serve as the foundation for the 2020 count. The four main components built into the design of the 2020 census include:

- Establishing where to count people
- Motivating people to respond to the survey
- Following up on responses and nonresponses
- Tabulating and disseminating the results

The first elements in the census design involved developing an expanded national address list and associated geospatial database or set of maps. Having such tools enabled staff to determine the exact physical locations of all the street addresses at which

How does a country as large as the US—with an estimated population of more than 330 million residents—accurately measure its population size as well as where each person lives? Taking advantage of lessons learned, the US Census Bureau staff focused on the design and modernization of the 2020 census to capture the desired data. GIS technology played a crucial role in studying each of these components and identified improvements that resulted in significant transformations of the 2020 census. For example, in 2010, the bureau had to hire 150,000 people to conduct precensus work to validate addresses to send the survey. In 2020, the bureau had to hire only 32,000 workers to go out into the field, which helped the bureau avoid more than $185 million in costs in comparison with the 2010 census. Access to GIS satellite imagery and map viewers made that happen.

*"Our primary goal is to count everyone once and in the right place."*

**—Deirdre Dalpiaz Bishop**
*Chief of the Geography Division of the US Census Bureau*

census staff should be inviting individuals to respond to the census.

The process of building the national address list took place throughout the decade. For the 2010 census, the Census Bureau hired about 150,000 people to walk around every block in the nation to validate their address list. As GIS technology advanced, staff had confidence that they could handle much of the work in the office, using a combination of satellite imagery and housing unit counts from the bureau's address file to help determine which areas of the country were still accurate and which areas required a personal visit to further validate the address list.

Staff examined 11.1 million census blocks in the nation, a unit of work about the area of one city block. Approximately 150 people did this work and validated 65 percent of the nation's addresses in the office. The remaining 35 percent required traveling to the actual address site. Based on the current trajectory, it is possible that the 2030 census will require very little in-field verification work. The census team also used GIS technology to design a map viewer that allowed the public to better understand where census representatives would be visiting to validate the address list and where they would not.

The In-Field Address Canvassing (IFAC) Viewer shows staff where census block addresses have been validated.

The bureau built and maintains a nationwide set of boundaries including legal, administrative, and statistical boundaries. To accomplish its task, the census works with more than 40,000 units of government to ensure that the bureau maintains accurate and up-to-date boundaries and street features in the database. Over the past few decades, the bureau has moved from a paper-based process to digital submission to conduct the Boundary and Annexation Survey (BAS). This has provided state and local government partners working with census staff a straightforward way to respond to the BAS. Customized coding scripts and tools based on GIS technology were used to help process incoming data and information, update the national database, and perform quality control checks. In 2020, the bureau processed more than 130,000 updates using these customized tools and scripts.

At the end of the decade, census staff conducted an operation called the Geographic Areas Reconciliation Program (GARP). GARP was the bureau's largest geospatial quality control operation. Its aim was to ensure that the boundaries of approximately 14 million unique geographic areas are aligned so that the census blocks align with the block groups, census tracts, counties, states, and the nation. This undertaking also includes congressional districts, state legislative districts, and voting districts. All boundaries must be aligned to ensure the accurate dissemination of geographic and statistical data.

Once a good address list and the geospatial data are in place, census staff must determine the best way to invite people to respond to the census survey. An invitation in the mail would be ideal, but not every part of the country receives mail delivery. GIS analysts mapped areas with mail delivery, making them eligible for a census form by mail (95 percent).

The other 5 percent of the survey is conducted using another methodology—sending an enumerator to drop off the invitation at the door or do the actual interview. Additionally, during the COVID-19 pandemic, people were at home in front of their computers and could complete the census online when their schedule permitted.

In the 2000 census, staff were able to mail an invitation to only 80 percent of residents in the country. In 2010, that percentage rose to 91 percent. By 2020, the percentage was up to more than 95 percent. This increase is due to GIS technology and the more sophisticated tools that allow the Census Bureau to integrate addressing services such as E-911 emergency services. This tool helped bureau managers and the public see which areas of the country should receive an invitation in the mail or would be visited in a traditional door-to-door manner. In 2020, more than 152 million addresses were in the census universe.

Multiple communication channels are available for completing a census form. Self-responders have proven to be more cost effective and efficient than sending staff to knock on doors. Partnerships with more than 1,000 national organizations and more than 398,000 community partners nationwide encouraged residents to complete the form. More than 8,500 local complete-count committees and local groups formed to reach out to people living in their communities. All these partners served as trusted messengers to encourage the public to self-respond to the census.

The Response Outreach Area Mapper (ROAM) application was developed to make it easier to identify hard-to-survey areas and provide a socioeconomic and demographic characteristic profile of these areas using American Community Survey (ACS) estimates available in the Planning Database. Learning about each hard-to-survey area allows the US Census Bureau to create a tailored communication and partnership campaign and to plan for field resources,

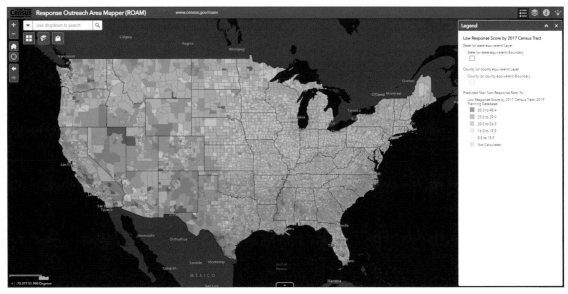

The Response Outreach Area Mapper app modeled areas that were likely to have low self-response rates.

including hiring staff with specific language skills. These and other efforts can improve response rates.

ROAM helps identify people living in census tracts that are the least likely to self-respond. This prediction was based on information from the bureau's ACS and the 2010 census dataset to model low response scores. Because of the COVID-19 stay-at-home policies in 2020, bureau staff were not able to do as much face-to-face education of the public as in previous census years. Nevertheless, the tool performed as anticipated and will continue to be used in the future to drive participation. The bureau received 99 million self-responses, which represents over 67 percent of the addresses in the national database. Of those, 80 percent responded online.

Enumerators were assigned to the addresses of the 33 percent of the population that did not respond in the first phase. This operation is called the Non-Response Follow-Up (NRFU). Because of COVID-19, this task was delayed until August 2020, but the census still completed the work by mid-October. During peak operations, 240,000 enumerators collected data in the field. To manage this massive operation, the bureau used its Field Operational Control System (FOCS). Managers used FOCS to manage the workload and make manual or on-demand case assignments to enumerators in certain geographic locations. The managers could view the remaining workload to see where they were on track and where they needed to boost the number of resources. They could also use the system's proximity function to ensure that enumerators' assignments were close to their homes. Enumerators were provided iPhones to conduct the interview—unlike in 2010, when they were armed with pencils and address lists and paper questionnaires. Initial expectations were that enumerators

*"The 2020 Census was the first time the decennial census used the internet in collecting responses. We were the first country to implement what we call non-ID processing, allowing respondents to answer the census without a unique identification code, by simply entering their home address."*

**—Deirdre Dalpiaz Bishop**
*Chief of the Geography Division of the US Census Bureau*

would be able to complete 1.55 cases per hour. In fact, they were able to complete 1.92 cases per hour. For the 2010 census, the bureau established 494 local offices. In 2020, the bureau opened only 248 area census offices. Although there were areas of the nation that performed exceptionally well, Louisiana and Mississippi lagged because of hurricanes. The COVID-19 pandemic also stood out on the map, as did the Navajo Nation areas in which the pandemic hit hard.

The final task for the Census Bureau is to ensure that all responses are associated with their correct geographic locations in the National Address List. The Census Bureau's national geospatial database ensures that when statistics are released, they are all tabulated to the correct geographic location, and that the bureau has counted everyone once, and only once, and in the right location.

Location has always built the foundation for the census and the census-taking. But this decade, the use of geography and GIS was woven through the entire design of the 2020 census, positively impacting all of the bureau's work.

ADDITIONAL BENEFITS

# Bridging the gap: Sharing data in the city of Thomasville, Georgia

**Community profile**

- City of Thomasville, Georgia
- Population of Thomasville (US census 2019): 18,539
- Nature of the project: Interdepartmental collaboration

**Community fact:** Situated at the end of the railroad line, Thomasville was accessible from the north and, during the late 1800s, became known as the "Winter Resort of the South." At the beginning of this era, Northerners and other visitors would come to Thomasville for their health, breathing the pine-scented air as a curative for pulmonary ailments. Many of Thomasville's luxurious hotels regularly hosted America's wealthiest families.

> *"City departments run independently in many ways, much like an island. We plan and work on our daily tasks and respond to the customer needs specific to that department. We needed a way to bridge departmental islands and improve project coordination."*

> **—Chris White**
> *Executive director of public utilities for City of Thomasville*

All too often, field crews tear up a newly paved road for a water main replacement, fiberoptic cable, or another reason. Such inefficiencies are expensive, prompting city leaders in Thomasville, Georgia, to explore ways to achieve a better solution by building bridges—bridges not made of steel cables and concrete but of data. The goal was to implement a software solution to improve efficiency and coordination among city departments such as building, engineering, planning and zoning, gas, water, wastewater, engineering, and public works. City officials knew employees were spending nearly $25,000 on 14 development projects using a siloed software platform and a paper folder to track staff input. By eliminating these inefficiencies, the city expects to see a 30 percent increase in employee productivity and a cost savings of approximately $7,500. The city also calculated that the water, gas, and wastewater departments were spending 456 hours each year looking through paperwork to find work history data. With the implementation of its new software apps, the city estimates a 25 percent productivity gain overall, with a cost savings of just under $20,000. Based on the current project schedule, the city expects to achieve an ROI after just three to five years.

Staff at the City of Thomasville have been implementing the new solutions in small, manageable chunks since 2016. The first phase focused on the departments involved in the building permit process: building, engineering, and planning and zoning. The second phase expanded to the gas, water, wastewater, and engineering departments. The third phase, which is ongoing, includes public works and engineering.

Before implementing the new solutions, the building department used another siloed software system to issue permits, conduct inspections, and enforce code. "The building department was the only agency using this system, so our communication with engineering and planning and zoning consisted of checklists in a folder, phone calls, emails, and spreadsheets," said Mark Harmon, chief building officer. "The process was cumbersome and unreliable."

During the first phase of implementation, the project team developed cases that incorporated workflows from the building, engineering, and planning and zoning departments. It was a seamless process to translate current workflows into a digital platform.

Each department added its own procedures—such as documenting significant conversations with applicants—so everyone could maintain situational awareness of the case.

The cases did more than just replace the old checklist folders. They significantly reduced redundant emails and phone calls between departments, and they allowed staff to easily run reports and access information at the push of a button.

The city engineer also needed a solution to improve coordination and communication with utility providers on infrastructure projects. City staff created a case for capital improvement projects (CIP).

"The engineering department is responsible for maintenance activities within city rights-of-way and delivery of infrastructure improvement within those rights-of-way," explained Wayne Newsome, city engineer. "The city owns and maintains most of the utilities occupying our street rights-of-way, so it's vitally important that utility infrastructure work is properly coordinated and scheduled in advance of planned street improvements and resurfacing projects."

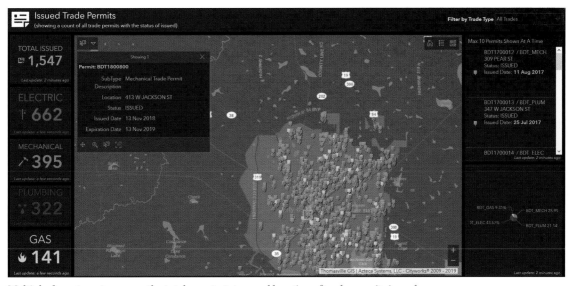

Multiple departments can see the total count, status, and location of trade permits issued.

The CIP case captures major project milestones, from concept development to final infrastructure updates, in the GIS. The workflow incorporates the utility review process into the plan design process to help the utility and engineering departments eliminate conflicts and plan associated work.

Now, both departments have one central location for CIP information, where they can easily access the status and associated work for any project.

Communicating a common operating view across an organization does not mean using only one interface to view the data. The City of Thomasville uses several tools and solutions to consume data and map services and conduct spatial analysis. For example, this system allows the city's code enforcement officer to view the number and location of active cases by type. Similarly, the chief building officer can easily view a dynamic summary of all active trade permits or residential and commercial permits, which increases the value of data by allowing increased flexibility in sharing information across the organization and community.

At the early stages of implementation, city staff developed benchmarks for measuring ROI over a 10-year period. These ROI categories include paper reduction, business process efficiency, work order efficiency, and the elimination of software platforms. The city has eliminated the use of one legacy software, and leaders planned to discontinue support for another system as well.

The success of each of these implementation efforts ultimately lies in the hands of the end users. City employees who use the technologies every day play a critical role in customer service, process improvements, and operational success. The city's mission statement is to "create and deliver exceptional service to our community through a culture of safety, courtesy, professionalism, and efficiency," and the departments are staffed to do just that.

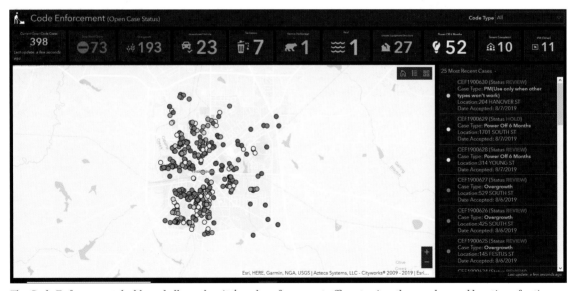

The Code Enforcement dashboard allows the city's code enforcement officer to view the number and location of active cases by type.

GIS creates one source of verified information for the city during all phases of construction, which helps staff improve productivity and manage capital improvements around the community.

---

ADDITIONAL BENEFITS

# Denton Municipal Electric's mobile workflow reduces manual processing

## Community profile

- Denton Municipal Electric (DME), Denton, Texas
- Customers of DME: 55,000
- Nature of the project: Eliminating paper workflows

**Community fact:** Since 1905, Denton Municipal Electric has been a community-owned, not-for-profit public power utility.

One of DME's strategic goals is to increase customer satisfaction. DME utility dispatch handles many types of work requests for several divisions of the city. The divisions had varying degrees of automation and no common system. Staff handled too much paper, had too many workflows, and took too long to respond to customers.

The cumbersome workflows required dispatchers to manually reenter 4,000 paperwork requests from the various systems each year, often causing long delays. Those delays were especially troublesome

> DME supplies electricity to 55,000 utility customers in the greater Denton, Texas, area. DME also dispatches other city services with differing workflows. The volume of paperwork from the various city services created delays in serving customers. DME needed to manage the various work requests efficiently and respond to its customers promptly. The mobile workforce management solution reduced manual processing by 60 percent.

during power outages. Requests from the 811 DigAlert system for locating underground utility cables took particularly long to be manually processed. DME needed consistency, efficiency, and real-time visibility of work status to provide the best service.

DME implemented the mobile workforce management system for work spanning numerous city divisions, including electric, water, and streets. Staff used all aspects of the GIS capabilities, including distribution of information online. Work requests are now rapidly and uniformly sent to rugged laptops in service vehicles.

The enterprise solution is linked to existing systems, producing efficiency gains both in day-to-day operations and during critical emergencies. Many information sources, including GIS assets, 811 requests, outages, customer calls, and crew locations, allow mobile employees to work more effectively. This time-

Denton Municipal Electric reduced manual processing by 60 percent using GIS.

Field crews are equipped with mobile tools that allow them to process work requests electronically.

ly information even allows workers to restore power outages more quickly. Work requests are processed electronically, providing real-time visibility of the work status throughout the organization and reducing delays. This workflow transformation gives DME instant access to location intelligence for all work locations.

The former paper-based workflow often took days to process. Since the utility's digital transformation, workflows are now completed in hours. Work requests providing location intelligence allow workers to minimize drive time and organize their work most effectively. End users applaud the mobile workforce management system for speeding processing time and eliminating redundant requests. Viewing crew locations in real time bolstered worker safety, and the new situational awareness improved DME's response time in emergency situations by an average of 15 percent.

The new workflow consistency improved operational efficiency by an estimated 10 percent. Simply replacing paper requests with electronic processing dramatically reduced data entry errors. DME immediately noticed better data quality by capturing work notes at their source. By quantifying the workflow, DME now has the tools to better monitor its business activity and continually improve the resultant levels of customer service.

*"This is a big deal for us. We've seen a large improvement for a relatively small investment. The ROI will continue to increase over time; it will continue to grow."*

**—Sandra Allsup**
*Electric systems applications supervisor at DEM*

ADDITIONAL BENEFITS

# Chapter 6
# GENERATING REVENUE

Each year, when a government looks at the budget requests that come in from various departments, it's faced with the same question: How are we going to pay for this year's infrastructure and services? The first step is to look at the revenue streams and determine whether funding will be up or down. Looking at location with respect to revenue streams may not be a next obvious step. But location and the demographics of a community can open new insights into where revenue is being generated, which parts of the community use the services, which communities have been left behind, which neighborhoods are faced with potential delays in payments, and many other revenue-to-location variables.

GIS is being used to ensure that revenue collections are optimized, to determine the fair rate at which individuals and businesses are taxed, to perform geo-audits to find escaped monies, and to calculate usage of services based on neighborhoods. Government professionals such as public works departments have been able to calculate land area–based fees to ensure the amount collected is equitable and accurate. Also, GIS has been used to justify grants and federal funding. Financial and business license program managers have been able to identify unlicensed businesses and their associated taxes. Counties and utilities have demonstrated where their jurisdiction's allocated funding was miscalculated. Transportation planners have found means to tax drone flights and to levy fines on displaced e-scooters and bikes.

Understanding the connection between the source of revenue and its location and demographic makeup has rapidly become a new way of understanding the economics of our communities. Underrepresenting a census count in a block group or having errors in the assignment of jurisdiction boundaries in a census tract can be the difference between securing tens of thousands of dollars annually from federal funding or missing out. Understanding a community's geography and its makeup can equal sustained revenue.

# Tippecanoe County, Indiana: Examining government processes to collect all revenue due

**Community profile**

- Office of the County Assessor, Tippecanoe County, Indiana
- Population of Tippecanoe County (US census 2019): 195,732
- Nature of the project: Generating tax revenues with GIS

**Community fact:** Tippecanoe is more than likely derived from the Miami Native American name for buffalo fish.

Tippecanoe County conducts property assessments annually. In 2020, property values went up substantially, causing concern among county residents. The first year the new system was in place, James Werner, project manager in the Office of the County Assessor, and his team examined the county's current processes in depth. Team members looked for optimal ways to ensure that the county was collecting every dollar owed, while keeping in mind that assessments needed to be able to withstand appeals and challenges from the public and business community.

Property taxes in Tippecanoe County function as a tiered system. The tiered system charges owner-occupied properties 1 percent, rental property and farms 2 percent, and commercial-industrial properties 3 percent. The app that was developed allows the county to filter data by taxing district so an individual taxing district or school district can see how much value was added in their specific area.

Between 2019 and 2020, Tippecanoe County, Indiana, identified $1.86 billion in additional property value. This resulted in an uptick in actual revenues based on a 3 percent increase in value. This increase resulted in more than $3 million in increased revenue. The county took advantage of GIS technology to:

Collect data through apps while in the field to calculate property values more precisely
Compare property sales versus assessed value
Validate assessments equitably among neighborhoods
Analyze GIS data to determine whether the county's assessment is equal to or within a relative range of its sales value

Property values and sales prices in Tippecanoe County have been increasing, as they have in the current real estate market across the country. The team focused on determining the fair market value of property in the county based on current sales activities and comparable sales (comps). They use a tool called Beacon to draw current sales information. The tool is open to staff and the public.

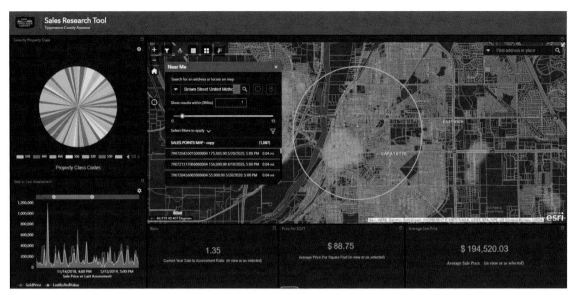

The county analyzes current property sales activities and comparable sales to determine the fair market value of property.

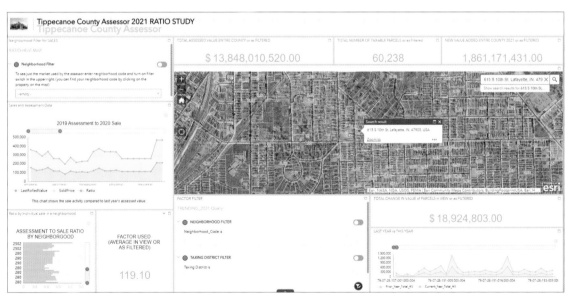

By conducting more accurate property assessments, the county was able to identify an additional $1.86 billion in property value between 2019 and 2020.

The county assessors focused on the accuracy of the data they were using to bill individual property owners. They looked at items such as improvements or social and cultural amenities being built in the area that increase property value and ultimately the sales price. Adjustments to the property tax rolls were made based on the most current data available on these sales comps, yielding a high valuation for taxing each property.

Data on increasing revenue streams was viewed across multiple departments. The total revenue increases derive from several sources, including school taxes, fees, and other revenue streams based on the property value or other information in the assessor's database.

The county has found that clear communication with the public is crucial to establishing a common understanding of what services citizens should expect to receive and illustrating how assessment increases are calculated for the year. Mapping has proved to be particularly useful in helping residents and property owners understand assigned fees.

*"All the data we collected went into the final map. I found the system very easy to use and appreciated the easy and intuitive use of the software. GIS is no longer a field where the layman user cannot do anything without an expert. The average person can create maps without technicians or consultants."*

—James Werner
*Project manager, Office of the County Assessor*

GIS apps, maps, stories, and other solutions in Tippecanoe County are used to support a wide variety of services, such as public health, emergency services including police and fire support, water and resource conservation, elections, communications, public works projects, and road and bridge projects. Werner and his team have a responsibility to sustain revenues for the county, which in turn are used to pay for coun-

The county tracks total assessment value year over year.

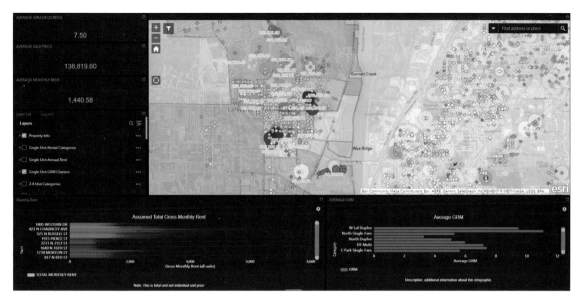

Dashboards and analysis tools allow assessors to investigate property information by property and location.

ty operations and other much needed government functions.

In a relatively short time, the county staff have learned a lot about working with GIS. The technology has proved that it is not unduly expensive, nor did it require multiple change orders. Werner and his team have found the system that makes data easily accessible to a basic user. The ability to easily create a map changes the dynamics of capturing data, enabling the county to collect the greatest and fairest amount of revenues to support county services.

*"We regularly show our commissioners what new GIS tools and apps we are using to generate new property assessments. This background information helps explain to the public why their property values (and their property taxes) have increased over the years."*

**—James Werner**
*Project manager, Office of the County Assessor*

ADDITIONAL BENEFITS

# Converting parking to housing: Identifying land area for 110,000 new homes in England

**Community profile**

- England, United Kingdom
- Population of England: 66.4 million
- Nature of the project: Parking and affordable housing

**Community fact:** Research commissioned by the National Housing Federation in 2019 found there was a shortfall of four million homes in England.

The availability of affordable housing is a pressing concern throughout the United Kingdom. Urban growth has sprung up in and around most cities and towns. Many of the current land parcels have been devoted to car parking for new consumer and retail development. At the same time, transportation is undergoing major changes with the introduction of electric and hybrid vehicles as well as autonomous cars and trucks. To better understand how development trends now will affect future growth patterns, the consulting firm Knight Frank was appointed by the Ministry of Housing, Communities & Local Government to conduct a national research study on this topic.

It is the government of the United Kingdom's policy that no new gasoline-powered cars will be sold after 2033. Personal car ownership is projected to drop significantly with growing environmental concerns and the development of autonomous vehicles. What happens to all the land that was specifically built for car parking? A significant land footprint will become available over the coming decades. The nation's Min-

A new study produced in England highlights the scale of potential development for land tied up across England's car parks (parking lots). Using GIS technology, the consulting firm Knight Frank mapped the precise location and extent of England's 103,000 public and private surface car parks. Government-owned surface car parks could yield 2.1 million homes, or a seven years' supply of housing at the government's stated target of 300,000 homes per year. It is estimated that the United Kingdom could net as much as £6 billion in land receipts (property taxes) for the Treasury by converting car parks to high-density housing.

istry for Housing, Communities & Local Government has set a target of constructing 300,000 new houses per year, which is a sizable target. It is relying on the private sector to help deliver much of the needed housing.

The ministry commissioned the Knight Frank study to determine how to best respond to these development challenges. GIS played a fundamental role in this study; in fact, it would not have been possible to conduct this data analysis without geospatial technology.

Knight Frank's study also established that two-thirds of the public sector–owned car parks do not provide meaningful access to high street retail, and

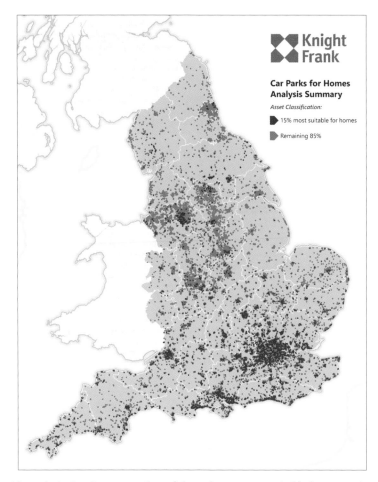

A countrywide analysis visualizes car parks and those that are most suitable for conversion to housing.

that 91 percent of public-sector surface car parks have another car park within a five-minute walk. Crucially, this means that there is enough scope to release the land for building new homes while maintaining easy access to car parking services.

The study found that selecting just 15 percent of public sector–owned car parks that are best suited for housing had the potential to deliver more than 110,000 new homes in areas with higher public transport connectivity. If sold to support building affordable housing, they could raise £6 billion in land receipts for HM Treasury.

Ian McGuinness, head of geospatial at Knight Frank, commented: "The study shines a light on the sheer scale of the opportunity to deliver much needed housing on government-owned land. What we have learned from this new research has evolved our own understanding of this market and the opportunity for government departments to work together to deliver housing. Through this work, the Ministry of Housing, Communities & Local Government has created the first detailed picture of which central government departments own the country's car parks."

All rights reserved

Using online mapping tools, the Ministry of Housing, Communities & Local Government (MHCLG) analyzes suitability of car parks for housing.

*"The geospatial data collected provided both a granular and big-picture perspective. This research made us look at all asset types and raised considerations on development land opportunity and how government departments could pool data resources. Modeling resulting sales values suggested financial return to the public sector far exceeding estimates originally put to industry by the Geospatial Commission on the untapped potential of such approaches."*

**—Ian McGuinness**
*Head of geospatial at Knight Frank*

McGuinness continued, "The pace of development of autonomous vehicles means we should already be thinking about the scale, location, and utility of space currently tied up to privately owned vehicles. The figures are compelling—76 percent of respondents on the National Travel Attitudes Survey agree we should reduce car use for the sake of the environment. One study estimates personal car ownership could drop as much as 80 percent over as little as 15 years.

"We recognize the challenges for town centers due to retail restructuring and the impacts of COVID-19. These car park locations can be an opportunity to enhance the vitality of town centers but also create value in more peripheral locations where purpose-designed development solutions will also help address climate change objectives."

Stuart Baillie, head of planning at Knight Frank, also noted: "Given the express need for housing and the mounting pressure on our green spaces and conservation assets, it is imperative that all brownfields and underutilized land is properly assessed for its economic development potential." By using GIS technology to map land holdings, government leaders can better realize the highest and best use of existing land parcels while achieving long-term housing goals for residents throughout England.

**ADDITIONAL BENEFITS**

# Capturing a bird's-eye view: Stafford County, Virginia, uses drone technology for economic development

## Community profile
- Stafford County, Virginia
- Population of Stafford County (US census 2019): 155,882
- Nature of the project: Drones

**Community fact:** Established in 1664, Stafford is perhaps most famously known as the boyhood home of George Washington.

Stafford County is the second-fastest-growing jurisdiction in Virginia, located on the Interstate 95 (I-95) corridor, south of the greater Washington, D.C., region. The area has considerable opportunities for new development. To better foster new economic development in the county, local executives and managers explored the possibilities of drone technology.

In 2018, the Stafford County Sheriff's Office decided to purchase three drones at a cost of nearly $220,000. At the same time, the GIS team purchased drone mapping software, which cost $2,501. The GIS team estimates that little more than one drone flyover recoups the combined cost of the initial software and annual maintenance fee compared with securing the services from an outside vendor. Access to drone technology and the unique data that can be captured by drones also reduced the number of flyovers necessary to generate imagery required for guiding the construction of the I-95 exchange.

New technology is often seen as a budget breaker, but Stafford County, Virginia, has demonstrated that investing in new technology can help generate new funding sources as well as save money through collaboration with other departments and organizations. The Virginia Telecommunication Initiative (VATI) extends broadband service to currently unserved areas, and, applying GIS technology, the Stafford County IT department was able to secure a VATI grant of $875,000. The GIS team provided data needed for the proposal as well as implementation after the award was made.

The project has become a catalyst for other economic development projects in the county, especially the Downtown Stafford initiative, a visionary redevelopment plan. The county's economic development and IT departments took advantage of the drones' data for their own projects. The sheriff's office already had a robust unpiloted aircraft system (UAS) division, so the GIS team only needed to purchase drone mapping software to process raw imagery into an orthophoto mosaic to serve as a base data layer for this initiative. With a construction project of the magnitude of the I-95 exchange, the county's

The county-owned drones can capture needed imagery data for redevelopment efforts.

departments needed to have current data for ongoing decision-making purposes.

The project has provided Stafford County with a cost-effective solution to targeted and timely aerial orthophoto 2D and 3D products. Working in cooperation with the sheriff's office UAS team, the GIS department creates orthophoto mosaics on a quarterly basis for immediate use by many county departments. Defined regions flown over by the drones include the Interstate 95/Courthouse Road interchange up to US 1/Courthouse Road. This has aided greatly in the development of the county's Downtown Stafford master plan. Another key region that is promoted by the economic development department is the Stafford Regional Airport/Interstate 95 commercial corridor, which has also benefited greatly from the new tools.

The sheriff's office is responsible for maintenance and upkeep of the equipment. The office also has responsibility for any liability issues that might arise. Having access to data gathered from the drone fly-overs allows the GIS team to process its own imagery rather than hiring a consultant. This makes it easier to schedule time for the drones to fly over the territory and capture needed aerial photography. Having ready access to in-house resources saves hours on the sheriff's end. Another side benefit is that staff in the sheriff's office gain experience flying in large contiguous areas, unlike the smaller, less-defined areas determined by real-time situations or investigations they normally do.

Stafford County has fostered a strong working partnership with the sheriff's office's UAS team that

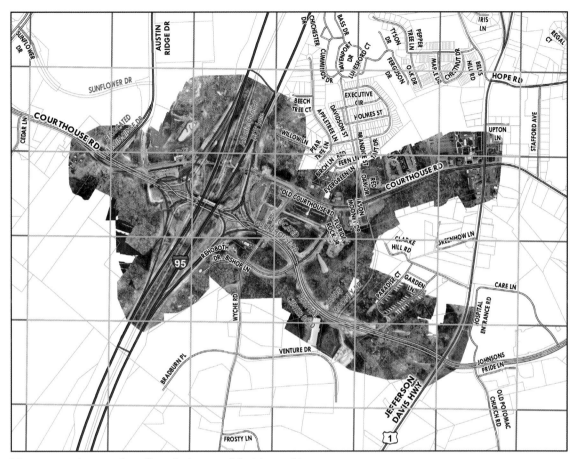

More accurate imagery data allows for improved decision-making.

has translated into the county's sharing new GIS applications, such as easy access dashboards, traffic camera applications, and maps for the traffic division. The GIS team has built an image catalog with change analysis capabilities. This GIS workflow takes place on a quarterly basis, with the GIS team maintaining the image catalog for the program. Having such recent data assures users that they can have confidence in the data received for their projects. The images captured are available to all departments and can be used in a variety of ways, serving a larger purpose for the county.

The recent VATI extends broadband service to unserved areas. VATI prepares communities to build, use, and capitalize on telecommunications infrastructure with the goal of creating strong, competitive communities. The GIS team aided the IT department in securing a VATI grant of $875,000 to support the Downtown Stafford initiative and lure new economic development projects and businesses to the area. The GIS team assisted with the proposal and post-award implementation. Funds from the grant supported providing maps to site selection officers identifying coverage propagation areas, broken down by potential

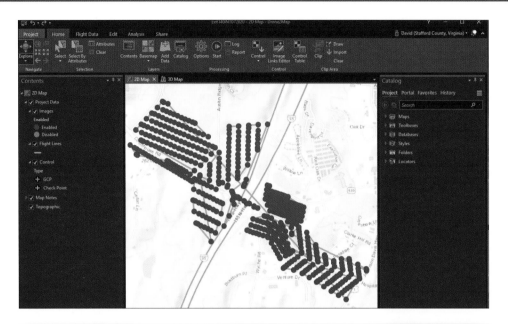

Managing data capture by drones in a GIS allows for decreased processing time and ensures accurate flight paths.

speed and location, in the five regions to be served; identifying supporting infrastructure such as poles and small cells; and securing individual addresses.

As part of the county's standard operating procedures, the GIS team makes a practice of acquiring orthophotography for the whole county every other year. The ability to use in-house resources makes this a cost-effective method for targeted updated aerials in real time at greater than 3-inch resolution. Even commercially available satellite imagery is prone to cloud cover, and its resolution is greater than 6-inch resolution. The county uses a table to analyze the cost per tile, using county-owned drones versus hiring consultants.

Having resources at the ready provides government departments with opportunities to generate new revenue such as VATI funding and also to experience cost savings through the collaboration of department staff on projects of mutual benefit.

## Table 1. The costs of drone-based orthophotography in Stafford County, Virginia

Cost per tile—6 inch resolution (0.5 foot GSD)

| 6 inch resolution tile | Cost per 2,500' × 2,500' tile |
| --- | --- |
| 5001+ | $26.67 |
| 501–5000 | $38.88 |
| 250–499 | $52.79 |
| 100–249 | $89.11 |

Assumes contiguous areas
Ranges not listed, can be provided by custom quote
Includes creation of new ortho-suitable DEM
Options available for custom quotes below the minimum tile range

Cost per tile—3 inch resolution (0.25 foot GSD) (1"=100)

| 3 inch resolution (0.25 foot GSD) (1"=100) | Cost per 1,250' × 1,250' tile |
| --- | --- |
| 2500+ | $14.79 |
| 500–2499 | $37.63 |
| 150–499 | $51.82 |
| 70-149 | $95.15 |

Assumes contiguous areas
Ranges not listed, can be provided by custom quote
Includes creation of new ortho-suitable DEM
Cost per tile—3 inch resolution (0.25 foot GSD)
Options available for custom quotes below the minimum tile range

Source: Virginia Geographic Information Network (VGIN).

ADDITIONAL BENEFITS

# Chapter 7
# INCREASING EFFICIENCY

The application of location-based thinking has demonstrated numerous measurable benefits with respect to increased efficiency. In fact, improvements in efficiency are perhaps second only to automation of workflows in documented ROI. Efficiency is a companion benefit to increased productivity. Rarely do organizations recognize measured benefits in one area without recognizing return in the other.

In government services, efficiency is typically measured in capital or operating improvements. Efficiency is realized in time savings, maximized materials management, or optimizing capital or operating expenditures. Although productivity benefits recognize individual employee outputs, efficiency often measures optimization of resources. For example, optimizing the routing of solid waste pickup has resulted in reductions in the number of vehicles and drivers required to accomplish the same task within the same amount of time across a larger geography. This same review of efficiency often yields returns on savings from items such as fuel and maintenance costs.

Applying GIS to modern workflows has demonstrated the value of optimizing response times, responding to calls for service such as emergency response or pothole patching or simple public information inquiries. More recent documentation of increased efficiencies has been derived from routing election poll workers to pick up voter ballots, optimizing food distribution to at-risk families, improving health equity in neighborhoods with socially vulnerable populations, and optimizing the distribution of COVID-19 or flu vaccinations.

# Maricopa County Department of Transportation: Road Information Tool

## Community profile

- Department of Transportation, Maricopa County, Arizona
- Population of Maricopa County (US census 2019): 4,485,414
- Nature of the project: Organizing and maintaining GIS data

**Community fact:** Maricopa County covers 9,224 square miles, making it larger than four US states. Serving so many square miles, the county's transportation system includes 2,524 miles of roadway, 436 bridges and structures, 172 traffic signals, and 59,056 traffic signs.

Twenty years ago, the GIS team and the Maricopa County Department of Transportation (MCDOT) developed an internal application—the Roadrunner—for the inventory, analysis, and reporting of transportation infrastructure assets. MCDOT maintains an extensive computerized system for inventory, asset management, and geographic information related to roads, structures, ditches, and other pertinent information. When Roadrunner reached the end of its technical usefulness, it was replaced by the Road Information Tool (RIT).

RIT and its predecessor Roadrunner use a linear referencing system, a method of storing geographic locations by using relative positions (known as events) along a measured linear feature. Distance measures

The Maricopa County GIS team and MCDOT worked together to redesign the county's Roadrunner app and replace it with the RIT, which organizes large datasets for MCDOT using GIS technology. The app also made it possible to capture data so that it could be easily accessible and ready for use by stakeholders. However, maintaining and updating the app's geodatabases required numerous time-consuming processes. In making the design changes, the county was able to automate and improve many of the maintenance processes and recover 80 percent of the time allocated for two GIS staff members to manage the program.

are used to locate events along the line—for example, mile markers on highways can take a driver to an interchange where a turn needs to be made. Roadrunner's system consists of two major data elements: the events associated with the linear road segments and the routes and reference points that constitute the linear referencing system.

Events are maintained by MCDOT's staff and include assets and information such as striping, surface type, ownership, bike lanes, right-of-way (ROW), and street width. MCDOT's staff is informed of new assets or updates through a variety of sources, such as construction as-built plans, maintenance schedules, or

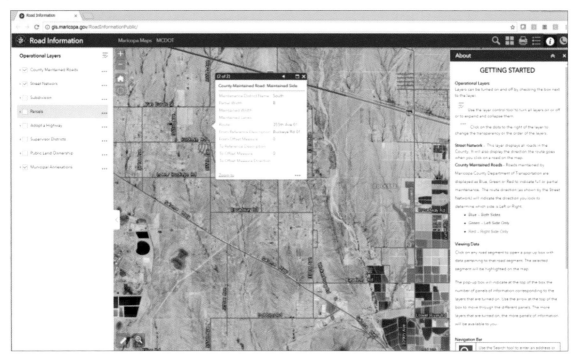

The Road Information Tool provides easy access to road asset data.

intergovernmental agreements. After event changes are identified, they are input into RIT using their corresponding route and reference point information.

Two processes are involved in maintaining RIT data. Although MCDOT staff manage the events, the GIS team manages the routes and reference data to support the updated linear referencing app. These two data sources are the product of an enterprise transportation geodatabase. In addition to the route feature class, the milepost and street centerline features are also maintained in the transportation geodatabase. Through numerous processes, these features are used to create the reference table.

MCDOT staff are responsible for daily data maintenance. To maintain a high level of spatial and attribute accuracy, the RIT transportation database is compared daily against other departmental data using geoprocessing tools. The resulting comparison

identifies new street segments or discrepancies in existing data. To correct the street centerline and route feature classes, manual edits are made to the associated attribute tables and spatial features. Both the street and route features are digitized to best match the center of the street using Maricopa County's most recent aerial photography.

The GIS team manages bimonthly data maintenance. Every other month, the route and street edits are uploaded to the Roadrunner database through the creation of a reference table and a copy of the current route features. The reference table is a collection of route intersections and other nonroute intersections such as mile markers. Each intersection or point represents a distance along a certain route. Through a system of manual and automated processes, each reference point is reviewed for its validity. To assure existing Roadrunner events are not orphaned, previ-

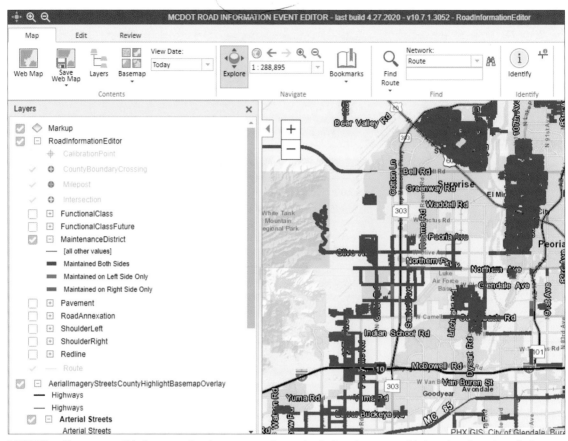

MCDOT staff are responsible for managing the events, or the method of storing geographic locations by using relative position.

ous reference point information is transferred from version to version. This process can require considerable manual review that sometimes requires visual comparison between versions. Once the reference table is finalized, it is synced with the Roadrunner's tables, and the corresponding events are updated to reflect any reference point changes. With the migration to RIT, this process was streamlined so that bimonthly maintenance was reduced to a few days.

The original Roadrunner app provided a system of inventorying many assets that are critical to multiple MCDOT departments. Although Roadrunner was im-

portant to the day-to-day operations of MCDOT, the system also required numerous time-consuming data maintenance processes. These processes resulted in an underlying linear referencing system that is static. With the migration to RIT, many of these processes are being improved and automated. With Roadrunner, each bimonthly update involved the review of more than 150,000 reference points and, on average, took more than a week to review and transfer to the production database. The amount of staff time managing these tasks manually took upward of 80 percent of the time for two GIS analysts.

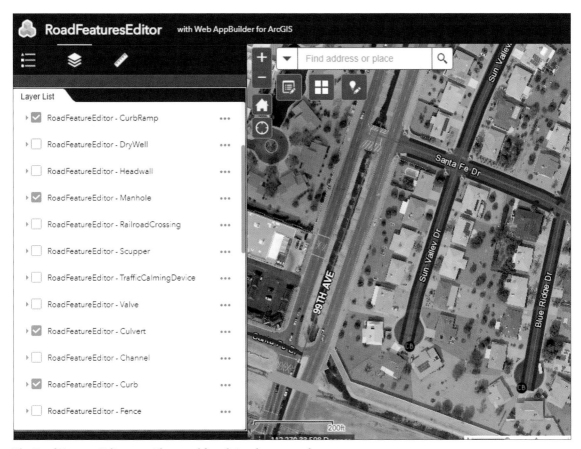

The Road Features Editor provides a tool for editing data on road assets.

RIT data is widely used for various MCDOT business functions. MCDOT Roadway Maintenance Division uses RIT and its counterpart, Cartegraph, to plan and complete work orders on MCDOT's assets. The Real Estate Department keeps track of right-of-way spatial information available through RIT. The Finance Department relies heavily on RIT's inventory of roadway infrastructure to submit its annual Governmental Accounting Standards Board (GASB) financial report. RIT supports other projects such as the Transportation System Plan by providing roadway attribute data to support modeling and analysis. RIT is more of an asset inventory than an asset management system.

The former manages information about fixed assets, whereas the latter manages information about activity such as work orders, projects, and seasonal maintenance of fixed assets.

The Roads and Highways desktop application is the front-end "thick" client for user interaction with RIT data. It allows users to enter, update, view, and report roadway information. However, the system needs changes to accommodate new data reporting requirements. This information is important for correctly reporting the valuation of roadways for the annual GASB audit.

One view into road information ensures that DOT, GIS, and other department staff are operating from the same information.

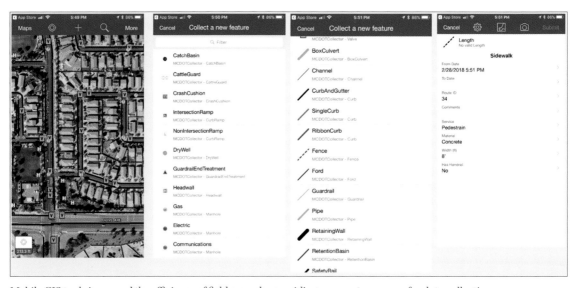

Mobile GIS tools improved the efficiency of field crews by providing an easy-to-use app for data collection.

*"Updating Roadrunner with RIT was a very collaborative effort from a business standpoint, not just an IT standpoint. It helped that the director and executive managers were able to use the app directly."*

**—Steve Hossack**
GIS software architect, Data Management and GIS, for MCDOT

The MCDOT RIT system plays a vital role in producing important roadway and ancillary information for Maricopa County. It is imperative that the RIT system has simple, stable, and efficient data entry and update mechanisms for MCDOT technicians to achieve timely, accurate, and high-quality roadway data. One example of the streamlined data collection effort it achieved was the data entry by technicians through the implementation of a mobile GIS app to collect the data. GIS technology has brought tremendous change to the way MCDOT and other departments manage their workloads, bringing new efficiencies to county operations. MCDOT previously had only 5 percent usage of GIS technology by its divisions. It is now one of the heaviest users of GIS technology, with an approximately 90 percent adoption rate of the technology.

---

ADDITIONAL BENEFITS

# Answers to your local government questions: City of Johns Creek, Georgia

## Community profile

- City of Johns Creek, Georgia
- Population of Johns Creek (US census 2019): 84,310
- City's annual budget: $63.2 million
- Nature of the project: GIS integration with a virtual assistant

**Community fact:** Johns Creek was the first city in the world to use open data with Amazon Alexa, a voice-based artificial intelligence (AI)-powered digital assistant. In 2019, for the second consecutive year, Johns Creek was recognized by winning Amazon's "City on a Cloud" Innovation Challenge award.

In response to residents' increasing requests for data and information, the City of Johns Creek, Georgia, decided to build an open data hub. Using AI, the city tied an open data portal to an Alexa speaker providing answers to more than 200 of the city's most asked questions, saving valuable staff time and expanding residents' access to information and data when they need it. The AI system has shown a 60 percent success rate in directing callers to the right answer with the system's technology. The city has also succeeded in reducing the amount of wait time for answers to questions.

Local governments generate a tremendous amount of data but using it effectively to increase efficiency can be a challenge. Residents want greater transparency so that they can understand how and where public dollars are spent. As Johns Creek is a relatively young city, its staff have an entrepreneurial spirit and are willing to take chances to solve city issues. When Nick O'Day, the city's chief data officer, came aboard, one of his main challenges was to establish a comprehensive open data portal.

Johns Creek's GIS system serves as a central repository for storing geodata that the city uses for spatial analysis and the creation of maps. In building the hub site, the city decided to include dashboards and other applications. Using these, a resident may search for information, such as where 911 calls are being made, by neighborhood. However, web traffic was lower than anticipated at first. People did not realize that the portal existed or that residents could access the resource directly.

While attending an industry conference, city staff learned that a voice-activated Alexa system can be tied into open data.

From that point forward, the city has continued to develop new tools in the same vein. Essentially, the city is using the new technology to push for a deeper level of understanding and greater access for people who may not be technically savvy but still have data needs. Building the Alexa solution has made it much easier for citizens to get answers to their questions.

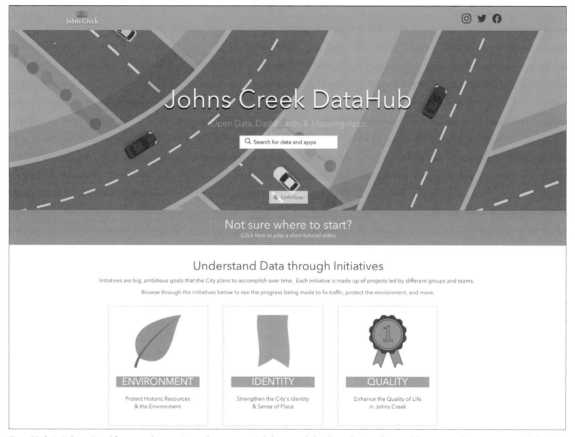

DataHub is Johns Creek's central repository for geospatial data and the foundation for enabling virtual assistant capabilities.

> *"That was an aha moment for us. The idea behind it was to use the easiest way of communicating, namely just asking a question and linking people directly into our open data."*

**—Nick O'Day**
Chief data officer for City of Johns Creek

The portal contains 200 questions that residents can pose and receive automated answers. The system may include more questions as residents' needs change. Fifty of the 200 questions make use of geographic data. Most of the questions people ask are the ones that focus on community issues that impact them directly. The top three topics residents have questions about are zoning, fire and EMT, and police calls. The other 150 questions cover numerous topics, such as When is the next council meeting? Where is city hall located? What jobs are available? The focus is on questions that have easy answers, since the system does not connect the caller to a live person nor is there a phone interface.

The city included 200 questions that residents can pose to their virtual assistant and receive automated answers, 50 of which use geographic data.

The system allows residents to access information and data 24 hours a day, 7 days a week. However, it is used differently during the day than at night. A separate script is available at night. If an individual has a true emergency, the caller will be sent directly to 911.

The city's overall goal is to reduce the amount of time residents spend trying to get an answer, potentially eliminating the need for the public to call or email. "We want to make the access to our information as easy as possible, both in terms of timeliness and level of effort," explained O'Day. The city intends to forge a deeper understanding about what information is available on the portal sites. Residents will be able to find the information to educate themselves about local government processes and become more interested in them. City staff members also have begun using the portal for their own information needs, which was an unexpected result but speeds up the process of getting information to users.

The core of all these products is open data. GIS technology acts as a data hub, helping to connect the information. On the other end, the city can pull data to test the utility of new applications. The city introduced an operations dashboard to monitor call center traffic to see how much utility has been generated. Through monitoring and capture of data, public executives and managers can determine what data to use for the city and help elected officials make the best decisions.

Since launching in 2017, the new system has grown considerably. The after-hours call center soon followed. In 2018, the city introduced a web-based chatbot. In 2020, the city introduced a daytime call center that allows for the same functionality as the virtual assistant. The city has undertaken a steady march of new apps, all using the same technology as city staff continually work to build new products. The city now has multiple communication channels, including the Alexa AI app, the call center, chatbot, and other innovations that came later. O'Day said, "They did not occur to me to be natural extensions of what we had done already but they actually were."

The open data hub has helped city officials and community residents communicate while also demonstrating to the public how innovative the municipality is. Johns Creek is a highly entrepreneurial community, and residents frequently provide feedback to city staff on other innovations to consider. The city has had other communities reach out to bring these new apps to market as a service to the industry. "It reinforces my personal philosophy that regardless of whatever political issues you have going on in your city, so long as the people that work there are really trying to do the best thing for their constituents, you are going to have a good outcome," said O'Day.

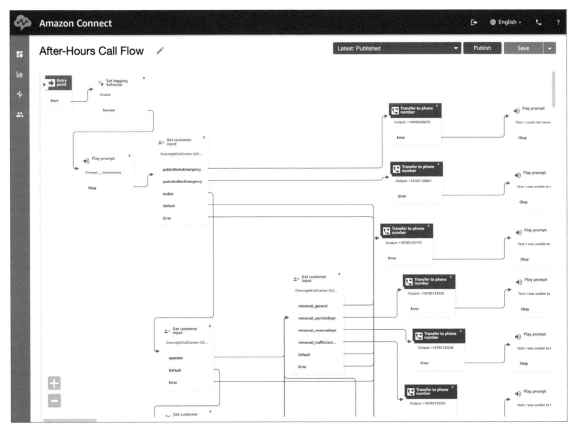

Since launching in 2017, the new system has grown considerably. The after-hours call center quickly followed the initial launch. In 2020, the city introduced a daytime call center that allows for the same functionality as the virtual assistant.

ADDITIONAL BENEFITS

# Data collection in Santa Barbara, California, strengthens with the use of a mobile GIS workflow

**Community profile**

- City of Santa Barbara, California
- Population of Santa Barbara (US census 2018): 91,350
- Nature of project: Field collection and workflow

**Community fact:** The oldest human fossils found in the US were excavated about 30 miles from downtown Santa Barbara.

City staff determined that Santa Barbara needed to modernize its legacy system and existing workflow to enable a new process of collecting field data and performing analysis of the city's large network of water meters. The meter replacement project—including an ambitious goal of replacing all 27,500 of the city's water meters in five years—presented an ideal opportunity for the city to strengthen the accuracy of its location data.

In its legacy system, the real-time location of all meters was not adequately captured, and the system did not provide the level of accuracy required to sufficiently identify the location of individual meters. One parcel could have multiple meters on the site. This was due in part to the meters being directly correlated to a parcel. There was uncertainty about the data's accuracy when multiple meters were present in a parcel.

Since water meters were often located within one foot of each other, the city's team needed a new solution that would provide a higher level of accuracy. The

The City of Santa Barbara, California, supplies water to approximately 95,000 residents. Considering California's proneness to droughts, state water suppliers face operational challenges surrounding water conservation, water-loss prevention, and system maintenance. An analysis of the city's water system demonstrated that the introduction of field-based workflow adaptions increased efficiency by 50 percent, delivering faster response times and increasing customer satisfaction.

*"We were using the parcel number to get a general idea of the location of our meters. But in circumstances where multiple water meters are located on a single parcel, knowing which meter was associated with a particular location was especially difficult."*

—**Theresa Lancy**
Water distribution supervisor for City of Santa Barbara

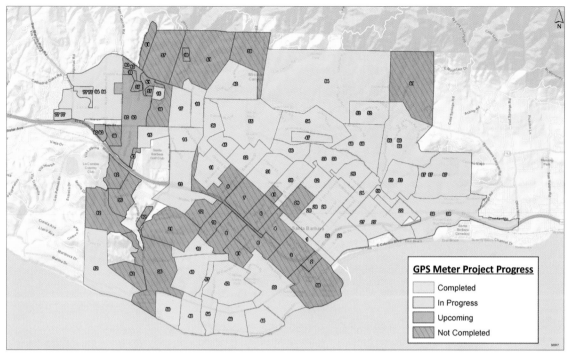

Citywide map provides insight into progress on meter replacement project.

City staff are empowered with mobile GIS tools to quickly capture information and track meter replacement efforts.

City of Santa Barbara explored several mobile apps to help meet its immediate need for an improved field data collection workflow.

The system that was selected enabled employees in the field to remotely edit and use updated web maps simultaneously. Field and office staff had a shared view of the water meter data. The city's team can now create data in the field and provide staff with the means to produce more efficient and accurate data collection. The city has achieved a more efficient real-time data collection workflow with centimeter-level accuracy so that individual meters formerly sharing a parcel can now be uniquely identified.

In addition, Santa Barbara's field personnel are no longer required to manually set up and dismantle the temporary survey base station. "Because the cost and effort involved was fairly minimal, it just made a

Efficient data capture in the field means quicker data processing in the back office and faster response times to citizen requests.

lot more sense to go ahead and set up our own base station," said Theresa Lancy, water distribution supervisor. "We also thought there could be other groups in the city that would use this system."

To date, the city has mapped 75 percent of its water meters. This information will be vital for future efforts to implement automated metering. The city is confident it will achieve its goal of replacing all of Santa Barbara's 27,500 water meters within five years; it has already increased its rate of water meter data collection by 50 percent. The new GIS-based work-flows have proved to be user-friendly, enabling field

*"Once we found something that could interface directly with a map, this solution was an obvious choice. It was so much easier to use. I foresee this becoming an integral part of how we capture information, both in records and operationally."*

**—Theresa Lancy**
Water distribution supervisor for City of Santa Barbara

personnel to expand their project scope, with the capability to map new hydrant and valve installations in addition to the city's water meters.

Faster response times have improved customer service for the citizens of Santa Barbara. The new solution is supporting a newly established goal to replace 2 percent of the city's 300 water main miles per year. Lancy and her team have reason to be optimistic about achieving that goal.

"Drought conditions certainly challenge municipalities like ours," Lancy said. "Efficiently maintaining our system is vital. Leaks need to be located quickly and addressed promptly. Having the right tools to identify, locate, and document repairs means better customer service and reliability—which is very important to us."

ADDITIONAL BENEFITS

# Chapter 8
# AUTOMATING WORKFLOWS

In many disciplines, the automation of workflows creates organizations that are more competitive, productive, profitable, and able to contain or reduce costs. Think Ford Motor Company and the assembly line or how a mobile app modernized 311. These same principles can be applied to government workflows and processes with GIS as the accelerator for a digital transformation. Rethinking, reengineering, and reinventing our processes, from field inspections to streamlined permitting to citizen engagement, has allowed us to see continuous improvements in performing our work. And the automation of workflows carries with it additional and immediate benefits via cost savings, time savings, productivity, and efficiency.

The first and often most tangible foray into automation is the automating of data creation, analysis, and outputs. GIS connects the steps in the processes by linking data and analysis to a geographic tag, bringing seemingly unrelated datasets together based on location. Today, the automation process is seeing a boost from three major data trends: data hubs that provide open access to an organization's data repository, dashboards for data-driven decisions, and data-connected employees and citizens.

Governments of all sizes and complexity can benefit from location-based process reengineering. Simple field data collection can feed central repositories and business systems, field workers can reduce time in the field through access to information on-site, routine analysis and queries can be automated, citizen inquires can be handled through GIS-based personal assistant queries, and a departmental hub can provide 24/7 access to government services. Soon, machine learning and artificial intelligence will begin to automate and predict workloads such as pavement management, snowplowing, and environmental impact reviews.

# Assessment field visits: Reexamining workflows for better results in Crawford County, Pennsylvania

**Community profile**
- Crawford County, Pennsylvania
- Population of Crawford County (US census 2019): 84,629
- Nature of the project: Field data collection

**Community fact:** Crawford County was established in 1800 and named for Colonel William Crawford, an American soldier and surveyor who worked as a western land agent for George Washington. Crawford fought in the French and Indian Wars and the American Revolutionary War.

Crawford County has had a GIS program in place since 2003. The GIS team started working with the county's assessor's office to determine whether they could use GIS technology to enhance the data being collected. The intent was to help county staff do their jobs more efficiently and accurately. At that time, the team spent a large portion of time doing prep work. Before venturing out for site visits, assessment personnel had to produce a paper map to determine where sites were located and load up a physical camera, paper and pen, property cards, permits, and other similar data. Then they went to each site to take pictures. The existing system made it hard to be efficient.

After several discussions, the county's management team decided to create a data collection app that included a few custom domains. The new app makes it easier to record site data quickly rather than

The assessor's office in Crawford County, Pennsylvania, has proved the saying "Saving time is saving money" true, at least in that county. The city has moved from a manual workflow system where the average workday was seven hours long. That average has been reduced to five and half hours. In the past, site inspectors spent 100 days a year in the field. That total has dropped to 50 days of fieldwork, while staff continue to do the same amount of work. The annual cost of assessors in the field was $28,000 a year. Since the newly automated workflow was implemented, the cost of fieldwork has dropped to $11,000 a year. The county's total savings since converting to the new workflow system is $17,000.

spend a lot of time typing up the data at the office after a site visit. The different department teams were able to synchronize land parcels so that the datasets were using the same type of data. The team uses Android tablets and has information at their fingertips when they need it. The app allows pictures to be captured, but the server is not large enough to house all the high-resolution pictures taken in the field, so field crews use tablets instead.

The county uses an enterprise server that allows different departments and divisions to access county

spatial analysis. Geotagged photos also can be used as a point tool. This means county staff can run data from combined geodatabases.

The app drops a point where the picture was taken, time-stamps it, and even notes the direction the photographer was facing when taking the picture. Having this data available has helped reduce prep time enormously. What used to take an hour and half to two hours now takes 15 minutes. Other added benefits for the county include adding a survey tool to the public website. Users of the system can submit new 911 data, such as street addresses for new housing units. The public can use the app to submit assessment reviews. Assessors are happy because they have been able to go out to their vehicles with a lighter workload to get more done, and the county administration is happy because of the cost savings, the efficiency, and the accuracy of the work.

The county's chief goal was to be more efficient and save money. Field staff went from carrying around heavy and bulky tools to bringing along a tablet that weighs just a few pounds. As a result, the daily number of sites team members can visit is roughly double the number before the implementation of the new system. Information on the sites is updated immediately. Staff are also happy not to be spending two to three days transposing their information into the system upon return to the office.

Because GIS is a function in the county, not a department, it has been important to communicate its value to county policy makers. The new app was designed to demonstrate the value of GIS to county commissioners.

County staff had a learning curve to overcome during implementation of the new system. After working out a few bugs, county leaders realized they needed to create a system that works best for them. As a result, other county departments adopted their

County staff use the GIS app to quickly record site data rather than spend time typing up the data at the office after a site visit.

data rather than maintaining multiple datasets on different on-site servers. Staff members can take pictures with the tablet that can be geotagged. That data can be transferred immediately to the office for

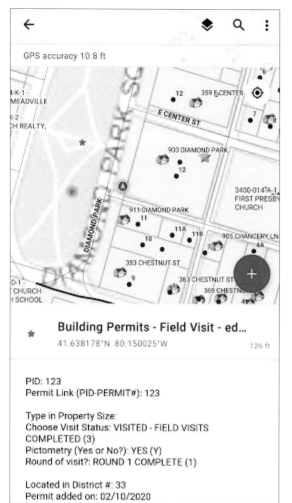
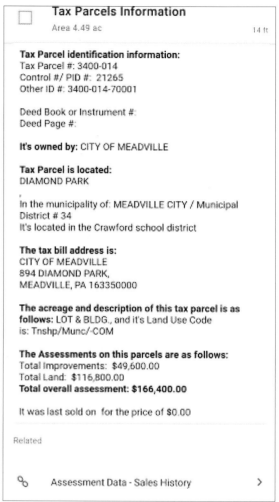

Capturing data via the mobile GIS tool takes field crews only 15 minutes, versus the previous hour and a half to two hours.

own apps. The public safety office uses the data collection app with GPS to establish a marker for a site for 911 purposes, resulting in 100 percent accuracy in finding new addresses and driveway access. The county's conservation district uses the app to capture data from recreational lakes with docks to keep track of permit locations.

The introduction of crowdsourcing as an element of data collection also makes more data readily available. There are many other approaches that can be used for realigning workflows that staff have not yet considered. Using GIS can help the county use other data tools to provide greater public access and more efficient office operations. The more information that can be collected, updated, and kept accurate, the better for the community.

Staff across the county can access the parcel information.

> *"[Crawford County is] very rural without a lot of money. GIS has been a haven for our county. The payout has been incredible for us, and we are still growing at every opportunity we see. We are helping our community and keeping our tax dollars lower."*

**—Phil Baranyai**
*GIS manager for Crawford County*

---

ADDITIONAL BENEFITS

# Preserving agricultural land in the state of Delaware

**Community profile**

- Department of Agriculture, State of Delaware
- Population of Delaware (US census 2019): 973,764
- Nature of the project: Agricultural land preservation

**Community fact:** Corn is Delaware's top crop, which is grown over two-fifths of the state's cultivated land.

The DDA has been preserving farmland for over 20 years. The DDA's agriculture land preservation program uses a competitive bidding process in which easements are purchased at an average 56 percent discount off the appraised value. This allows farmers to make extra money off their land while continuing to farm it. The DDA holds permanent agricultural easements on 866 farms covering 122,000 acres of Delaware land. Additionally, the DDA holds 425 temporary 10-year easements on another 55,000 acres.

In the past, DDA inspectors employed a manual workflow to conduct on-site visits. They used paper maps to decipher property boundaries, recorded inspection notes on laptops, and used digital cameras to take photos of the properties, writing down each property ID number on a piece of paper and photographing that before every inspection to keep the photos organized. The inspections are not complicated, but manually managing all the related data and photos had become challenging and costly.

After inspectors finished a set of hundreds of assessments, they manually organized the photos by property ID, renamed each photo so it contained an

As part of Delaware's agriculture preservation program, the Delaware Department of Agriculture (DDA) sends inspectors to meet with easement landowners to confirm that the owners follow development restrictions. To upgrade workflow processes, DDA leadership explored the use of GIS technology to streamline inspections and automate reports. With the new technology, the inspectors were completing their site visits about twice as fast as they did with the old workflow. This increase in efficiency was attributed to having data, real-time location, mapping, and photo capture all in one device.

ID number, and placed all the photos from each property into a folder. Inspectors then put the inspection results, photos, and captions into a report template, which contained a property map that had to be centered and edited to show the photo locations.

This process took hundreds of hours each year. Managing the data and photos manually as well as creating individual reports for each property was tedious. Inspectors were not able to complete their reports until months after the inspections took place, generating a severe time lag. The workflow was clearly in need of an upgrade, and the staff members were asking for improvements.

Looking for a low-cost upgrade, DDA's GIS coordinator, Jimmy Kroon, determined that he could

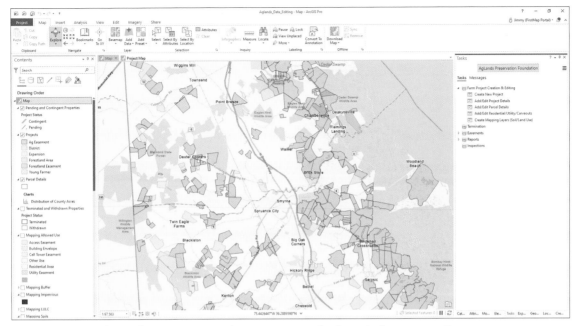

Using GIS, DDA staff streamline inspections and automate reports for the agriculture preservation program.

use mobile data collection to automate the reports. The enterprise GIS team at Delaware's Department of Technology and Information (DTI) assisted with designing a new geodatabase and offered to host it. To get started, Kroon and DTI's GIS team designed a geodatabase that would support data-driven map

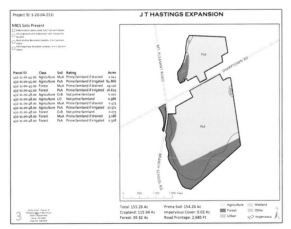

Example of department's mapping analysis of a property's proposed expansion.

documents for individual inspection reports. Then the team designed the geodatabase as the backbone of the operation.

It took less than an hour for Kroon to train the inspectors on how to use the new solution. Within a week, DDA inspectors began using the new mobile app to conduct a set of 306 farm inspections.

They reported that the app was easy to use. Having easement boundaries on a mobile map with real-time location details helped the inspectors get oriented quickly in the field. They liked being able to capture all inspection data and photos using a single device. Offline capabilities made rural inspections easier because the inspectors didn't have to search for mobile service to upload their data. In the first year alone, DDA used the new solution to inspect and generate reports for 730 easements throughout the state of Delaware.

After implementation of the new mobile app, the DDA looked back at the process and calculated

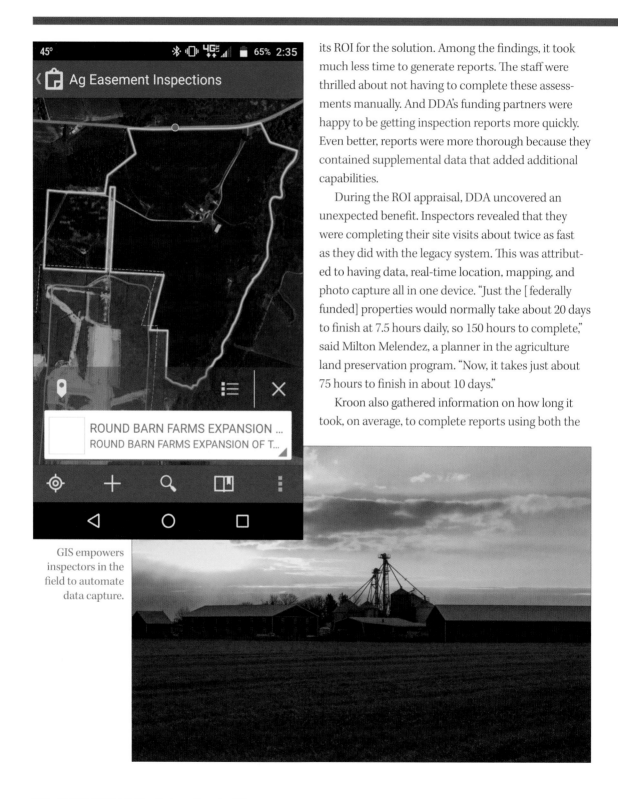

GIS empowers inspectors in the field to automate data capture.

its ROI for the solution. Among the findings, it took much less time to generate reports. The staff were thrilled about not having to complete these assessments manually. And DDA's funding partners were happy to be getting inspection reports more quickly. Even better, reports were more thorough because they contained supplemental data that added additional capabilities.

During the ROI appraisal, DDA uncovered an unexpected benefit. Inspectors revealed that they were completing their site visits about twice as fast as they did with the legacy system. This was attributed to having data, real-time location, mapping, and photo capture all in one device. "Just the [federally funded] properties would normally take about 20 days to finish at 7.5 hours daily, so 150 hours to complete," said Milton Melendez, a planner in the agriculture land preservation program. "Now, it takes just about 75 hours to finish in about 10 days."

Kroon also gathered information on how long it took, on average, to complete reports using both the old and new workflows, and DTI's enterprise GIS team helped estimate how long it took to create the solution. Additional costs, including purchasing new smartphones and a new cellular service plan with data, were also included in the detailed ROI report. In the end, DDA reaped clear benefits from the new workflow. Setting up the solution required a one-time investment of 41 hours, and now DDA saves nearly 500 hours annually—75 percent of the time it used to take—on completing inspections. Generalizing employee costs for everyone involved in the inspections—including their average salary, health care and fringe benefits, and overhead expenses—DDA saved $22,710 in the first year and is slated to save more than $25,000 in each ensuing year.

Delaware's agricultural land preservation program has been in operation for several years. During that time, the most significant milestone the DDA faced in implementation was building out its geodatabase structure. Once that was designed and properly tested, everything else has been a matter of making simple improvements and small adjustments, such as the reporting format.

One of the biggest benefits for the program has been the ability to share information quickly between field crews who are out collecting data and to send data instantly to policy makers and other personnel in state and federal agencies. This capacity has been useful in daily operations. DDA did not anticipate how rapidly the amount of time required to process new applications would decrease. That too has been a vast improvement afforded by the program. For the program's administrators, perhaps the best part was finding people who didn't think of themselves as GIS users but came to use it successfully as part of this project.

*"The process of creating ROI for a project really demonstrated how costly employee time is. It costs far more than items we think of as 'expensive,' such as mobile devices and data service, but I think it's also overlooked because it's a sunk cost. This project has created a lasting impression on me and is applicable to all aspects of our operations at the Department of Agriculture. I was recently promoted to be our department administrator. In this role, I oversee all daily operations and budgets, and this has really shaped my thinking as a manager. With all the focus on budget reductions, exercises such as this are a great example of how DDA is saving money using GIS."*

—**Austin Short**
Delaware deputy secretary of agriculture

**ADDITIONAL BENEFITS**

# Survey app allows Massachusetts to perform watershed inspections in half the time

**Community profile**

- Division of Water Supply Protection, Department of Conservation and Recreation (DCR), Commonwealth of Massachusetts
- Population of Massachusetts (US census 2019): 6,892,503
- Nature of the project: Field data collection and reporting

**Community fact:** Massachusetts's Department of Conservation and Recreation is steward of one of the largest state park systems in the country. It manages 450,000 acres of forests, parks, greenways, historic sites and landscapes, reservoirs and watersheds, seashores, lakes, and ponds.

> **The Massachusetts Department of Conservation and Recreation Division of Water Supply Protection is responsible for protecting the drinking water supply for the residents of Massachusetts, primarily in Greater Boston. Its programs promote water quality and conservation through water resources policy and planning efforts. By moving to a GIS survey, the department was able to reduce the time it took to process watershed inspections by 50 percent.**

One of the Division of Water Supply Protection's many responsibilities is performing routine inspections of more than 150 watershed preservation restrictions. Creating these critical monitoring reports has long involved a cumbersome, paper-based workflow. The department must keep these reports on record to refer to if a landowner has questions or for future monitoring visits. The reports can also be used in legal proceedings if there is ever a violation on a property, so they need to be consistent, easy to read, and, most importantly, accurate.

About two years ago, Danielle Almeida, watershed preservation restriction coordinator, and Erica Tefft, GIS coordinator for the department, began the process of converting the paper-based workflow to a more efficient, templatized digital process that leaves less room for error and takes half the time.

They first decided what they wanted the final report template to look like. Then they outlined what information they wanted to collect and how they wanted it to be collected. Tefft then used a GIS app to create a survey around those requirements. Now the staff performing the inspections can collect the required information and export it to a Microsoft Word document that requires no additional modifications. The final report includes text-based information as well as photos and description tables.

Using the GIS-based service app, they have cut the time it takes to perform the entire inspection workflow from 10 hours per property to 5 hours. That includes doing the premonitoring prep work, going out to do the inspection, and then writing the report.

> *"I think it's been great for me as a user and the program coordinator. I really like how quickly the report comes together and the finished product that they have for our records."*
>
> **—Danielle Almeida**
> Watershed preservation restriction coordinator

Tefft said that staff in other groups within their division are seeing the benefits of this GIS app and asking how they can use these tools to streamline their work. "They say, 'Hey, I can really use this for this project,' or 'Wow, it'd be really great if I didn't ever have to write that report again.' So, I would say over time, as other people within our division see how these products can be used, I'll get a lot of interest in how other people can start leveraging these for themselves," she said. As a result, the division has already started developing additional projects that use the same GIS survey technology to streamline other inefficient, paper-based workflows.

ADDITIONAL BENEFITS

# Chapter 9
# MANAGING RESOURCES

Resource management can mean different things to different professions—infrastructure, facility, human, and natural resource management, to name a few. From a perspective of sustaining infrastructure and services, resource management can focus on the management of crews, time, equipment, materials, and money. By contrast, the preservation and conservation of natural resources seeks to sustain land, water, air, minerals, habitats, and wildlife. Governments are charged with balancing both sets of resources. In the end, resource management provides an opportunity to ensure resiliency, sustainability, and services that contribute to a better quality of life.

GIS has played a major role in preserving and conserving our natural resources for decades. Understanding the location and makeup of an ecosystem provides insight into sustaining our forests, oceans, deserts, and open spaces. We have witnessed the value of location-based thinking to bring back declining habitats, restore and protect endangered species, and mitigate against wildfires and flooding. GIS has also paved the way for research in alternative energy siting and generation while providing a foundation for scientific research at the intersections of the built and natural environments.

Shifting toward the day-to-day operations of most governments, GIS has played a critical role in asset management, helping to design, inventory, and maintain control over our infrastructure. GIS allows us to maximize the productivity and efficiency of our human capital while at the same time assisting in forecasting and controlling the use of materials and funding. With this technology, governments better understand where their resources are, where maintenance needs to be performed, and where gaps in service delivery need to be addressed. Today's GIS recognizes that a building or facility is grounded in a series of physical locations. Management of the interiors of buildings paves the way for space management, work order management, facilities maintenance, and controlling interior climates based on occupancy to control costs.

GIS-centric resource management results in a better understanding of the interdependencies of ecosystems. Location plays an important role in business and operation continuity, providing superior allocation of resources where they are needed. Resource managers are benefiting and will continue to benefit from spatial analytical models that can be applied in a digital twin, model patterns of locations on the earth where natural resources are at risk, and predict need, based on current trends, through artificial intelligence and machine learning.

# COVID-19 pandemic: The City of Glendale, California, uses operations dashboards for business continuity

## Community profile
- Glendale Fire Department, California
- Population of Glendale (US census 2019): 252,381
- Nature of the project: Business continuity

**Community fact:** In its early days in the 1900s, the Glendale fire service was all volunteer. To pay for the equipment needed to fight fires, insurance companies used fire marks, metal plaques marked with the emblem of the insurance company, affixed to the front of insured buildings. If a business caught on fire, the volunteers would respond to extinguish the fire. The insurance company would then pay the volunteers for saving the building. If a business didn't have a fire mark displayed, the volunteers wouldn't put out the fire.

COVID-19 has placed firefighters across the country at an elevated risk of contracting the disease. Emergency personnel regularly interact with residents in need of assistance who may be infected with COVID-19. Given the close quarters in which firefighters operate, the potential for exposure and the danger of spreading the virus to others in the department have presented serious challenges for the city.

Beginning in March 2020, Glendale was affected by the community spread of COVID-19 as the pandemic threatened over 200,000 residents. The fire department was not immune to those direct impacts. When a Glendale firefighter contracted COVID-19, 16 team

> The Glendale Fire Department has taken on unprecedented challenges as part of the department's response to the COVID-19 pandemic. As one of 30 fire departments in Los Angeles County, California, Glendale participates in a mutual-aid response and coordination effort to keep firefighters safe and effective. During the pandemic, GIS technology has provided new tools via a dashboard to support business continuity. The ability to analyze geospatial data helps the city better manage resources, assign tasks, and protect firefighters throughout a nine-city area.

*"Some of the fear we had was that we may have departments that are completely taken out of the system, not able to respond to calls and serve their community."*

**—Silvio Lanzas**
Glendale fire chief

members who had contact with him were immediately taken off their truck and placed into quarantine for two weeks. Losing that many firefighters because of a single positive test could be devastating to the effectiveness of any fire department and potentially elevate the risk to the community it serves. The consequence of one positive case illustrates why Los Angeles Coun-

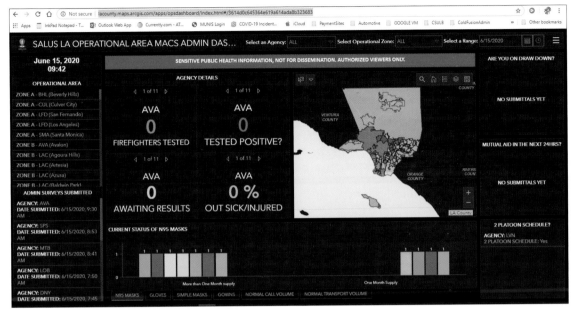

Operations dashboard tracks fire department staff tested for COVID-19 so fire chiefs can monitor staffing levels while maintaining operations.

ty fire chiefs were wary of how quickly their forces might be depleted.

To help keep firefighters and the communities they serve better informed and safe against the impacts of the growing public health emergency, the fire department needed to fast-track the deployment of GIS operations dashboards for business continuity purposes. Glendale Fire Chief Silvio Lanzas recognized the potential for large-scale information sharing in near real time, which could help unite the county's 30 fire departments in response to a major crisis.

Lanzas examined several real-world examples of operations dashboards being used by fellow emergency responders to support readiness, response, recovery, and continuity. He realized that this technology could save lives and help keep employees ready to continue to serve the public. For this reason, the fire department used dashboards as the core of its operational response and business continuity efforts.

The city was able to provide the support needed to configure and deploy two new dashboards in under a week.

Operations dashboards allowed the department to better visualize the present and future threats that the growing pandemic presented. A dashboard provides important insights into the status and capacity of each fire station location, including:

- How many staff work at a location
- What skill sets staff at those locations have
- What facilities are located nearby
- Who lives in a given neighborhood that may need extra support, such as the elderly or people with disabilities

Understanding the staffing levels at each location provides a data-driven decision tool in allocating teams during an event that requires mutual aid. The department needed a solution that could keep staff informed of any impacts an agency was experiencing from the outbreak and how that could directly affect the communities it serves.

The common operating platform was used to share information and help keep the 30 fire chiefs and staff informed on any effects an agency was having or presumed to have because of COVID-19. If one fire department was out of commission, the entire region could be negatively affected because someone else would have to respond to those calls.

"At the beginning of the application design process, we created web-based forms to capture the specific data elements on COVID-19 from our 30 fellow fire departments," said Oscar Barrera, city resource specialist in GIS at the City of Glendale. The coalition of fire departments was then able to share data among all the departments. The fire department quickly es-

A GIS survey app allows departments across the county to report resource needs, including personal protective equipment inventory and staffing levels.

tablished a new workflow to aggregate and upload the survey data submitted by representatives from each of the 30 county departments. Additionally, firefighters have been used in the field to designate the location of all active COVID-19 cases among staff members with whom they have had contact.

Department staff took advantage of the out-of-the-box functionality of the dashboards, customizing them to meet the city's specific requirements and using them as the template for the launch of their own dashboards to support business continuity. The first dashboard was created in coordination with the three hospitals that service the Glendale area. It provides a near real-time visualization of active COVID-19 case data throughout the department's jurisdiction.

The second dashboard developed provides a near real-time visualization of operational readiness indicators, collected from survey forms submitted by the county's fire departments every day. This includes firefighters' shifts, calls for service, personal protective equipment (PPE) inventory levels, and medical leave or quarantine. This data provided the fire chiefs with greater awareness of workforce capacity and well-being, which is an essential component of resilience and continuity.

A deeper understanding of how the countywide force's operational readiness is impacted by COVID-19—and the direct and indirect threats it faces—has been crucial to ensuring that local communities are adequately covered and always protected.

"I think personally it's been a game changer," Lanzas said. "We have done a better job of keeping our firefighters healthy, which ultimately means we can continue serving the public. This pandemic, when it first started, had the potential to truly wipe out entire swaths of our workforce. I think through the collaboration and the GIS technology that we've used, [we've been able to] stay ahead of the curve."

Fire department staff monitor staffing levels across the community.

The project demonstrates the value of managing resources by tapping into the power of collaboration and working with other fire agencies in Los Angeles County to come up with a means of capturing information from all the participating agencies, centralizing the information, and distributing it to the other participating agencies in as close to real time as possible.

*"We have 30 fire departments in Los Angeles County, and we've always done a decent job of sharing information, but nothing like I've seen through this. This dashboard and GIS technology helped bring us together as fire service leaders."*

**Silvio Lanzas**
Glendale fire chief

ADDITIONAL BENEFITS

# Preparing for elections in Maricopa County, Arizona

## Community profile

- Elections Department, Maricopa County, Arizona
- Population of Maricopa County (US census 2019): 4,485,414
- Nature of the project: Business continuity

**Community fact:** Maricopa County is the second-largest voting jurisdiction in the United States and represents more than 60 percent of Arizona's registered voters.

Maricopa County personnel discussed making changes in their election processes to determine how to get the best results for the community. The decision was made to invest more in GIS to help officials make more informed decisions. In 2019, officials began planning for elections using mapping to determine where citizens currently lived and where they were likely to vote. The primary goal was to make the best use of the county's resources to make the election successful.

These decisions were made pre-COVID-19, but the data already gathered lent itself well to the task of identifying where new polling locations should go. GIS data provides leaders and management staff the ability to analyze the best places for poll locations on Election Day. Staff used a dot density map from previous in-person voters to assist in placement of new sites and consolidation of polling locations. For the primary election in 2019, election officials selected 100 locations, and for the general election, 175 sites.

The need to get out the vote and make participating in this civic duty accessible and transparent for citizens has been the topic of much discussion. For election officials in Maricopa County, Arizona, letting people know where they need to go to vote and selecting where polling stations should be located within the community are important civic issues. GIS technology has helped election officials make more informed decisions on the placement of polling sites.

*"We were creating dot density maps to find clusters of voters in a certain area. That tool was very important for our database architects to help get the data out and present it spatially. Gathering and crunching data made it possible to show [it to] election directors to help them make their decisions."*

**—Gary Bilotta**
GIS director of the Elections Department

Maricopa County has had GIS technology since 2000, and the technology has become more ingrained in elections over time, improving resource allocations through the ability to make smart decisions. The best outcome for the citizens was not reflected in a traditional ROI but rather in the fact that, after the polls

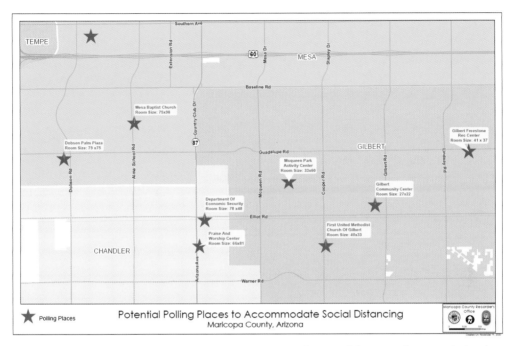

**Potential Polling Places to Accommodate Social Distancing**
Maricopa County, Arizona

★ Polling Places

Election staff identify additional polling locations to accommodate social distancing for voters during the 2020 election.

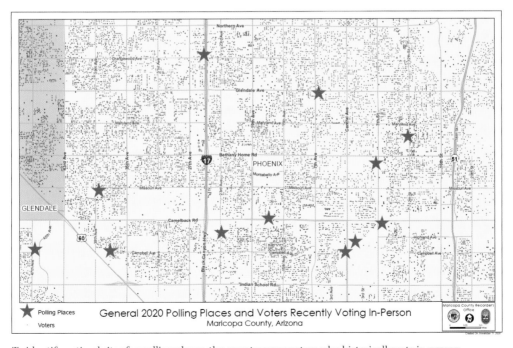

**General 2020 Polling Places and Voters Recently Voting In-Person**
Maricopa County, Arizona

★ Polling Places

★ Voters

To identify optimal sites for polling places, the county maps voters who historically vote in person.

closed and the election was over, Maricopa County's results were transparent to voters.

The county continues to mine its election data regularly, working with the team at least twice a month to discuss what is needed. Data collection efforts have been ongoing, and mapping and data analysis have been critical for development of a greatly improved process. The largest milestone for the project occurred seven days before the 2020 election, when because of COVID-19, staff had to scramble to find suitable new locations for polling stations. Having data already collected and available made it possible for staff to determine which locations would encourage voters to come out.

*"We were pleasantly surprised with the outcome of the election, especially given the craziness of COVID-19. Taking an in-depth look at the data in order to share the story helped guide us to good decisions. And it was a successful effort."*

**—Gary Bilotta**
GIS director of the Elections Department

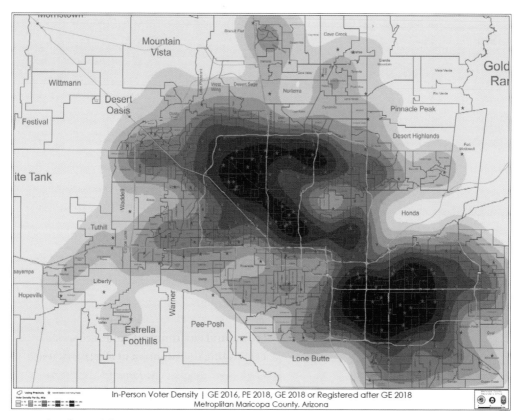

In-Person Voter Density | GE 2016, PE 2018, GE 2018 or Registered after GE 2018
Metroplitan Maricopa County, Arizona

Having foundational data on voters and population density allowed the county to quickly adapt when COVID-19 protocols affected in-person voting.

ADDITIONAL BENEFITS

# Using GIS to link sustainability goals with electric resources in the city of Palo Alto

**Community profile**

- City of Palo Alto, California
- Population of Palo Alto (2018 US census): 66,292
- Nature of the project: Addressing climate change through electrical vehicles

**Community fact:** Per capita, Palo Alto is America's electric car capital. In 2017, one in three vehicles purchased in Palo Alto was electric—the highest adoption rate in the country, according to data from the International Council on Clean Transportation (ICCT).

Sustainability has been a critical issue for the city of Palo Alto, California, since the 1990s when the city began to set goals for reducing its carbon footprint. A significant portion of Palo Alto's greenhouse emissions come from the transportation sector, notably cars and other motor vehicles. To cut carbon emissions, the city has actively encouraged residents to take alternative modes of transportation and switch from gas vehicles to electric vehicles (EVs). Although good for reducing emissions overall, EVs need electric charging stations to fuel them. A resident or business wanting to install charging stations must obtain a permit from the city and ensure there is sufficient electrical panel capacity on the premises. If there is a need to increase electrical supply to the premises, City of Palo Alto Utilities (CPAU), the city-owned and -operated municipal

Palo Alto reduced greenhouse gas (GHG) emissions by an estimated 36 percent in 2018, relative to a 1990 baseline, or 56.5 percent if you count carbon offsets. In 2016, the city council adopted the goal of 80 percent GHG reduction by 2030, calculated using the 1990 baseline, and a draft Sustainability and Climate Action Plan (S/CAP) framework. This ambitious goal is 20 years ahead of the State of California's target of 80 percent by 2050. In 2017, the city council accepted a 2018–2020 Sustainability Implementation Plan, which focuses on two key sustainability concerns, $CO_2$ and $H_2O$ (GHGs and water), and four action areas: energy, mobility, electric vehicles, and water. In early 2020, the city launched a 2020 S/CAP Update to help meet its sustainability goals. The city proposed goals and key actions in seven areas: energy, mobility, electric vehicles, water, climate adaptation and sea level rise, the natural environment, and zero waste. Facilitating the adoption of electric vehicles is a key strategy in reducing fossil fuel use and associated GHG emissions of the community. GIS technology will aid in meeting Palo Alto's ambitious S/CAP goals.

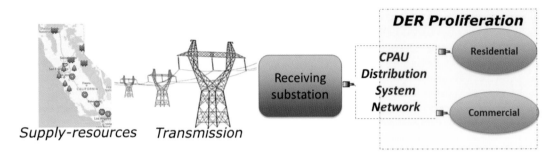

Electrical service to a home.

electric utility, would need to facilitate it by upgrading the customer's service lines and associated utility systems, such as a distribution transformer.

An electrical transformer typically serves 10 homes without EVs. With EVs, it may only serve five homes because of the higher electrical loads of homes with EVs. Currently, it takes about eight hours to fully charge most EVs. Thus, it is important to have the proper size transformer to serve customers reliably and safely.

With 25,000 households owning approximately 4,500 EVs, one in seven homes in Palo Alto has an EV. With EV ownership expected to increase, CPAU reached out to IT department staff and began an evaluation of the locations where there were clusters of homes with EVs. The locations of EVs registered in Palo Alto were obtained by CPAU from the Department of Motor Vehicles, under strict confidential and nondisclosure conditions for the sole purpose of electrical distribution system evaluation and planning.

Using the spatial data of homes with EVs and using CPAU's transformer-to-homes connectivity database (which contains information on homes that are connected to the same transformer), the team mapped the system. The GIS division geocoded the data created by and for the GIS inventory and matched this data with EV locations and the connectivity map. Among the data collected were house and street addresses,

electric meter locations with transformer connectivity, and the number of house meters drawing energy from a given transformer.

The green circles in the map in the figure denote the transformer locations, and the size of the circle illustrates the number of homes with EVs connected to that transformer. The symbol of the car denotes that the home has a registered EV. CPAU staff were able to closely monitor the transformer loading for larger circles. If deemed necessary, CPAU would install a second transformer nearby and reconnect some of the homes with EVs to the new transformer, thus reducing the load on the first transformer to safe levels. The assessment provided a quick way to see which transformers in the city needed upgrades or maintenance.

Transformer upgrades cost money—a lot of money. Having good locational data for analysis allows staff to more accurately determine the transformers that need upgrades and to lower overall cost. In the future, this information may also be used to find good locations to install public EV chargers.

Having an up-to-date and expansive geodatabase for data is key. Analysis of GIS appears in the form of a map, which helps engineers and policy makers make better decisions. These tools enable a higher ROI by allowing the city to make strategic investments

Analysis helps the city understand the number of electric vehicles connected to the electric utility transformer.

determining when and where maintenance is needed to extend the life of key assets.

At present, Palo Alto has 4,500 electric vehicles, equivalent to 7 percent of the 52,000 vehicles registered in the city. City leaders hope to increase that percentage to 80 percent by 2030. The GIS tool allows staff to explore different directions the city could take and offers more flexibility with other strategic decisions as they arise.

*"The new tool allows the city to take a surgical approach in making strategic decisions rather than working with a hammer."*

**—Jay Sivarajah**
GIS program manager in information technology

The CPAU provides an analysis of where energy is being drawn down throughout the city, which serves as an important communications tool. Having such data easily accessible makes replication of the tool for other purposes possible. Likewise, the liability risks to the city are more controlled because the data is cleaned before being used. Among the key questions that Palo Alto staff wanted data to analyze include:

- Where are people using power?
- Are residents converting to renewable energy resources, such as solar?

As part of its long-term effort to reduce carbon, Palo Alto has adopted a smart-communities approach. As Palo Alto has one of the highest EV adoption rates in the US, the GIS system allows community leaders to achieve GHG reduction goals at lower cost and in a more reliable and customer-friendly manner.

ADDITIONAL BENEFITS

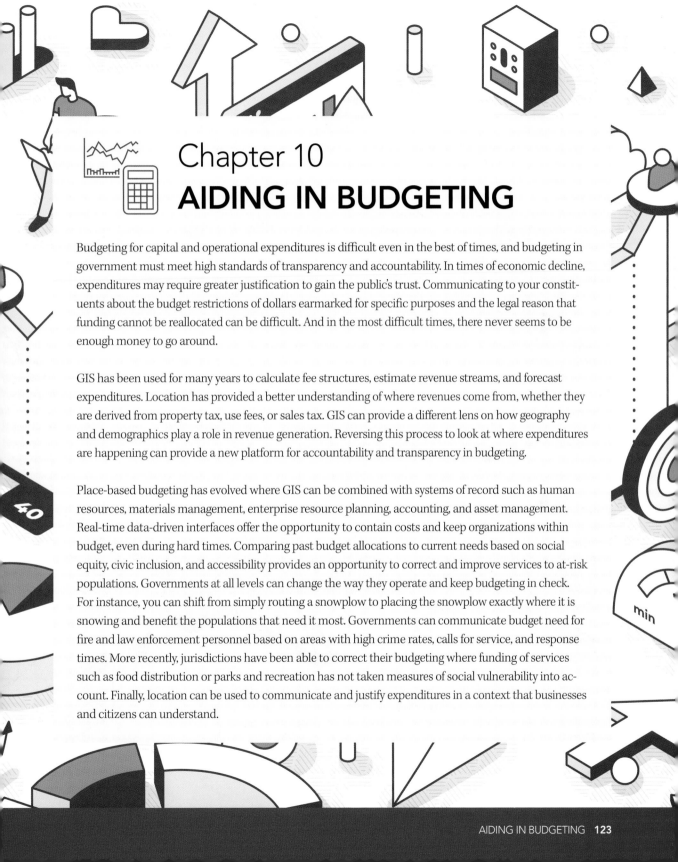

# Chapter 10
# AIDING IN BUDGETING

Budgeting for capital and operational expenditures is difficult even in the best of times, and budgeting in government must meet high standards of transparency and accountability. In times of economic decline, expenditures may require greater justification to gain the public's trust. Communicating to your constituents about the budget restrictions of dollars earmarked for specific purposes and the legal reason that funding cannot be reallocated can be difficult. And in the most difficult times, there never seems to be enough money to go around.

GIS has been used for many years to calculate fee structures, estimate revenue streams, and forecast expenditures. Location has provided a better understanding of where revenues come from, whether they are derived from property tax, use fees, or sales tax. GIS can provide a different lens on how geography and demographics play a role in revenue generation. Reversing this process to look at where expenditures are happening can provide a new platform for accountability and transparency in budgeting.

Place-based budgeting has evolved where GIS can be combined with systems of record such as human resources, materials management, enterprise resource planning, accounting, and asset management. Real-time data-driven interfaces offer the opportunity to contain costs and keep organizations within budget, even during hard times. Comparing past budget allocations to current needs based on social equity, civic inclusion, and accessibility provides an opportunity to correct and improve services to at-risk populations. Governments at all levels can change the way they operate and keep budgeting in check. For instance, you can shift from simply routing a snowplow to placing the snowplow exactly where it is snowing and benefit the populations that need it most. Governments can communicate budget need for fire and law enforcement personnel based on areas with high crime rates, calls for service, and response times. More recently, jurisdictions have been able to correct their budgeting where funding of services such as food distribution or parks and recreation has not taken measures of social vulnerability into account. Finally, location can be used to communicate and justify expenditures in a context that businesses and citizens can understand.

# Mapping GIS data for better public health in Brownsville, Texas

## Community profile

- City of Brownsville, Texas
- Population of Brownsville (US census 2019): 183,392
- Nature of project: Public health and disease vectors

**Community fact:** The Port of Brownsville has become a major economic hub for south Texas, where shipments arrive from other parts of the United States, Mexico, and around the world. Brownsville's economy is based mainly on its international trade with Mexico, and it is home to one of the fastest growing manufacturing sectors in the nation.

The GIS data collected through the city's mobile app has enabled the Brownsville Public Health Department to analyze data and devise an approach to determine how best to achieve four main goals for keeping residents safe and healthy in the event of a virus outbreak:

- Virus containment
- Introduction of preventive practices
- Increased community awareness
- Lifestyle and demographic data

Brownsville is in a subtropical climate zone, an environment ripe for hosting viruses and disease vectors such as mosquitoes. City leaders have considerable experience in containing viral outbreaks such as the Zika virus, chikungunya virus, and the dengue and West Nile viruses. Having faced such public health threats before, the public health department staff and

> Investing in an effective, proactive surveillance initiative can yield tremendous results in terms of combating disease and virus transmissions. The City of Brownsville undertook a public health initiative designed to collect and maintain more accurate data by using a variety of GIS tools, including mobile apps, drones, and story mapping. By planning ahead and having the right GIS tools available, the city's initiative helped secure $247,686 in external grant funding to expand the reach of the initiative and protect the public.

community volunteers collected GIS data on mosquito vector abundance and incidence. The objective was to describe the various species of mosquitoes found in vector surveillance, quantify their prevalence, and identify any associations with temporal or weather-related variations.

A Brownsville and Cameron County investigation plotted requests from residents who identified vector breeding areas and checked those against current trap plots to correlate any possible trends. GIS was used to plot species types and quantities and create a predictive model of areas of concern for floods or possible arboviral disease spread. Mosquito data was plotted with the US Environmental Protection Agency (EPA) Aedes mosquito project to identify areas of increased Aedes aegypti, which has correlated with speciation of mosquitoes.

City staff are responsible for vector control surveillance and response.

Through Brownsville's mobile app, citizens can report where they are finding mosquito breeding site conditions such as illegal dumping, tire dumping, and standing water. Mapping such locations accurately has allowed the city to plot trap placements and track placements and hot spots to continue or change vector variations. The city can track where the breeding grounds for mosquitoes and other insects are, as well as what treatments appear to be working in destroying viable breeding grounds throughout the city and county.

Brownsville's solution to such challenges has been to remain focused on working toward meeting city goals for using GIS technology to help solve issues related to controlling mosquitoes and insects in the prevention of acquired infectious diseases. Based on Brownsville's successful track record, the city also went after supplemental funding for staff and

*"Having our own public health department provides the city with the ability to take things to a new level to meet the needs of our community. You have to continue to flex and evolve. Using GIS data as a tool to share with the community leaders and residents adds tremendous value at the local level."*

**—Noel Bernal**
City manager for the City of Brownsville

resources to fight virus strains including COVID-19. When the city and other local health departments in the region lagged in fighting COVID-19, Brownsville leaders applied for additional funding from the EPA and the Centers for Disease Control and Prevention (CDC).

With GIS, the city can target areas for resource allocation, including spraying ponds for mosquito abatement.

Having GIS data on hand and readily available allowed the city to secure grant funding to fight current and future virus strains. By harnessing the power of GIS into a handheld device, the city has been able to aggregate more information using apps on smartphones, which most residents own. Having such data has allowed city staff to better map where cases of the viruses are being identified.

Brownsville learned several lessons about needs for data and analysis. Residents built the initiative based on experience with the Zika virus outbreak and then applied it to COVID-19, providing weekly reports to the mayor. This new approach to public health has permeated the culture of the organization, encouraging greater innovation within the city. As a result, the city is much more data-driven and makes more decisions with insights from academic researchers and practitioners.

The city has also created dashboards for sharing public health data with residents. Much of the information generated is available on the Brownsville Department of Public Health dashboard, originally built during the Zika outbreak. Given these foundational tools and capabilities, Brownsville was able to pivot quickly during the COVID-19 pandemic.

*"We have been able to better allocate our resources for combating COVID-19 as a result of our GIS portal. We also augmented staff by securing other grants to help expand our system."*

—**Noel Bernal**
City manager for the City of Brownsville

ADDITIONAL BENEFITS

# Lending a helping hand: Residents gather GIS data for improved broadband access in Potter County, Pennsylvania

## Community profile
- Potter County, Pennsylvania
- Population of Potter County (US census 2019): 16,526
- Nature of the project: Planning and budgeting for broadband access

**Community fact:** Today, almost 300,000 acres, more than 40 percent of the land in Potter County, is owned by the Commonwealth of Pennsylvania.

In 2019, the county teamed up with adjacent Tioga County to conduct a survey of community residents to determine where they wanted their public tax dollars to be spent. Improved access to broadband and cellular service came in a close second behind roads.

The county needs good connectivity throughout its broadband network. However, demand from Potter County residents for high-speed internet service intersected with the county's limited financial resources. Initially, service providers in the area did not see enough demand to justify building new infrastructure to extend internet services.

After discussions, county leaders decided to use GIS technology to plan and develop a budget to support the expansion of broadband coverage. This effort included conducting a citizen survey to gain more data points to address the coverage gaps. The maps show where services are located. These reports are

Potter County, is the fifth least populous county in the state of Pennsylvania. Community leaders and staff in this largely rural county know that broadband services are needed for residents to compete in today's global economy. The cost to provide broadband service is high—from $30,000 to $40,000 per square mile. Potter County averages 5.8 homes per mile, but most vendors require a minimum of 28 homes per mile just to cover installation costs. The county has used GIS technology and crowdsourcing to identify gaps in coverage, planning to use this information to negotiate with service providers.

shared with potential partners to help fill the coverage gaps. If requested, results of speed tests are made available to show ROI.

With so many 5G networks coming online, the demand for greater and faster access will continue to grow. To meet this demand, Potter County leaders decided to involve residents, businesses, schools, churches, and neighborhood groups in gathering GIS data, crowdsourcing information from residents on their broadband speed or lack thereof. GIS data is uploaded to a dashboard for the community to review and see gaps in coverage. Reducing the cost

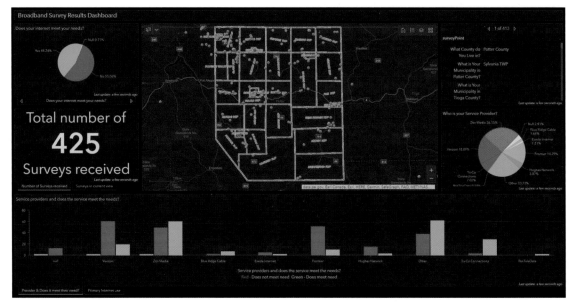

Results from the survey were displayed on a dashboard to provide insight into gaps in service across the community.

per square mile is the key to bringing service to those who need it. The county plans to use this information to negotiate with area service providers and identify where the need is greatest.

*"Potter County developed a dashboard that is fed by survey results. The survey is perpetually open and shared with the decision-makers in our area. It has evolved into a living and breathing report for county leaders, employees, and community residents."*

**—William Hunt**
Planning and GIS director for
Potter County

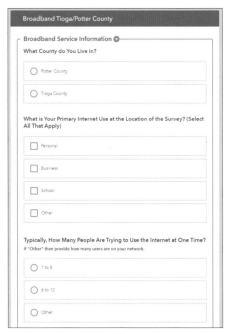

The mobile GIS survey allows the county to collect baseline data on current use, speed, and bandwidth and the need for services from households across the community.

The global economy has become increasingly dependent on internet services. The COVID-19 pandemic clearly demonstrated that large numbers of people could work remotely at home, children could be taught outside a school building, and family and friends could stay connected via webcams. Providing broadband serves to address the digital divide, offers access to telemedicine, and provides economic opportunities for web-based businesses. The pandemic exposed gaps in coverage that have caused tremendous communication issues, limitations on health equity, a reduction of economic opportunities, and other major problems related to the shift to online education. Extending broadband services to communities of color as well as small and rural communities without large budgets has become a national priority. In rural Pennsylvania, Potter County is addressing this issue by engaging residents to crowdsource GIS data to identify gaps in coverage.

ADDITIONAL BENEFITS

# GIS dashboard reengineers planning at Texas state parks

**Community profile**

- Department of Parks and Wildlife, State of Texas
- Population of Texas (US census 2019): 29,183,290
- Nature of the project: Parks management

**Community fact:** In 1983, the Texas legislature passed the Wildlife Conservation Act, authorizing the Department of Parks and Wildlife to manage fish and wildlife resources in all Texas counties. The department operates 95 state parks and historic sites, 51 wildlife management areas, eight fish hatcheries, and numerous field offices statewide.

In the Texas Department of Parks and Wildlife, regional directors and park managers have long been proponents of using data to guide their decisions. But data has not always been easy to use. Each month, the department would send out an email with a financials spreadsheet, sharing data for the most recent month as well as for the same month the previous year. That spreadsheet provided a valuable snapshot, but until recently, any deeper analysis had to be done manually—for example, copying and pasting data from previous spreadsheets.

Such manual analysis might be feasible when looking at historical trends, but it was often too time consuming when it came to dynamic decision-making. For example, a park manager trying to decide the best allocation of limited maintenance funds would want to know which camping loops or facilities serve the most visitors—and are tied to the most revenue. In such a case, a park manager would likely have been

The Texas State Park Insights Viewer, developed using GIS, brings together revenue, visitation, and capital construction data into an intuitive dashboard that enables employees and decision-makers to conduct the kind of detailed analysis that was previously impractical.

forced to review old spreadsheets and make a rough estimate. Also, such spreadsheets tended to become data silos. With different divisions and programs within the agency using their own copies of the spreadsheet to do their own analysis, they often ended up looking at very different data. There was no single source of information.

That's when the department turned to GIS to build its Park Insights Viewer, which now serves as that single source of information. It brings together revenue, visitation, and capital construction data into an intuitive dashboard that allows regional directors, park managers, and other employees to conduct the kind of detailed analysis that wasn't practical before.

The idea for the dashboard came when the department's infrastructure division asked for a tool that would allow it to calculate how much revenue would be lost if a certain campground or camping loop were shut down for construction. For example, the division might have three construction projects on tap for the fiscal year. The challenge is to figure out when to schedule each project to minimize the potential loss of revenue. Such analysis, which would entail running

The Park Insights Viewer allows Texas state parks staff to monitor visitation, revenue generation, and construction across state parks.

multiple scenarios, would have been arduous to the point of impracticality without the dashboard.

The dashboard also makes analysis more intuitive by presenting data on a map. Although engineers might use a spreadsheet to determine the cost of a new facility, seeing the location of that facility on a map would help them understand the potential impact of construction. "Bottom line, the useful information provided in Park Insights Viewer has allowed us to make informed decisions quicker than ever before," said Reagan Faught, State Parks region 2 director for the Texas Parks and Wildlife Department.

ADDITIONAL BENEFITS

# Conclusion
## Leaning forward: Embracing GIS as a critical infrastructure

GIS is made up of two guiding principles. First, GIS is a concept—an acknowledgment that location brings a unique perspective to organize data and information and apply spatial thinking to provide new insights. The second principle is that GIS is a technology—it allows organizations to build and connect data based on geographic tags and provides a system to apply spatial thinking. The ROI presented in this book occurred because these organizations accepted the concept of a location strategy and applied GIS technology to help achieve it.

Essentially, these organizations recognized GIS as a critical infrastructure. And much like other infrastructure systems—transportation, utilities, broadband, and water networks—this critical system must be maintained and adapted to meet changing demographics and integrate new technologies as they emerge. If they are not maintained, these systems often reach crisis level. When this occurs with technology, the common phrase is the need to "modernize information technology." This is the politically correct way to say that some organizations have embraced technology to help advance their organizations while not necessarily keeping these systems up to date. One of the major steps in realizing ROI from GIS is to keep pace with advancements and treat technology systems as critical infrastructure.

### Keeping pace with GIS ensures the benefits keep coming

If organizations do not keep pace with advances in GIS data, capabilities, and applications through a comprehensive strategy, they can be left at a disadvantage. We have seen the negative impacts of not maintaining critical GIS infrastructure many times. Take, for example, evacuation planning and communication on road closures ahead of a natural disaster. Back in 2016, as Tropical Storm Colin made its way toward land, the nation watched as Pinellas County, Florida, rolled out its locationcentric plans and Ready Pinellas apps, well in advance of the first sirens sounding. In a region challenged by extreme weather and storms, communities in Florida must have the technology infrastructure in place to respond quickly. It can make the difference between lives saved and lives lost. Pinellas County is a positive testament to advancing through lessons learned and being ready for storm surges and climate-change impacts.

Unfortunately, we have seen examples in which state and local governments have not been prepared in the same way and have struggled to keep their citizens safe when disasters hit. Information products must be pushed out to the community before it is too late for them to be effective. When GIS is prioritized as a critical system in an organization, staff can adapt more quickly, rapidly scaling up to meet the new demands of residents and being prepared to pivot when new advances are made.

### How IT advancements are transforming organizations

With each iteration of *Measuring Up: The Business Case for GIS* (this is the third volume, after all), we are reminded how combining IT principles with GIS principles can create new opportunities to realize an even greater ROI. We cannot ignore that the capabilities of GIS, and the benefits derived, have always been interconnected with, and enhanced by, peer technologies such as the Internet of Things, blockchain, mobile devices, digital twins, and cloud computing. The ability for GIS to connect to systems of record such as financial data, billing, customer relationship management (CRM), and enterprise resource planning (ERP) provides unprecedented visibility into our options to develop better policies and allocate resources more equitably. Data coming from consumer applications such as Waze can be combined with traditional traffic data collected by local governments to change how communities relieve congestion and adjust to mobility needs. Real-time data from human movement feeds can provide visibility into patterns and trends of how public facilities, parks, and transit are being used so adjustments can be made in equitable budgeting and resource allocation.

The stories in this book were collected to demonstrate best practices and hopefully inspire you to replicate these results in your own organization. The most consistent and significant ROI stems from applying GIS in the following application areas:

- **Field mobility**—GIS empowers staff to collect information in the field for immediate use by management and back-office personnel. Today's mobile solutions offer routing and workforce management capabilities that improve productivity, automate workflows, avoid costs, and save time.
- **Real-time awareness**—GIS helps manage, process, and analyze data coming from sensors and human movement feeds through IoT that can reduce trips made to the field and provide insights at unprecedented speeds. Real-time awareness is leading to major time savings, improved efficiency, and increased accuracy.
- **Performance management**—with GIS, decision-makers have up-to-the-minute insights into their operations from real-time data feeds and systems of record information. Dashboards are giving organizations increased efficiency, cost savings,

resource management, revenue generation, and time savings.

- **Civic engagement**—powered by GIS, new information hubs and storytelling tools create closer bonds between governments and their communities. These collaboration tools are helping small businesses thrive in economic shifts by having citizens report businesses that are still operating. They also provide resources for citizens to access social services or jobs. Increasingly, civic data hubs are providing a whole new experience in self-service government. Their benefits include opportunities for cost avoidance, aid in budgeting, improved productivity, and increased revenue streams.

## How emerging trends in GIS will change the benefits received

Although GIS is typically known for helping organizations achieve and improve field mobility, real-time awareness, performance management, and civic engagement, there are new approaches and advances in GIS technology that we must also keep an eye on. There are always early adopters and pioneering organizations that seize the opportunity to embrace new capabilities, functions, and integrations with peer technologies as they become available. These are organizations that we should commend and aspire to emulate. This volume of *Measuring Up: The Business Case for GIS* has highlighted several pioneering organizations—such as the governments of Glendale, California; Potter County, Pennsylvania; and Johns Creek, Georgia—that have embraced cutting-edge GIS capabilities and seen tremendous payoffs.

These organizations have recognized that GIS is no longer a technology just for large organizations. This generation of GIS technology can afford governments of all sizes the opportunity to innovate. Nick O'Day, chief data officer for the City of Johns Creek, Georgia, said it best: "We were looking at the major cities across the country, the New Yorks and LAs and San Franciscos of the world, at what they were doing with the same technology we had access to, and thinking, 'Why can't we do that?'" This next generation of GIS users embraces artificial intelligence (AI), machine learning, drone data capture, augmented reality, and virtual reality and combines these concepts with GIS to rethink and reimagine how their organizations might evolve and modernize. They are leading the way and setting the standards.

Our hope is that these organizations are not alone. Advances in GIS are ready for the leaders of today to embrace and move forward. The business value of GIS comes when you ask how an existing process can be improved, how a workflow can be automated, or how a work procedure can be eliminated altogether. GIS advancements that organizations are starting to embrace include:

- **Artificial intelligence and machine learning**—using GIS data as the connective thread, organizations are making strategic inroads with AI, especially machine learning, to automate processes, improve predictive modeling, model traffic patterns, predict housing needs, prioritize road maintenance, and more. Automation, productivity, and cost savings will be tremendous.
- **Digital twins**—GIS visualization and 3D modeling are giving organizations the ability to better verify public policy decisions in real time and in real-world contexts. Organizations are creating digital twins—virtual representations of the real world, including physical objects, processes, relationships, and behaviors—to enable better real-time visualization, provide advanced analysis and automation of predictions, and allow for information sharing and collaboration. To address the challenges of major social problems such as homelessness and housing affordability, these models can allow governments to test their ideas and understand the interdependencies and impacts of their decisions. Decision-making will receive the biggest boost from digital twins. Cost avoidance, aid in budgeting, and cost savings from missteps in policy will yield the greatest benefits.

As we prepare for a world impacted by climate change and inequity on one hand, and disruptive technologies such as autonomous vehicles and drone delivery on the other, GIS is poised to assist organizations with their most pressing challenges. What GIS is and what it will provide are improvements in processes for everyday workloads. The ROI from the applications of GIS will continue to deliver in the areas of saving money, saving time, cost avoidance, revenue generation, aid in budgeting, increased efficiency, improved productivity, workflow automation, resource management, and improved accuracy. GIS is, and should continue to be, regarded as a critical infrastructure within organizations, because the quantified benefits of GIS are real.

# Afterword
## Closing thoughts

The stories featured in *Measuring Up,* volume 3, showcase how governments at all levels can make greater use of GIS in their daily operations and civic engagement efforts. Use of GIS has become widespread as the technology can be adapted for many purposes. Whether it is to determine where car parks can be easily converted to affordable housing (England) or the use of artificial intelligence for responding to questions from the public (Johns Creek, Georgia), there is no topic that is not location-based and would not benefit from location intelligence.

GIS is a powerful tool, but technology alone cannot solve all challenges facing governments. Consider what it takes to build a house. Saws, hammers, drills, tape measures, and many other tools are required on a construction site. But just as a carpenter needs blueprints to begin building a house, governments need to identify their challenges and create strategic plans for responding to their challenges. It is then that the true power of GIS takes the stage as leaders, executives, managers, and other stakeholders can better understand the effects of their decisions. Datasets, mobile apps, storytelling maps, and other GIS tools help communicate the outcomes of data-driven decision-making in a matter of hours, instead of the weeks or days it might have taken before.

Connecting with governments to find out about how other communities are using GIS technology is key to a successful system. *Measuring Up,* volume 3, is one step toward learning how GIS can make a difference in your community. If you want to learn more about GIS, reach out to Esri or ICMA to connect with your peers.

**—ICMA and Esri**